SUNY Series in Philosophy
Robert Cummings Neville, Editor

Chuang-Tzu
for
Spiritual Transformation

Chuang-Tzu
for
Spiritual Transformation

An Analysis of the Inner Chapters

ROBERT E. ALLINSON

State University of New York Press

Published by
State University of New York Press, Albany

© 1989 State University of New York

For information, address State University of New York
Press, State University Plaza, Albany, N.Y., 12246

Library of Congress Cataloging-in-Publication Data

Allinson, Robert E., 1942-
    Chuang-Tzu for spiritual transformation: an analysis of the inner
chapters / Robert E. Allinson.
        p. cm. — (SUNY series in philosophy)
    Includes index.
    ISBN 0-88706-967-3.   ISBN 0-88706-969-X (pbk.)
    1. Chuang-tzu. Nan-hua ching.   I. Title.
BL1900.C576A45 1989
299'.51482 — dc19   88-19974
                                                             CIP

10 9 8 7 6 5 4 3 2 1

Contents

I dedicate this book to my wife, Irénè Grafton Allinson,
who originally urged me to write this book and has been
a source of inspiration all along the way.

Foreword

Studies of Chuang Tzu in English have reached gratifying standards of quality and quantity. Two recent books by Wu Kuang-ming and an issue of the *Journal of Chinese Philosophy* (13/4) are evidence of this. The present outstanding volume by Robert Allinson builds on those studies and initiates a new direction.

Professor Allinson builds on the earlier work, especially that of Wu, by accepting the interpretation that Chuang Tzu used language metaphorically and elliptically to evoke an existential response, a response that cannot be commanded by direct imperatives or elicited by plain normative description. His new direction for understanding Chuang Tzu is his comprehensive and detailed argument that Chuang Tzu was advocating an ideal of sageliness. Whereas many interpreters have claimed that Chuang Tzu used his metaphorical language to defend a relativism, Allinson shows with convincing mastery that Chuang Tzu had a position, namely, the importance of achieving the ideal of sageliness.

To make his point, Professor Allinson has not only to examine the relevant texts and comment on the other major interpreters. He has also to relate his line of argument to a theory of hermeneutics. In so doing, he brings the discussion of Chuang Tzu into the heart of contemporary Western philosophy. Furthermore, his interpretation of Chuang Tzu makes the sage thoroughly intelligible to a Western audience, not an inscrutable oriental with a perverse use of language but a spiritual philosopher closer to Augustine than to masters of the Zen kōan.

Professor Allinson's book, like his many articles, thus contributes to the growing body of literature that is creating an effective dialogue between Chinese and Western philosophy. Such a dialogue cannot take place on the ground determined by either side. It must be a new creation resulting from a long process of interpretation back and forth. The sophistication of this book demonstrates that the dialogue has worked and that we are in a new era of substantive comparative philosophy.

Some Westerners, lamenting the decline of popular appreciation of the classics of European thought, dismiss comparative philosophy

1

as constrained to take the worst of both worlds. This is historically shortsighted. Early Christian thought, for instance, was comparative philosophy, combining Jewish, Zoroastrian, and Greek traditions. Early modern philosophy arose from a comparative base of scholasticism and humanistic science. The reality of our own world is that the Western traditions have encountered the Chinese and Indian, and sophistication with regard to any requires sophistication with regard to all. Professor Allinson's book contributes to that sophistication.

Like his earlier papers on Taoism, this book of Allinson's takes Taoist thinking to be a world-philosophy, on a par with that of Plato and Aristotle. His techniques of analysis have come mainly from the styles of thought honed in the Western tradition. But he has subjected those techniques to tutelage from the Taoist texts themselves, sensitizing them to East Asian ways of thinking. The result is a monograph accessible to Western philosophers on their own terms, but sensitive to the inner workings of Chuang Tzu's text and style of thought. This is a model of straightforward philosophical analysis that engages a classic too often thought to be too opaque for critical study.

"Becoming a sage" is a soteriological theme, and it occurs frequently in many kinds of Chinese thought, Taoist, Confucian, and Buddhist. Modern Western philosophy, by contrast, rather sharply distinguishes analytical philosophy from soteriological religion, and the roots of that distinction go back to the medieval period when thinkers who were both analytically philosophical and religiously concerned for salvation emphasized a distinction between natural reason (philosophy) and revealed faith (religion). The distinction between reason and faith does not occur in anything like that form in Chinese thinking. As a consequence of this situation, many Western philosophers dismiss Chuang Tzu with the other Chinese philosophers as mere religious thinkers.

Paradoxically, part of the uniqueness of Chuang Tzu is that he, of all people, dismisses the immediacy of both faith and reason. Every commitment is turned around, relativized, and made ironic. Even more than Nietzsche, Chuang Tzu was a secular philosopher, and therefore more telling for our secular age in discussions of the soteriological warrant of sagehood. Allinson points up the demystified and demythologized relevance of Chuang Tzu. In so doing, he also makes a substantial contribution to the philosophy of religion.

It is my very great pleasure to introduce this volume, a treat both of scholarship and imaginative argument.

ROBERT CUMMINGS NEVILLE
Boston University

Preface

The *Chuang-Tzu* is a treasure trove of philosophic wisdom. At the same time, it is a most obscure work. There is no apparent linear development of philosophical argument. In addition, many of its internal passages seem to be non sequiturs from each other. To make matters worse, it is replete with internal passages which are themselves so obscure that they defy any kind of rational analysis. And the whole of it is cast in such a literary mold that it may discourage the reader from ferreting out any philosophical theme.

In this work, I hope to accomplish at least two ends. First, I have endeavored to set out one major philosophical task with which the work as a whole is concerned: this is the task of self-transformation. Secondly, I have endeavored to show that the disconnectedness of the text and the highly oblique literary form of the text have a systematic correlation with the technical means of accomplishing the goal of self-transformation.

In order to accomplish the goals which I have set out, I have had to devote considerable space to demonstrating that the text is not a relativistic tract. The view that the *Chuang-Tzu* is a work of relativism has, in my opinion, prevented scholars from attempting to penetrate to a core philosophic aim that is present in the text and at the same time has prevented an analysis of the systematic methodology to be found in the text.

All in all, one might say that I have attempted to bring out a hidden logic in the text. To this end, I may be accused by some of logicizing the text. Against this accusation, I will have to allow my arguments to stand by themselves. It is not that I think that the text is simply a systematic strategy for achieving the goals of self-transformation. I think, however, that there is a method in the apparent madness of the text.

What other choices do we have? Some might adopt a middle course and argue that a self-transformation theme exists alongside the relativistic theme; some might argue that one theme is emphasized as the major theme; others might argue that the other is more major. The

3

problem with this approach is that the two themes—if we wish to argue that the text contains both—are not wholly consonant with each other. In fact, unless we can specify what relation they bear to each other, they contradict each other and cancel each other out. In this case, instead of having two themes, we have none.

The other major option is to refuse to consider any central textual focus and treat the text as an historical collection of different viewpoints, most probably composed by diverse authors, and thus relieving oneself of the responsibility of alleging that either there is any central theme or that whatever themes can be found have to cohere with each other. In this instance, the text becomes valued more as a collection of literary vignettes and philosophical drolleries to be relished as one might savour an historical literary antique for its turn of phrase and its capacity to represent the existing philosophical viewpoints existent at the time of its composition.

It seems to me, that regardless of the fact of multiple composition and brilliant flights of literary invention, that there is a core meaning structure to be found in the text which reveals a direct connection between the relativistic seeming statements and the consistent *nisus* towards self-transformation. Whether or not this is blurred and distorted by the multiple authorship, it seems undeniable that it exists especially within the framework of the genuine, inner chapters. Therefore, I have taken the text as it stands as a philosophical work to be examined in its own right and on its own merits quite apart from the questions of multiple authorship or whether the views represented are ones which can be found in various historical schools of philosophy at the time. By doing this, we can, in fact, discover a *Chuang-Tzu* which exhibits a step by step, coherent argument structure consisting of sophisticated techniques to effect a transformation of consciousness on the part of the reader. It is the purpose of this work to show the unity and the coherence of the inner chapters of the *Chuang-Tzu* are such that it deserves to be examined as a philosophical work and an artistic masterpiece of the first order in which form and content are interwoven thematically just as one finds in Plato's *Symposium*. It is hoped that this work can serve as a contribution to the development of the same systematic study of texts in Chinese philosophy as one is accustomed to find in Western philosophy.

What is more, the techniques of textual interpretation introduced here for the first time can also apply to the art of interpreting and commenting upon Western philosophical texts as well as Chinese ones. Definitions and comparative definitions of myth, legend, archetype, paradox and others introduced here are of relevance for Literary criticism and the study of world literature in general. This book is therefore also offered as a work in cross-cultural philosophical and literary hermeneutics which can have value for the general reader in addition to the philosopher and those interested in Chinese philosophy and Chuang Tzu.

Introduction

The *Chuang-Tzu* is no ordinary book. Arthur Waley, who taught himself Chinese and became one of the most gifted English language translators of Chinese literature, referred to the *Chuang-Tzu* as, ". . . one of the most entertaining as well as one of the profoundest books in the world."[1] Because, however, of its obscurity, antique allusions, seemingly self-contradictory passages and literary railleries existing side by side with philosophical revelations, it has defied attempts to reduce it to clear-cut prose paraphrase explanations. Despite this lack of any systematic or even partially systematic explanation of the main themes or the methodology of the *Chuang-Tzu* it has nonetheless exercised an undeniable fascination with literati over the ages.

What I have attempted to do in this companion reader to the *Chuang-Tzu* is to call attention to the major, underlying theme of the text, that of spiritual transformation. In order to do so, I have concentrated on the first seven or inner chapters, which are considered to be genuine. If I have included material from the mixed and the outer chapters, it is only by way of expanding upon the themes already present in the first seven chapters. If material from the mixed and outer chapters is at odds with the material from the genuine chapters, I take that as one of the clear indicators that it is spurious. One of the key features of this book on the *Chuang-Tzu* is that it pays close attention to the distinction between the material presented in the genuine and the non-genuine chapters. The absence of a strict line of demarcation between the genuine and the non-genuine chapters has, I think, obscured the fact that an underlying theme of spiritual transformation is at the heart of the text.

What I propose in this present volume is to select out for special attention both underlying themes and basic methodologies employed to elucidate those themes in the inner chapters of the *Chuang-Tzu*. The key focus for the themes which I will examine is the master purpose of spiritual transformation, in which all of the themes in one way or another fit and into which all of the methodologies figure.

In what follows, I have attempted to analyze the literary forms and conventions utilized within the body of the text of the *Chuang-*

Tzu, the key metaphors employed in the text, and the anecdotal argument form of the text as a means of facilitating and charting the course of progress of spiritual transformation within the reader. My essential argument is that the majority of the seemingly self-contradictory passages, the non sequiturs, the seemingly oblique or purely humorous literary references, including the use or purposeful misuse of historical personages and philosophical enemies like Confucius as interlocutors, one and all have the intention of silencing the analytical thinking reflexes of the reader and simultaneously empowering the reader's dormant intuitive or holistic mental functions. In the process of crippling and paralyzing the instant reflex of the mind to think analytically, the *Chuang-Tzu* displays a glittering array of linguistic techniques and literary devices which reveal the ever increasing levels of complexity required to break through the ever increasing resistance of the intellectual habits of the reader and at the same time catalogue the ever increasing levels of personal realization which are achieved in the course of the process of spiritual transformation.

The intended outcome of the *Chuang-Tzu* is to some extent prefigured in the title of the first of the seven inner (genuine) chapters, which has been rendered in English as "Happy Wandering" (Jane English and Gia-fu Fung) or "Going Rambling without a Destination" (A. C. Graham). While I have adopted such translations myself to avoid an awkward locution of my own devising, such translations, although they are linguistically suitable, are philosophically misleading. The 'wandering' refers to the absolute freedom of the *mind* to move in any direction that it fancies, a level of freedom that is possible only after achieving a state of transcendence or transcendental happiness. This state, which can only be achieved in turn by spiritual transformation, is one in which the mind can move in uninhibited ways because it is not bound by the limitations of any particular standpoint. The problem with the literal meanings implied by "Happy Wandering" or "Going Rambling without a Destination" is that they both imply the possibility of a purely egoistic pastime which is not suited to the level of freedom under discussion.[2] It is extremely difficult to describe the condition referred to in a short, idiomatic English phrase that still captures the philosophical meaning. Keeping in mind that the chapter headings are in any case all later additions, if one were to strive for a philosophical and not merely a linguistic equivalent of the Chinese, one might be better off considering the translation, "The Transcendental Happiness Walk."

How does spiritual transformation either relate to or differ from religious transformation? Spiritual transformation does not depend upon the belief in any system of putative truths. It does not require faith in a specific form of religion or adherence to any set of religious practices. It does not imply a supreme being or worship in any pre-scribed form, nor does it point to the authority of any particular revealed scripture. It is also unlike religious transformation if by religious trans-formation one has in mind the model of religious conversion. Spiritual transformation does not require a belief in any set of ideas such as a particular manifestation of a deity or a set of doctrines concerning the soul or an afterlife or even a code of ethical practices. In addition, spiritual transformation is unlike conversion because it is not basically a deep-seated emotional experience.

Spiritual transformation is perhaps best likened to a change in one's level of consciousness. It is an experience one undergoes which is transforming of one's personality and one's perspective. One sees in a different way than one saw before the transformation. It is not so much a change in a particular belief or viewpoint as it is a change which takes one beyond all viewpoints. The attitude of one's mind is altered, hence the term spiritual transformation.

How does spiritual transformation relate to or differ from mysti-cal transformation? Spiritual transformation is unlike mystical trans-formation, because there is no sense of becoming one with the cosmos. One does not lose one's identity in some kind of undifferentiated uni-fication with the all. Such a state in which all distinctions vanish is what Hegel criticized Schelling as endorsing (Schelling's night in which all cows are black). If one means by mystical transformation a state in which all distinctions merge with all others, then the state of spiritual transformation is by no means a state of mystical transformation.

Spiritual transformation is also unlike mystical transformation because there is no special, secret knowledge which one must learn or to which only a special and select group of initiates is privy. The state of spiritual transformation which is the core message of the *Chuang-Tzu* is equally available to all and is not dependent upon either the special understanding of hidden truths or the special practice of cer-tain exercises, techniques of breathing, or meditation.

Spiritual transformation is unlike philosophical explanation, because it is not a deduction from a previously accepted premise. In this sense, because it is not a logical deduction, it may be said not to be an intellectual act. It is noetic, but it is not intellectual. It is perhaps best likened to the experience of sudden insight, the "aha" experience in which we suddenly understand something which we previously could not fathom. In this case, however, the "aha" experience is not an understanding of one particular resistant problem but a sudden understanding of how one's whole thinking process had been mis-directed. In philosophical language it is an awakening from one's dog-matic slumbers.

Spiritual transformation is unlike psychological insight because it is at once broader than and inclusive of psychological insight. It shares in common with psychological insight the feeling of freedom from what had been previously burdening one. It differs from psychological insight in that it does not refer to any particular piece of self-knowledge which had been constricting one's vision. Rather, it refers to the mind's freedom from any and all mental blocks. In addition, spiritual transformation differs from psychological insight in that it does not simply remove emotional blocks, which owe their origins to emotional conflicts, but removes an entire mental block, much as a writer might suddenly become free from a writer's block.

A further distinction to be drawn between spiritual transformation and psychological insight is that spiritual transformation is in no way reducible to some observable, empirical process. What occurs in the process of spiritual transformation may have some psycho-physical parallels, but what is relevant here is the validity of the viewpoint that is obtained by the transformation and not the measuring of whatever accompanying brain-wave patterns there may be.

It could be argued that I am interpreting the text of the *Chuang-Tzu* as if it were one lengthy, extended kōan in the literature of Zen. While such an argument is of necessity historically backwards, since Zen (or Ch'an) arises much later in history, there is some justice to the argument that I am interpreting the fragments that make up the *corpus* of the *Chuang-Tzu* as an extended kōan or series of kōans. Since Zen has been argued to be the legitimate heir of Taoism, it would not be surprising to find that certain characteristics of the child were to be found in the genetic make-up of the parent.[2]

The *Chuang-Tzu* is, however, not merely one long, extended kōan (or series of kōans), since it also engages in philosophical argument. In addition, the text as a whole may be taken as a chart of spiritual progress. The literary conceits and linguistic techniques which make up the text of the *Chuang-Tzu* seem systematically and artfully arranged both to indicate the different levels of spiritual development which lie before us and to show which linguistic devices are appropriately applied to these differing and ascending levels. While the *Chuang-Tzu* is, to be sure, a textual kōan, it is at the same time much more.

If we do not choose to approach the literary bones of the text in the manner of a contemporary oracle-literary bone reader, so as to perceive the intricate patterning of wisecracks and complex configurations that demonstrate to us both that the text is a riddle and that the riddle possesses an answer, then what other options for textual interpretation or commentary are open to us? In A. C. Graham's *Chuang Tzu: The Inner Chapters* (London: 1981), as with his work as a whole, e.g., *Studies in Chinese Philosophy and Philosophical Literature* (Singapore: 1986), we find the text of the *Chuang-Tzu* divided up with respect to possible or probable differing authorship by varying philosophical schools. This approach, in a broad manner of speaking, may be taken as representing a sophisticated extension of an historian of religions' approach to ancient texts.[4] Such an approach, while possessing a strong degree of historical accuracy, makes it difficult if not impossible to analyze the text as a single line of philosophical development which aims at inducing as well as describing different levels of spiritual development.

The problem with the history of religions' approach to a text in A. C. Graham's sophisticated development (which has more in common with comparative religion than with the history of religions narrowly construed) is that one is tempted to look for textual contradictions as representing the viewpoint of differing historical schools, rather than considering the possibility that contradictions are part and parcel of a general, systematic textual theme. The tendency not to come to grips with thematic (rather than comparative) bases for contradictions can even influence one's reading of the inner chapters (which are agreed to be the works of one author), as we will see when we examine Graham's treatment of the butterfly and the Great Sage dream anecdotes.

If several passages from different chapters, or even within the same chapter, contradict each other, then one whose commentary format is fashioned after the history of religions' approach can easily explain away such contradictions as being the result of authorship by different writers. The end-result of such an approach is that we miss an intra-textual systematic connectedness in which certain contradictions form part of a series of related strategies.

If we accept the history of religions' approach we not only weaken the possibility of finding an overall textual theme, but moreover we are left with a congeries of assorted sayings which at best possess a certain historical value and a sampling of literary flights which at best satisfy an aesthetic palate. Whatever is left over can be lumped together in the general conceptual wastebasket known as "mysticism" by the reader who is already predisposed in this direction. Such a categorization automatically exempts any refractory passages from conceptual analysis, since they are (*ex hypothesi*) designed only to confuse the reader who does not possess the requisite mystical knowledge to know at once to what they refer; they can be dismissed as a secret language which is understood only by those who have been instructed in the special meaning of the passages. From an historian of religion's standpoint, the statements to be found within the *Chuang-Tzu* either would be penned by different hands or would be of purely antiquarian or literary value. Whatever statements are left over would make up a private language for certain privileged mystical cognoscenti.

In seeing the text both as a manual to and a description of the process of spiritual transformation, I am assuming that there is a single, major theme that is to be found in the text and that the varying types of statements that one finds in the text all relate in various ways to the development of this theme. Whether or not the text is by a single hand (and it assuredly is not), the point is that the text can be construed and has a history of being construed as a philosophical text which is part of a philosophical tradition. The notion that the text has a single theme is, of course, strongly qualified by the selection of what is considered to be authentic and inauthentic material. The major criterion for authenticity is how close the material comes, both in form and in content, to reflecting and amplifying the major theme that is outlined in the first seven chapters. Thus, it does not matter greatly, in the end, that some of the material has been put together by later disciples of Chuang Chou any more than it matters greatly that all of Aristotle's works are taken from lecture notes by his students. The criterion of authenticity lies more with coherence with the core message of the inner chapters than with anything else.

In a word, our starting and finishing point is the text and not the "real meaning intended by the author." Since we have no access to the intentions of the author (and in any event this would be at best a kind of psychological anthropology), what we do have and what we can work with is the text at hand. The attempt to discover the "real intentions" of the author may be likened to the attempt to employ methods borrowed from the psychologist, the literary biographer and the historian to figure out what Shakespeare "really meant" in Hamlet's soliloquy rather than attending to the written text before us.

If we can discover a major theme that seems to be the over-all thematic governing principle of the text, then our task will be to see how the various portions of the text function so as to communicate the different aspects of this theme. The major objective of the text is to facilitate and to describe spiritual transformation. The accent is equally on what one is transformed *from* and what one is transformed *to*. One is transformed from the mental prison of differing and competing conceptual belief systems, but this does not imply that one is transformed to some kind of skeptical relativism. Rather, the mind is opened so that one can act from a higher level of mentation which, as is argued below in detail, is an epistemologically superior framework.

What I have singled out for special treatment in what is to follow is the unique functioning of literary forms and anecdotal arguments in bringing about the special kind of transformation that then becomes the object of philosophical understanding and discussion. I would like to add one caveat. In the course of my argument, I have made free use of metaphorical language such as the "right hemisphere of the brain." I would ask the reader to distinguish my use of language from the use of such brain-talk as might appear in the language of cognitive psychologists. In the end, cognitive psychologists might be interested in reducing all mental acts to brain functions, but this is not at all my interest or intention. The aspect of transformation in which I am interested is the purely mental aspect, and this aspect has no physical referent. It may be possible to trace some physical correlate but this would be more of an epiphenomenon than a cause of the mental change. Therefore, that with which the *Chuang-Tzu* is concerned is not that which could be induced by purely physical means, such as stimulating different areas of the brain by implanting electrodes. The purely physicalistic or reductionistic hypothesis assumes that understanding mental concepts plays no special role in the process of transformation. But from a philosophical point of view, one is interested in the superiority of the viewpoint that is obtained after the transformation—a superiority which cannot be attested to by pointing at which neurons have been activated.

In order to persuade the reader to examine the text as a work invoking spiritual transformation, I have had to remove one very restrictive preconception which has proved highly successful in making the text resistant to such an analysis, namely, that when everything is said and done, the bottom line of *Chuang-Tzu* interpretation is that Chuang Tzu is a relativist. If this is the attitude with which one approaches the text, there is a disincentive to burrow beneath the surface material of the text in order to spell out the strategic functioning of the seemingly contradictory bits and pieces that make up the corpus of the *Chuang-Tzu*. If I am successful in convincing the reader that the text is not simply a relativistic *tour de passe passe*, then he or she may be disposed to follow out my plan of how the text works transformatively. My interest has largely been to expose the watch works that lie behind the watch face of the display. Such an exposure is not, to be sure, required in order to tell the time. The work can function as a transformatory work even if one is not aware of the techniques which are being employed to bring about the transformation. However, one must at least be open to the possibility that the text is not a relativistic *divertissement* of relativism before one is ready to allow it to function as a transformative text.

I must also ask the reader to understand that certain technical terms in the *Chuang-Tzu* (just as in the *Critique of Pure Reason*) are not always used in the same sense. The Chinese term 'hwa' (化), which is translated as 'transformation,' is used in the *Chuang-Tzu* in some contexts to refer to the worldly transformation of things. However, as I argue below, this is not the major reference of the term 'transformation' but a derivative and metaphorical reference. Things are transformed in our proper understanding of them. The worldly processes of transformation are merely signals to the mind or metaphors which stand for the higher transformation which is intended.

Nor is the transformation a worldly flux which one views from the safe distance of philosophical spectatorship. Such an interpretation implies a disinterest in the *process* of transformation which is the very essence of the text. If we were meant to stand apart from or above the hurly-burly, there would be no need for the elaborate, concrete imagery of the world which informs the text of the *Chuang-Tzu*. The value of the text does not only lie in the end-goal that is to be reached, but in the rich methodology which is employed in the reaching of the goal.

To think otherwise, is, to my mind, to be left with two basic options. Either we view the *Chuang-Tzu* as a piece of charming mysticism which possesses an undeniable literary fascination but is of interest only as a curiosity piece for the dissection and delectation of serious Sinologues, or we consider it a minor philosophical work which, because of its great obscurity and incoherence, is a showpiece for the various and contradictory ideas that were co-temporary with its time of composition.

I have attempted to lift the *Chuang-Tzu* out of the realm of being either a collection of literary vignettes of historical value or a paradoxical and mystical congeries which would make of it a minor philosophical work. What is most distressing about this last alternative is that since mystics and minor philosophers of paradox have carte blanche to commit all sorts of logical fallacies, there is a disincentive to explore the possible systematic methodology contained in paradoxical language forms.

If what follows is successful, the *Chuang-Tzu* will neither be taken as a minor philosophical work nor as a dazzling mixture of literary and mystical sayings. It will assume its rightful place as a masterpiece of the first philosophical order. Chuang Tzu, in the end, will not be seen as a second rate philosopher or a minor poet but a philosopher of major status. This, to my mind, is more consonant with the historical fascination and influence his work has exercised over the centuries. To this end, this little book is dedicated.

1 On the Chirping of Birds

A large issue, which it will take the compass of this book to thoroughly clarify, is whether or not the *Chuang-Tzu* is an exercise in relativism.[1] It is a vital issue with which to begin, as the wrong initial assumption with regard to this question will seriously impede the proper understanding of all that follows.[2] At the outset, I would like to stake my claim that the *Chuang-Tzu* is not an exercise in relativism *simpliciter*.[3] While there is indeed a place for relativism in the *Chuang-Tzu*, I will argue that it is but a provisional place; relativism is specifically employed as a strategy for breaking down other views rather than representing a final point of view of its own.

One of the main lines of argument I will be advancing is logical; the other is textual. The logical argument is based on the argument from self-consistency. The *Chuang-Tzu* cannot be an exercise in relativism because to say so would be to imply that it could not present any view at all, including the relativistic one. The problem is that one cannot make sense of relativism put forward as a philosophical position. If all views are of only relative worth, then on what grounds can one commend one's own view if it be that of the relativist? Relativism is ultimately self-defeating; as Spinoza once put it, the consistent skeptic must remain dumb.

We could, nonetheless, argue that coherent or not, the *Chuang-Tzu* is an exercise in relativism. If relativism is philosophically incoherent, then so much the worse for the *Chuang-Tzu*. The problem with this approach is that it makes the *Chuang-Tzu* out to be the product of a third class mind. While this is logically possible, the richness of the text and the high regard in which the *Chuang-Tzu* has been held by both Chinese and Western scholars argues strongly against the possibility. Kuang-ming Wu, in his superb commentary, *Chuang-Tzu: World Philosopher at Play*, cites Fung Yu Lan's statement that, "It is only in Chuang Tzu's book that we have a well-developed philosophy [of Taoism]."[4] He also recounts the well known praise of H. G. Creel, who stated, "The *Chuang-Tzu* is in my estimation the finest philosophical work known to me, in any language. Its authors included some of the keenest minds the world has known."[5]

In the course of what follows, I hope to offer sufficient logical and textual grounds to convince the reader that the *Chuang-Tzu* is not a relativistic text. With respect to logical grounds, I will argue that Chuang-Tzu cannot extend the relativistic thesis to language without leaving himself without any means of communicating whatsoever. With respect to textual grounds, I will offer both indirect and direct textual evidence to support my claim that the *Chuang-Tzu* is not an exercise in relativism.

I would like to commence my discussion of relativism by focussing on the question of linguistic meaningfulness or meaninglessness. If language is relativistic with regard to meaning, then any word can mean anything at all, which means that all language is infinitely equivocal. Equivocity extended infinitely in all directions is in no way distinct from utter unintelligibility. The existence of some meaning is dependent upon the fixity of the medium of communication. We could not even state the thesis of relativism comprehensibly unless the words we employed possessed some significance. Significance in language is dependent upon some degree of fixity of meaning. In fine, no form of relativism can even be advanced unless language itself is, to some extent, non-relative.

In the famous second chapter of the *Chuang-Tzu*, "*Ch'i Wu Lun*," "A Discussion on the Equality of Things,"[6] the question of the meaningfulness or the meaninglessness of speech, whether oral or written, is raised in a highly poetic form:

> Words are not just wind. Words have something to say. But if what they have to say is not fixed, then do they really say something? Or do they say nothing? People suppose that words are different from the peeps of baby birds, but is there any difference or isn't there?[7]

The question which is being raised is, is there a difference between speech and the chirping of birds, or is there no difference at all? Simply understood, the analogy would appear to be forcing a choice between all or some language being meaningful and all language being meaningless. All that is required for language to be unlike the chirping of birds is that some language would be meaningful, not that all language would have to be meaningful.

If we presuppose for the moment that the *Chuang-Tzu* is an intelligible text, then on logical grounds there must be a difference between human language and bird chirping or else there would not even be a *Chuang-Tzu*. What after all is the status of the *Chuang-Tzu*? It cannot be a songbook for birds as it would be completely useless. Chuang Tzu, we have argued, is surely aware that his entire text makes no sense unless words possess significance. The only other option is that Chuang Tzu is sociopathically perverse and has written an entire book to torment us. The same arguments of the richness and the historical importance of the text that applied against assuming that Chuang Tzu was unaware of the inconsistency of the relativistic thesis apply here against assuming that Chuang Tzu was a perversely minded sociopath.[8]

However, in the translation of the same passage which is offered by A. C. Graham, there would seem to be the implication that there is no difference between human speech and the sound of birds:

> Saying is not blowing breath, saying says something; the only trouble is that what it says is *never* fixed. Do we really say something? Or have we never said anything? If you think it different from the twitter of fledglings, is there *proof* of the distinction? Or isn't there proof?[9]

The difference between Watson's version and Graham's version is subtle but important. In Watson's version, the question is raised as to whether or not the meaning of words is fixed. It is not taken for granted that it is not fixed. It is simply stated that *if* it is not fixed, then we may raise the question if words really say something or if they do not. In Graham's version, it is stated outright that the meaning of words is never fixed. What is hypothetical in Watson becomes categorical in Graham. From the categorical non-fixity of language in Graham's version, we are much more easily led to the probable conclusion that language is meaningless. In Watson's version, the conclusion is left more up in the air. In addition, by inserting the word 'proof' in his translation, Graham creates the impression that in order for us to believe that words are meaningful, we would require proof. This would further strengthen us in our skepticism (and/or the belief that Chuang Tzu is provoking us towards adopting a skeptical attitude), because it is more difficult to supply proof than merely to question, as Watson translates. The original Chinese is compatible with either version, so it is impossible to make a decision on strictly philological grounds.[10]

On logical grounds, it is *per impossibile* for the correct interpretation to be that there is no difference between bird sounds and speech or we could not even understand what quandary was being raised in the first place. The very existence of the question as a question and not a string of nonsense syllables presupposes that the question is intelligible. The statement of the question as meaningful or, if you like, the statement of the two options as a meaningful choice, requires that the language of its formulation be significant. This *eo ipso* rules out one of the alternatives as logically possible. If the *Chuang-Tzu* is saying something else, as Graham's translation and commentary seems to suggest, then Chuang Chou must be speaking absolute nonsense; at the very least, his position is reducible to something as elementary and self-refuting as early Greek sophism.[11]

One could point as a defense of the skeptical thesis, to the passage which refers to the antinomical irresolution of the debates between the Confucians and the Mohists. However, in Watson's rendition, this passage would appear to be a reference to words which are not used substantively, and hence it would support the thesis that words, if used properly, do have a substance to them. In any event, the passage cannot be reduced simply to this historical reference. This traditional style of understanding much of the *Chuang-Tzu* as expounding historically existent philosophical debates has become *de rigueur* in existing commentaries on the *Chuang-Tzu*.[12] But the historical reference is incidental, as the solution posed is unworkable even in its own terms if considered as a mere historical reference. In Chuang Tzu's terms, if all language is relativistic then the attempt to conceive this as a description of the futility of debates between Mohists and Confucians is equally absurd. One cannot understand this as a depiction of the futility of arguments (whether historical or contemporary) unless the language that frames the question is something other than pure nonsense. We may now turn to the remaining section of the chirping of birds passage:

> What does the Way depend upon, that we have true and false? What do words rely upon, that we have right and wrong? How can the Way go away and not exist? How can words exist and not be acceptable? When the Way relies on little accomplishments and words rely on vain show, then we have the rights and wrongs of the Confucians and Mo-ists. What the one calls right the other calls wrong; what one calls wrong the other calls right. But if we want to right their wrongs and wrong their rights, then the best thing to use is clarity.[13]

If both Confucianists and Mohists are wrong, then speech must be significant in order to make sense out of the term 'wrongly'. If, as Graham argues, the *Chuang-Tzu* is asserting the position that "there is neither right nor wrong," then this is unstatable and incomprehensible; the words 'wrong' and 'right' would lose all of their meaning if words are truly no different from bird sounds.

So far, I have been arguing that there is strong logical proof that language cannot be identical to the chirping of birds. The question remains, can we find textual evidence to support my thesis that Chuang Tzu is saying that speech differs from birds sounds? In the remainder of this chapter, I would like to show that there is both indirect and direct evidence to suggest that Chuang Tzu intends a difference to be taken between words and wind.

The argument which I will call the argument from indirect textual evidence is based upon the general linguistic formulation of the question. While this argument is not by itself strongly convincing, it bears consideration. The general formulation of the question is rhetorical. A rhetorical question is one which we normally employ when we consider that the answer to our question is obvious and in the affirmative. For example, if I ask, "Am I Robert or not?" I expect that the answer to this question is that obviously I am. From the general formulation of the questions that Chuang Tzu poses, we can assume that he takes the answer to be both obvious and affirmative—that language does possess a meaning.

The argument which I will call the argument from direct textual evidence is stronger than the argument from indirect textual evidence. The strongest piece of direct textual evidence is exactly that, namely, any unqualified assertion of what one claims the author is asserting. The second strongest piece of direct textual evidence is what I call the appeal to general textual coherency. This is the appeal to attend to the beginning and ending phrases in a passage which contains phrases that seemingly contradict the direct textual evidence. The beginning phrases in a passage are taken to reflect the general intention of the author. The ending phrases in a passage are taken to reflect the general conclusion of the author. The test of textual coherency will be satisfied when the beginning and the ending phrases of a passage cohere in meaning with each other. The *Chuang-Tzu* satisfies the test of general textual coherency when it is applied either internally to the passage in question or externally with regard to the previous and subsequent passages to the passage in question. The seeming contradictoriness of phrases which do not cohere with the direct textual evidence or the intention or the conclusion of a passage in the text will be fully explained in later chapters in this volume.

It is not difficult to find a case of direct textual evidence in the case of the chirping of birds. The very first sentence in the passage in question will suffice:

Words are not just wind.[14]
The second sentence supplies us with another piece of direct textual evidence:

They have something to say.[15]

In Graham's version, the first two sentences also provide us with two pieces of direct textual evidence:

Saying is not blowing breath;
saying says something.[16]

I take it that here we possess two unqualified assertions that language is significant. This is direct textual evidence. It is all the more significant because these two cases of direct textual evidence also qualify as cases of indirect textual evidence and form part of an argument of general textual coherency. With respect to indirect textual evidence, I find it highly significant that within the chirping of the birds section these are the only two sentences that are formulated in the declarative mode. In other words, these are in fact the only two statements that are direct in the sense of being univocal and declarative. All the other sentences in the chirping of birds passage are formulated in the interrogative mode. From a sentence formulated interrogatively we cannot claim to have a univocal understanding of the beliefs held by the utterer of the question. However, from a sentence uttered in a declarative mode we can claim to have a univocal understanding of what the utterer is asserting. The two cases of direct textual evidence also qualify as indirect textual evidence in that their linguistic formulation counts as evidence of their intention.

In addition, these two leading sentences form a part of a general argument of textual coherency. We can read the beginning and the ending of the passage taken together (excepting the middle section):

Words are not just wind. They have something to say. . . . If we want to right their wrongs and wrong their rights, then the best thing to use is clarity.[17]

There is a congruence here between the initial assertion, which we are taking to reflect the general intention of the author, and the last assertion, which we are taking to reflect the conclusion of the author. The conclusion affirms the intention. If words have something to say, then clarity can penetrate to their meaning. (I am for the moment conflating the Mohist-Confucian controversy with the issue of linguistic significance for the sake of the discussion.) This holds true regardless of the particulars of the translation. We may also apply Wing-tsit Chan's translation:

But if we are to decide on their several affirmations and denials, there is nothing better than to employ the light of reason.[18]

The main point is that the beginning and the end of the passage cohere with each other. If speech is intelligible, then there is some purpose to be gained by relying upon rationality. If words were wind, there would be little point in turning to the light of reason to attempt to resolve whatever controversies seemed to crop up.

To broaden the argument from textual coherency, we may bring in textual evidence from the immediately preceding and the immediately following passages. In the preceding passage, it is claimed that one does have a teacher (one's own mind). Following Watson:

> If a man follows the mind given him and makes it his teacher, then who can be without a teacher?[19]

That one can have a teacher implies that there is something that can be taught and hence some kind of intelligible message. This is an outright rejection of the skeptical conclusion of a thoroughgoing relativism. Clearly, there must be a meaningful inner dialogue if one is able to learn from oneself. That there is something meaningful is the substance of the passage that immediately precedes the chirping of the birds passage. This predisposes the reader to anticipate that the next passage will carry on with the presupposition of intelligibility. We move immediately from the concept that there can be a teaching to the first sentence of the chirping of the birds section:

> Words are not just wind.[20]

And next to:

> They have something to say.[21]

The only subsequent demurral (following Watson) is that *if* what they have to say is not fixed, *then* they may say something or nothing. All that we can logically derive from the discussion thus far is that if words did have a fixed meaning, then the question of whether or not they possessed significance would not have arisen. It is the fact that words are used in different senses that gives rise to conflicts. If we examine the passage immediately subsequent to the passage in question we find that the sage sees what is worthwhile in each point of view.[22] From this we may gather that each point of view is a partial understanding of the truth. It cannot be that all points of view are false or else he could not see what is true in each of them. If we can see how in certain cases both views can be seen as right or even how both can be seen as wrong, then the views seen must possess intelligibility. This is not the same as saying that both views are right or that both are wrong. It is only to say that both can be seen as right or wrong depending upon the standpoint that we take. Neither does this imply that all standpoints are equally valid, as the thoroughgoing relativist must maintain. For him all standpoints are equally valid, for he has no grounds to recommend one standpoint as over against another. But the sage can and does see the truth. In Watson's formulation, the subsequent passage clarifies this attribute of the sage:

> Where there is recognition of right there must be recognition of wrong; where there is recognition of wrong there must be recognition of right. Therefore, the sage does not proceed in such a way, but illuminates all in the light of Heaven.[23]

A relativism that applies to all things cannot have recourse to any sort of an alternative since relativism *ex hypothesi* relativizes all choices. If there is something that can be illumined, then *ipso facto* there is something that is of value. But this passage contains no sort of relativism that equalizes and hence reduces all values to each other.

The co-recognition of right and wrong is not the same thing as a statement that all points of view are equally wrong. It also does not follow from the co-recognition of right and wrong that there is no such thing as right. What is being said is that we must go beyond conventional standards of right and wrong, but what we go to is a higher right. We are not transcending to nowhere, where all points of view including the transcendent one are on an equal plane. If this were the case, there would be no transcendence or going beyond. The metaphor of Heaven implies that one is utilizing some frame of reference that transcends the ordinary; in order to arrive at this frame of reference I take it that one transcends or goes beyond one's ordinary way of thinking. In any event, there must be some transcendence or going beyond. This is the case whether one chooses to employ the language of transcendence or "the light of Heaven." It comes to the same thing. If the light of Heaven were not a better thing, then Chuang Tzu could have easily chosen the expression, 'The Darkness of Earth' instead. It is plain that Chuang Tzu considers the way of the sage to be a better way. And this is not the standpoint of a consistent relativist.

The immediately prior and the immediately subsequent passages meet the test of textual coherency. The passage immediately prior concerns itself primarily with the concept of the teacher. The passage in question concerns itself primarily with the concept of the meaning of the message (or the possibility of there being a teaching). The immediately subsequent passage refers primarily to the mode in which the sage finds the right way. All three passages have to do with the possibility of right understanding: the possibility of there being a teacher, something that is taught, and the way of understanding. All three passages cohere with each other and presuppose the significance of speech.

In conclusion, there is strong textual evidence, of both indirect and direct kinds, that supports the general conclusion that language is significant. There is no direct statement from Chuang Tzu that language is different from the chirping of birds, but when he asserted that language is different from wind (or hot air in the contemporary parlance) he took it for granted that we would be able to infer that language was also different from the chirping of birds. I intend to enlarge upon that difference in subsequent chapters. Here I would argue both on logical grounds and on the basis of textual evidence that the thrust of his meaning is that words *are* different from the chirping of birds.

2 Myths and Monsters: On the Art of Metaphor

There is much more to be said on the subject of relativism, and it is a topic to which we will return in order to pursue our argument that Chuang Tzu was not a relativist. It is time now, however, to turn to the opposite side of the coin. If Chuang Tzu is not a relativist, then how are we to make sense out of his frequently appearing relativizing statements? Simply put, we can argue that Chuang Tzu is attempting to force the reader to disengage the conceptual or analytic powers of his or her mind. To put it this way, however, is not complete. To make the argument complete we must show how, specifically, the choice of linguistic and literary forms is designed to disengage the conceptual or analytic functions of the mind and at the same time to engage the intuitive or aesthetic functions of the mind. Otherwise, we are left with an irrational leap from the inadequacy of logic to the adequacy of action that is based on something we know not what. In this chapter, I hope to show how Chuang Tzu has selected certain linguistic and literary forms so as to still the analytic function of the mind while awakening the intuitive function. In short, we will be preparing the ground for showing that no non-cognitive logical quantum jump is required in order to go from a standpoint that holds all standpoints to be valueless to a valued standpoint. By understanding the proper function of relativizing statements we will be able to understand how Chuang Tzu can seemingly say that which cannot be said and at the same time can lead us in a certain valued direction. I will argue that certain semantic and literary forms are chosen not simply because they paralyze the analytical or conceptual mental functions, but also because they at the same time empower the intuitive or aesthetic cognitive functions.

Let us return briefly to the passage regarding the chirping of birds. One thing that strikes us very strongly about this passage is its form of placing two logical alternatives next to each other without making it very clear which of the two, if either, is to be preferred. The two logical options appear to cancel each other out. We have argued in the previous chapter that from both logical and textual standpoints, the two answers given cannot be of equal value. If this is correct, then the question we must now address is, why is it that the issue is posed in this seemingly paradoxical fashion?

What I would like to propose is that in the chirping of birds passage we have a microcosm of the argument structure of the *Chuang-Tzu*. I am using the phrase "argument structure" advisedly. Clearly, this is not a direct form of an argument intending to prove something or another. On the other hand, it is not (I claim) a non-cognitive stream of communication or a purely literary contrivance with no argument design. I use the phrase "argument structure" to call attention to the fact that certain semantic and literary forms are used precisely because they have the power to convince the intuitive or aesthetic dimension of the mind. In this sense, they function as arguments.

In the *Chuang-Tzu*, there is precious little that is stated directly or univocally to be true. I take this to be by design, not by accident. It does not follow that nothing is true or that there is no form of communicating what is taken to be true. All that we can infer logically is that if there is something that is true, what is true cannot be stated directly. Likewise, if there is something that is not true, what is not true cannot be stated directly. This is not because the *Chuang-Tzu* is a mystical text, whatever that means. The overall reason for this use of language is a strategic one. The general objective of the *Chuang-Tzu* is the self-transformation of the reader. In subsequent chapters, I will point to some evidence for this statement. At the moment, we must take it on faith. The mode of self-transformation with which the *Chuang-Tzu* is concerned is that of subjective apprehension; to put it in another way, the alteration of subjective apprehension is the pathway to subjective transformation. If putative truths or falsehoods were simply stated in literal, direct forms, the danger is that these would most likely be apprehended as intellectual claims. An intellectual claim or statement about what is or is not the case would be understood as a form of theoretical knowledge claim, to be tested by the kinds of tests intellectual theories are to be tested by (for example, whether they are consistent with known scientific facts, whether they meet certain empirical tests and so on). Chuang-Tzu does not wish his philosophy to be understood as a purely intellectual theory and thus resorts to linguistic formulations that resist any clear-cut theoretical paraphrase.

It is one thing to say that univocal paraphrases are avoided so as to restrict the dangers of understanding statements on a strictly theoretical plane and another to argue for the choice of the exact forms that are utilized as serving a special type of strategic function. In what follows, I would like to select out certain linguistic and literary forms in order to display their strategic cognitive functions. As a sample of strategies, I will concentrate on double-headed (both-sided) questions, myths, monsters, and metaphors.

I use the term double-headed to refer to interrogatives that pose opposite alternatives in a rhetorical form. We may refer to the chirping of the birds passage since it is so familiar to us by now.

In the first chapter we discussed the rhetorical form of the question in terms of its indirect mode of taking sides. While this is true enough, the explicit or obvious aspect to the two-sided question is that it is *not* taking sides. Not only is it not taking sides, but by posing both sides as supposedly equally valid possibilities the question allows neither side consideration as a legitimate possibility. If both sides of the question exhaust the logical possibilities and each side is posed as equipossible to the other side, then there seems to be no *logical* answer to the question. I emphasize the term 'logical' because in the first chapter I took great pains to indicate that I considered there to be a definite answer to the question. But by posing the question in the form that it is posed, the logical possibilities of an answer cancel each other out. That there is no logical answer does not mean that there is no answer; it also does not follow that the answer to the question is an *illogical* answer. What does follow is that whatever answer there is to the question will not follow logically from the posing of the question.

What results from the double-headed question is conceptual paralysis. As both sides of the question cancel each other out, there is no answer on the conceptual level, but it does not follow that there is no answer whatsoever. In fact, the form of the question already disposes the mind in one direction. However, at the same time, the conceptual faculty of the mind is frustrated in its endeavor to sort out the answer in a logical form.

What results then is not simply conceptual paralysis. At the same time there is a conceptual paralysis, some other part of the mind is intrigued by the question. What is important about the level of intrigue that is aroused is that it is revelatory of two presuppositions. First, that there is an intrigue or curiosity that is aroused suggests that all of our mental faculties cannot be considered inadequate to the answering of the question that is posed. Second, and closely related to this fact, is that if cognitive intrigue or curiosity is aroused, this suggests that there might exist some dimension of the mind which, if properly aroused, might be able not only to answer the question that is raised, but also to understand why the question is raised in such a paradoxical form.

The double-headed question is, I believe, the most explicit of the four literary forms which I will undertake to analyze in its ability

to address the intuitive mental capacity and at the same time to paralyze the analytic mental capacity. While all four forms have this two-
sided function, only the double-headed question performs this function
so explicitly.

The two sides to the question may be referred to two separate
cognitive functions: the analytic or conceptual function and the intuitive or aesthetic function.[1] If we like, we may think of these two functions as correlated with the current scientific concept that the brain is
divided into two hemispheres.[2] That the aesthetic side is cognitively
capable (which we will elaborate below) is the reason why we understand something by the double-sided question, although initially we
do not quite know what it is that we understand. The side of the
question that is negatively posed is the side that addresses the analytic
functioning of the mind; the side of the question that is affirmatively
posed is the side that addresses the intuitive functioning of the mind.
That the entire double-sided question is posed rhetorically and is
accompanied by both logical and textual evidence of an affirmative
answer is suggestive of the fact that the answer, as a whole, will ultimately be in the affirmative.

The posing of the question on two sides then is the posing of the
questions on two levels: the analytic and the aesthetic. The function of
the self-negating question is to negate on one level while affirming on
another level. The negating function of the question we may refer to
as an attempt to disassociate the analytic function. The analytic function is satisfied by a simple negation. However, when the negation is
accompanied by an opposite affirmation, the analytic function is
paralyzed: it is disassociated. The entire function of the paradoxical
interrogative is disassociative on the analytic side, while it is associative
on the aesthetic side. The analytic faculty does not know what to do.
Its ordinary logical grasp of the question has been rendered impotent.
The aesthetic faculty has been simultaneously aroused. It grasps something but it is not able to state what it grasps in words. That the question is poetically framed, in its comparison of language with the chirping
of birds, arouses the aesthetic function, which is charmed and attracted
by the poetic imagery. One side of the mind is made to feel helpless;
the other side of the mind is aroused to action. The total function of
the poetically framed paradox is to still one side of the mind while
arousing the other.

The comparison of language with the chirping of birds is not an
isolated example of poetic paradox. The text of the Chuang-Tzu is
replete with such examples. My argument is that such linguistic formulations are not semantic accidents. In fact, I believe that they represent an essential component of what I call the argument structure of

the *Chuang-Tzu*. In what follows, I would like to examine this claim in detail by examining other examples of poetic devices which are in fact lesser forms of poetic paradoxes. In turn, I will examine the case of myth, the case of the use of grotesque creatures or monsters, and the case of metaphor and analogy in general. The case of the double-headed question is really a form of word monster, the meaning of which should become clear in the sequel.

The Case of Myth

The use of myth is extremely apparent in the *Chuang-Tzu*. In fact, the very beginning of chapter one of the *Chuang-Tzu* begins with a myth or what we may consider to be a mythlike story. This provides an interesting contrast with Plato, who often ends his dialogues in myth or introduces myth in the middle of his dialogues. While the general function of the myth is quite similar, the technique of beginning with myth or the mythical form is more effective.[3]

Before we analyze the specific content of the myth, which is of crucial import for the thematic message of the *Chuang-Tzu*, it is useful to consider why the myth is placed at the beginning of the text. When we analyze the content of the myth later on, we shall see a convergence between the meaning of the myth and the structural use of the myth in the composition of the argument structure.

I submit that there are at least two strategic reasons for the placing of the myth at the very beginning of the *Chuang-Tzu*. First and most obviously, there is an implicit message to the reader that what is to be said cannot be said directly. So far, the myth has this strategy in common with the double-sided interrogative. But the second and more unique function of the myth is that what it has to say is very clearly to be understood as not literally true. While this is apparent in the case of the double-sided interrogative as well, it is more obvious in the case of myth, as myths are understood as untrue stories. On the other hand, while in its very essence the myth is literally untrue, it is always understood to possess some truth value on another level. The myth, like the double-sided question, affirms while it simultaneously denies. Its simultaneous affirmation and negation is not as explicit as that of the double-sided interrogative, but it functions cognitively in precisely the same way. Its major difference lies in the power of its affirmation quality, which is far more effective than that of the double-sided question.

Whenever the mind becomes aware that a myth is being told, the first response is the relaxation of the analytic faculty. So far, this is in common with the negative side of the double-headed question. But it is more precise in that it is implicit in the very nature of myth that the myth is not to be taken as literally true. The conceptual faculty of the mind is being told to take a holiday: it is not needed here; there is no need of any truth criteria to evaluate the truth claim of what is to be said. The myth is entirely outside of the realm of truth-telling. However, as we shall see below, this is not strictly true.

As the analytic function of the mind is stilled, another dimension of the mind is called into being: the mind of the child. The mind of the child is our initial acquaintance with the intuitive or aesthetic cognitive power of the mind. The child's mind is what is accustomed to hearing myths and stories. The child's mind is excited by the prospect of hearing a story. In an adult reader of a philosophical text, the child's mind is called into being. The myth, like the double sided question, serves a double function: it turns off the adult critical mind, but it does not turn the mind off altogether. It turns on and excites the child's mind and prepares it to enjoy and to understand in some special way what is to follow.

When we are children we are told stories which, while entertaining, we also know are not literally true. But what we also know is that these stories frequently have some important moral that they are exemplifying. As adults, we carry over to the myth the truth-bearing quality of the children's story. A myth can be understood as a children's story for adults. In addition, as adults we are accustomed to thinking that a myth carries with it some kind of truth value, the reason why it continues to exist as a myth, to be told and re-told. A myth, in short, is an adult story for an entire civilization.

What we have said so far is that the critical faculties of the mind are suspended in the myth-telling period. While the critical faculties of the mind are suspended, however, the mind does not cease to function completely. There is a willing suspension of disbelief while at the same time there is a reminder on a primordial level that something is to be communicated which possesses some very important cognitive import. The form of the myth presentation has the function of transmitting to the conceptual mind that it need not worry about what is to be said. But what is to be said will have significant cognitive import nevertheless.

We are now prepared to answer the question with which we began this section: why is the form of the myth employed at the very outset of the *Chuang-Tzu*? From the very beginning, we are informed that the message to follow is not to be understood as some kind of literal truth. At the same time, we are informed that what is to be said will possess a highly significant truth value. In addition, an extremely important clue has been given to us about how to grasp the truth value of what is to be communicated. In order to apprehend the truth value of what is to be communicated, the reader must suspend the ordinary critical faculties of the mind at the *beginning*. This does not mean that these critical faculties will remain in suspension throughout the entire reading of the *Chuang-Tzu*: but it is important that they be suspended at the outset of the reading. A very important demand has been placed upon the reader, but this demand also carries with it the implicit promise that if we suspend our analytic judgment, we will be rewarded by being given something which carries with it a higher truth. At the same time, we are instructed in the means of apprehension of this higher truth. We are being told that if we keep our child's mind, we may be able to understand something which we will not be able to understand if we attempt to immediately translate what we are being told into the categories of the critical intellect.

In short, when myth is placed at the beginning of the text, the implicit message is that understanding must take place on a different level than through a customary reliance upon the conceptual intellect. By calling this other dimension of understanding into existence at the very outset of the book, the *Chuang-Tzu* comes out very strongly in favor of the primacy of the aesthetic mode of apprehension.

The use of myth, like the use of other literary devices which we will examine below, is not for the sake of literary indulgence. To pay little attention to the presentation vehicle of the content places us under severe danger of not understanding much of what is to follow. If we brush aside the literary beginnings to "get to the meat of the text" we will never find the meat. Or, if we do, we will have no capacity for recognizing it when we do or for being able to digest it and assimilate its nutritive value.

In nearly all important commentaries on the *Chuang-Tzu*, it has been customary to begin the important discussion of the *Chuang-Tzu* with chapter two. But by so doing we approach the text with one mental hand tied behind our backs. By understanding the significance of beginning where Chuang-Tzu in fact begins, we understand something of crucial importance: we now realize that whatever is to be understood must be understood in a different way than we normally attempt to understand. We are being asked to learn how to cognize preconceptually. While the myth cannot explain how we are to do this, it is plainly an invitation to try. In that which follows, I hope to make it very evident how the engaging of the aesthetic or preconceptual mind is a precondition for the proper understanding of the message of the *Chuang-Tzu*.

By implication, when we begin with the myth we are also being told something else. We are being told that there is a fundamental and inherent connection between our mode of understanding of the *Chuang-Tzu* and the message that is to be gleaned from the *Chuang-Tzu*. By explicitly placing the myth at the beginning, Chuang-Tzu stresses the connection between the literary form of the text and the content. When we begin to read we immediately search for the content, but here we are given the form instead. While the form may be reflective of the content (as we will discuss below), what is important about its placement is that it calls attention to itself. There is an adumbration of what I will argue to be the central objective of the *Chuang-Tzu*: there is a condition for understanding and that condition is the alteration of our mode of apprehension. In fact, the proper alteration of our understanding is the message of the *Chuang-Tzu*. This precondition will become explicitly worked out in the second chapter of the *Chuang-Tzu*. It is foreshadowed here in the literary choice of a starting point. The total merging of form and content will become more evident by the end of chapter two of the *Chuang-Tzu*.

At the beginning of the *Chuang-Tzu* we are being invited to practice what is, if you like, the theoretical aim of the text as a whole. The fundamental objective of the *Chuang-Tzu* lies in the area of self-transformation: we must ultimately transform our understanding. Of course, this cannot be done at once. It can only be the result of a process of following several stages. However, the end result, if the text is successful, will be dramatic. Here, at the start, the dramatic transformation is well foreshadowed. We must switch from the adult reader's critical stance to the childlike openness which is characteristic of the reader of or the listener to myth. We know that what we are about to be told is something that is not true in the ordinary sense in which we use that word, but we also know that it is intended to be true in some extraordinary sense. We know what we are to be told is not to be taken as totally false or meaningless. We are being mentally prepared for that eventual insight into the truth that all myths promise.

The starting point thus is extremely informative as a means of teaching us how to read the text that will follow. We know that the intention of the text is to relate that which is no ordinary truth. We know that what is to follow cannot be understood on the level of literal truth. But we also know that, just as our stories of childhood contained some important truth function, this adult story presages some important truth that is intended for the adult child's mind.

In technical language, the paradoxical double-headed interrogative is disassociative analytically while it is associative aesthetically. The technical designation of the mythical form is also disassociative-associative. However, the mythical form accomplishes its disassociation and association in a different way and also adds in a new element. It accomplishes its disassociation through its form of disengaging the analytic function. The analytic function is thus completely disassociated. Simultaneously, the aesthetic function is associated through its linkage with the mind of the child. The difference here is that the positive association is more strongly present than it is in the case of the double-headed question. It is more strongly present in that our mind is more prepared to assimilate some form of truth, and it knows that that assimilation will be intimately connected with the child's form of apprehension. We can call this added element the factor of gaining rapport with the child's mind. The complete technical designation for the mythical form is thus disassociation-association and the gaining of rapport.

To this we may add one final element in terms of the strategy of mythical formulation. Because the myth is placed at the very beginning of the book, not only is the child's mind engaged, but at the same time our normal reading pattern is interrupted. When we begin to read a philosophic text, we conventionally begin with a critical mind set. Another facet of disassociating this analytical tendency is its disassociation in the very first sentence of the text. Thus, not only is our mind being keyed to an attunement with a different mode of understanding, but our reading pattern as philosophical readers has been totally disrupted.

This final element of pattern interruption may not seem very different from the strategy of analytical disassociation, but its significance resides in its placement at the beginning. Our entire conscious set is interrupted. In terms of formal elements, this has a special significance. When we read entire works, we are accustomed to read in a certain pattern. Our custom in reading philosophical works is to read in a pattern involving the analytical powers of the mind as our primary vantage point. What we are being made to realize when myth is placed at the beginning is that our typical reading pattern is to be disrupted. We are being asked to read a philosophical text in a new way.

Our typical conscious pattern has been deflected. We are left disoriented, but we are not left without any pattern at all. We are left with the primordial pattern of myth. The entire text of the *Chuang-Tzu* is to be understood as a special kind of myth. The pattern of myth is one in which things are not either true or false in an ordinary sense; issues of truth and falsity are for the moment suspended. But it does not follow from this that the world of myth is a totally irrelevant world. It is a world in which we are magically ready to change our consciousness and, in fact, *in our readiness to understand this world, we have already changed our consciousness*. Our very anticipation of a change is the beginning of that change.

The formal disruption of our reading pattern has already changed our expectations. We do not yet know what it is that we can take to be true, but we do know that there is some truth that is to be communicated. The mythical starting point is a powerful starting point, for if we grasp its import we anticipate a level of truth that we know cannot be understood in a non-mythical form. Otherwise, there would have been no point in beginning with a myth in the first place.

The myth is the fundamental archetype in our discussion of the trilogy of myth, monsters, and metaphors. The understanding of the function of myth is an excellent preparation for the understanding of the function of the use of grotesque characters (monsters) and the use of metaphors or analogies in general. With the myth, the child's mind has been triggered. Just as the child's mind is opened wide when it hears the story form, "Once upon a time . . . ," the form of the myth is a trigger to open the adult mind to a special form of communication. To put it in prosaic terms, with the appearance of the form of myth the receptivity of the mind is fostered. The use of the myth is a subliminal or unconscious trigger to remind the adult of the receptivity he or she possessed as a child. In a philosophical context, the use of the myth as a strategic device opens the philosophical mind to the possibility that what is to follow is something that will be true in some special sense.

What the text will put forward as a philosophical truth is not something that is to be grasped at one go. The use of the myth at the beginning is a reminder to the adult reader that some preparation is needed before one can possibly hope to approach and assimilate the putative truth message. When we read a myth as adults, we cannot forget the fact that what we are reading is, after all, only a myth. However, we also realize that the form of the myth was indispensable for the growth of the mind of the child. We realize that as children we required some fictional form in order to arrive at some higher level of truth. We realize in retrospect that a fiction had to be told to us which we were to take as in some sense true in order to arrive at a level of understanding which we could, properly speaking, only possess when we became adults. As adults we can refer to childhood stories as myths or fables, but when we do so we also retrospectively recognize them as indispensable cognitive and pedagogical devices.

In precisely the same sense, our mind is thus being prepared for the promised higher message or philosophy of the Chuang-Tzu. After all, we are presupposing that we are reading philosophy and not escapist literature or children's stories. As philosophic readers, we expect that the form of what we are reading will play a systematic role in our understanding of the content. The myths and fairy tales we were told as children contradicted the facts that were around us. However, we accepted these myths and fairy tales as somehow important for the understanding of the world. The provisional acceptance of these contradictions required a special act of understanding in us even as children. In a work for adults, we are again being asked to provisionally accept on some level the truth value of that which contradicts our conventional standards of truth. We understand now, as adults, that we can discard the stories of childhood, but we also understand that they will always be necessary for the child's mind.

As adults reading myths, we read with the understanding that we are being told a story that will be told to us as true, but which we will later discard at a certain stage in our development. As adult readers of the *Chuang-Tzu*, we read the text as if we were philosophic children. We read the *Chuang-Tzu* with the tacit understanding that the truth is developmental and that we will come to it only in stages. We can thus consider the beginning of the *Chuang-Tzu* a *necessary fiction*.

The full meaning of the necessary fiction can only be understood in the sequel. To anticipate very briefly, as we read through the text of the *Chuang-Tzu* we will find that certain goals are posited, for example the goal of freedom or transcendence, that will be set forth as desired objectives for us to reach. But at a later stage in the *Chuang-Tzu* we will be told that we cannot strive to reach such goals. What we were told initially, that there was a goal to reach, will be revealed later on to be a fiction. But it will also be revealed as a necessary fiction, to prepare us for the state of realizing that there is no way in which we can strive to reach such a goal.

But this is to anticipate much of the argument that is to follow. Suffice it to say for the moment that our remembrance of our own development prepares us for the *Chuang-Tzu*, and the *Chuang-Tzu* in turn prepares us for philosophical development. The *Chuang-Tzu* begins with the form of the myth to prepare us for the journey of the mind, while at the same time it reminds us to be prepared for the understanding that whatever is to be said has but a provisional character to it which nonetheless includes the ultimacy of myth and metaphor in the making of philosophical understanding.

Metaphors and Analogies

As in the case of myth, the use of metaphors and analogies in the *Chuang-Tzu* is not an idle literary quirk of the text. In order to make the case more plain, I will subsume the case of analogies under the case of metaphor. In the case of a metaphor, what is stated is not something that has a univocal meaning, but it is not something stated that has no meaning at all. It is in the very fact that metaphors do not say exactly what is to be said that the conceptual mind is stymied in its effort to reduce the metaphorical equivalence to a univocal concept. On the other hand, something is definitely understood when one grasps the metaphorical equivalence. It is only that this grasping cannot be rendered in a prose reduction.

The metaphor then is a reduced myth or, if you like, a reduced double-headed interrogative. It differs from the double-headed interrogative in that its attempt to baffle the conceptual mind is not as blatant. The metaphor is a more acceptable version of disassociating the analytic mind. It is like the myth in that we are prepared in the case of metaphor to receive some truth content. It is weaker than the myth in that we do not as readily assume that any metaphor will possess some necessary truth value. On the other hand, it does possess an efficacy that the myth cannot possess for the highly resistant reader, who may not be willing to entertain the putative truth value or pedagogical function of the myth. The highly resistant reader may, however, be prepared to accept the possibility that a metaphorical equivalence may possess a truth value. The metaphor, then, is a second order myth for adults. Its advantage over the double-headed question is that its form is not necessarily paradoxical. Its disadvantage is that because it is more common it is more likely to be overlooked. Its advantage over the myth is that it may appeal to a more resistant reader. Its disadvantage is that it does not possess the same level of appeal to the child's receptivity to the possible truth value. It does, however, have an appeal to the intellectual reader who may be willing to consider the latent truth value that is contained in a metaphor or analogy. For this reason, metaphors and analogies abound in the text of the Chuang-Tzu.

As in the case of the myth or the double-headed question, if metaphor possesses some cognitive significance which cannot be put into a prose paraphrase, then the faculty of the mind which is being engaged is the preconceptual or aesthetic faculty. The engagement of the preconceptual or aesthetic faculty is more widely accepted in the case of metaphor than it has been in the case of myth or double-headed interrogatives (where it has not been understood at all). We often depict the direct assimilation of content in the case of metaphor as a pictorial understanding. While this may not be considered to be understanding on the level of concepts (as in the case of Hegel's differentiation) it nonetheless must be considered to be some form of cognition. While some might argue that the double-headed question or perhaps the myth involves no cognitive apprehension, I believe that most would agree that the understanding of a metaphor is certainly a cognitive act. Popularly, in Western philosophy, such a mode of understanding has been denigrated as a level of apprehension that is below the level of abstract understanding. The tradition of Plato, Kant and Hegel has been enormously influential in the West in terms of considering metaphorical understanding to be inferior to conceptual understanding.

The key issue here, however, is not the respective inferiority or superiority of metaphorical and conceptual understanding. What is important to note is the particularities of the act of metaphorical understanding. One feature of the aesthetic grasping of an idea is that the idea is grasped as a whole rather than as a part. Whether or not the idea can be rendered choate in terms of analytical concepts is not the point. If it could, presumably the metaphor would have no unique cognitive function at all. All that is needed for us to be willing to analyze the cognitive import of a metaphor is the recognition that some level of cognition is required, not that the same kind of cognition is present as is present in the act of understanding abstract concepts.

In terms of the *Chuang-Tzu*, the subliminal implication of the use of metaphor is that what is to be understood is to be understood not by the abstract intellect alone, but as a whole. In Hegelian terms, the idea is that the mind is simply able to see a picture. But the point here is that a picture is a pictorial representation of a whole, whereas an abstract concept is by definition only an abstracted part. The strategy behind the use of metaphor in the *Chuang-Tzu* is that the mind is being accustomed to see in pictures in order to engage its intuitive and holistic cognitive powers. If one considers the cognitive apprehension in the case of metaphor to be a microcosm of philosophical understanding for the message of the *Chuang-Tzu* as a whole, the use of metaphor can be seen as a preparation for holistic understanding. Just as in the case of the understanding of any particular metaphor, the cognitive act is a holistic grasp; if one wishes to cognize the message of the *Chuang-Tzu*, a holistic cognitive act will be required.

The use of metaphor is not, of course, unique to the *Chuang-Tzu*. What is fairly unique to the *Chuang-Tzu* is the predominance and the prevalence of the use of metaphor. We could, in fact, make a serious case for what we could call the metaphorical order of arguments in the *Chuang-Tzu*. The *Chuang-Tzu* is not presented in a clear-cut, linear form. This is not to say that it is not systematically presented. It is only to say that Chuang Tzu did not think that philosophical understanding could be obtained through communicating in linear argument forms. The use of a metaphorical order of arguments is itself an exercise in pattern interruption.[4]

To restrict our discussion to the use of metaphor in the first place requires our understanding that metaphors do not function as *explanations*. While it cannot be denied that the grasping of a metaphor involves a cognitive act of apprehension, what is important to note is that the cognitive level of apprehension is one of *understanding*, not explanation. If what is understood cannot be explained in terms of the analytical understanding, it does not follow that nothing has been understood. If we could translate a metaphor into a literal prose paraphrase without any cognitive remainder, we could then say that we have understood a metaphor through a conceptual or second-level order of processing. If, however, we cannot translate a metaphor into a literal prose paraphrase without a residue that cannot be conceptually understood, and we still understand something by that metaphor, then we can say that a metaphor is intelligible on a preconceptual level. If we are willing to grant that a metaphor can be understood although it cannot be translated completely into a prose equivalent, then we are saying that a metaphor can be cognized by a primary cognitive process.

What we are saying here is not terribly different from what we were saying earlier in terms of the understanding of a myth. In the case of a myth we know immediately that what is to be communicated is not "serious." In the case of the myth we have immediate access to the child's mental processing. This in fact is the way in which the myth possesses cognitive access. In the case of the metaphor, the adult mind also possesses an ingress to the *cognoscendum*. However, when the adult mind presses for an explanation of what has been cognized, no cognitive satisfaction can be obtained. In the case of metaphor the access to the primary cognitive process is visual, but the visual cannot be translated without remainder into concepts. While a metaphor requires an act of cognitive apprehension, this grasping of the meaning of a metaphor cannot be translated in cognitive equivalence into analytic concepts. What is lost in the attempt to provide a literal prose paraphrase for the metaphorical equivalence is precisely the *understanding* that occurs as a result of the apprehension of the meaning of the metaphor in the moment of grasping the metaphor. The understanding of the metaphor (which is shorthand for saying the understanding of the meaning of the metaphor) is a result of the engagement of the holistic or the intuitive cognitive capacity. When there is an attempt to reduce this understanding to a prose counterpart, the analytic or conceptual cognitive capacity is engaged. This analytic capacity is satisfied by explanations which correspond to known definitions or scientific evidence. The metaphor by itself provides no explanations. But it does not follow from this that the metaphor is a non-cognitive device or that its cognitive component can be encapsulated in a prose equivalent. The understanding that occurs in the apprehension of a metaphor, including a visual metaphor, is not visual. This is deceptive since the form of a metaphor is so often, although not always, visual. (A pun, for example, is a metaphor of sound). What the understanding of all metaphors has in common with the notion of pictorial understanding is that all metaphors, like pictures, must be grasped as a whole. It is the holistic comprehension which is required in order to cognize a metaphorical equivalence.

The importance of the holistic understanding cannot be overemphasized for the *Chuang-Tzu*. The overabundant use of metaphor is a significant clue to the importance of the holistic or intuitive capacity of comprehension in preparing the subject reader to assimilate the overall message of the *Chuang-Tzu*. That overall message, as we have suggested, has to do with the self-transformation of the reader. This is a topic which we will discuss in detail in ensuing chapters. For the present, I would only like to emphasize the significance of the strategic use of metaphor in bringing into play the appropriate cognitive capacity of the reader that will be required in order that the message of the *Chuang-Tzu* be transmitted.

If Chuang Tzu were to propose conceptual constructs alone, these could easily be debated on the level of concepts. By giving us metaphors, he provides an implicit warning that the message of the *Chuang-Tzu* is something that cannot be translated into analytic concepts without remainder. It does not follow that the message of the *Chuang-Tzu* is wholly transcendent. If it were wholly transcendent, we would not have the *Chuang-Tzu* at all.

Since we do have the *Chuang-Tzu*, we must understand it on its own terms. If we could translate the metaphor into a prose commentary, there would be no need for the *Chuang-Tzu*. If we cannot translate the metaphor into a literal prose commentary without losing an essential element of understanding, then we can say that the metaphor is intelligible on a pre-conceptual level or a level of understanding we can call a primary cognitive processing level.

As we have noted above, the access to the primary cognitive process has already been presaged in the use of myth. The myth is in fact the archetypical metaphor. Paradox, which we shall discuss in later chapters, is also a species of metaphor. What we shall discuss below is the use of the non-verbal metaphor which we have labeled "the use of monsters." Paradox can be seen as a verbal monster.

Monsters

We shall conclude this chapter with a brief discussion of the use of grotesque creatures as images or as interlocutors in the course of the *Chuang-Tzu*. The use of the term 'monster' is hyperbolic: many mythical creatures in the *Chuang-Tzu* (such as the great bird or the great fish of chapter one) are monstrous in that they are not natural (even if they are not frightening). The use of monsters is another case of the use of metaphors; it deserves special consideration, however, because of its unique cognitive function.

The use of the monster has two forms: one is in the form of the subject of the narrative; one is in the form of the narrator. At the very beginning of the *Chuang-Tzu*, two monsters are utilized as the subjects of the narrative in the telling of the myth: the great bird and the great fish. One immediately apparent feature of these monsters is that they are very easily visualized. This visual feature is something that these monsters will share with the narrator monsters that are employed later on.

The cognitive function of the image is that it is eidetic. It is seen immediately. The immediate pictorial representation of an image is cognitively like the "I see" of immediate apprehension. The clue that is planted at the very beginning of the *Chuang-Tzu* is that understanding the content of the *Chuang-Tzu* will be very much like seeing the picture images that are the subjects of the narrative.

When we encounter the monster as narrator, we come across a device which is similar to the double-headed interrogative. Our normal expectations of a philosophical interlocutor are shattered. Instead of a respected figure we are given important truths by old women, cripples, and even robbers. What happens is very much like what happens in the case of the double-headed question. Our analytic expectations are paralyzed. What is about to be said to us is not something that we will take seriously. On the other hand, the content of what is said is very serious and often very profound— even if it is put in a humorous way. While our conceptual mind cannot take it seriously, our intuitive mind cannot help but pay attention to what is being said. The content speaks for itself. In the moment of cancelling the analytic expectation, the content is given to the intuitive cognitive capacity. Unlike the double-headed question, we are (at least sometimes) quite certain of the meaning of what is imparted. What we are not certain of is how are we to take that meaning. All that we can be sure of is that we are not to take the meaning in our customary way. The meaning itself is not ambiguous; what ambiguity might exist is not intrinsic to the form of the presentation. In some cases the meaning might itself be difficult to grasp, but this has to do with the content of the meaning, not its form of presentation. In terms of the form of the presentation, the puzzling aspect lies solely in the message-bearer itself. The message-bearer shocks and upsets the conceptual faculty, but this prepares the mind for the appropriate assimilation of the message content. The message content is to be understood by the side of the mind that has been left undiminished in the cancellation of the analytic cognition.

But the intuitive or holistic understanding has not been left untouched; it has been engaged. The use of the monster as narrator has already engaged the intuitive side of the mind so that it is directly prepared for the apprehension of the content. The monster is a rich metaphor for it opens the mind for metaphorical understanding at the same time as it presents itself as a metaphor.

The monster as metaphor is like an expected interlocutor but unlike an expected interlocutor. In the use of the monster we do have an interlocutor or narrator. As there is a narrator function, we do expect that there will be a message that is to be transmitted. This is the likeness of the monster to the conventional narrator. The unlikeness is that the monster is an unexpected narrator. Thus the expectation that something serious will follow is interrupted; the use of monster as narrator is also a form of pattern interruption.

What is especially valuable about the monster is that the pattern is interrupted at precisely the same moment that the message is delivered. The association of the mind with the content of the message is complete. The mind is capable of grasping the message in its entirety because the conceptual barriers have been breached. The use of the monster as message-deliverer is a powerful affirmation of the intuitive cognitive capacity.

3 The Content of the Myth

Up until now, we have been preoccupied with the formal structural elements and the role they play in cognition. I would like to refer now to the content of the mythical subject matter.[1] Of necessity, this is but a selection from the abundance of mythical materials presented in the Chuang-Tzu. I would like to focus on the beginning of chapter one of the Chuang-Tzu because I believe that the choice of mythical subjects for treatment at the beginning of the text has powerful implications for the message of the text as a whole. I do not believe that the mythical creatures selected are selected at random. For the purposes of this chapter, I will intermesh mythical creatures with the use of small mammals, although the points made with each differ respectively. The thesis which I will be exploring in this chapter is that the selection of mythical materials has to do with the overall aim or goal of the Chuang-Tzu. The selection of small mammals and insects relates to the position the Chuang-Tzu will take on the question of valuation. Thus the selection of story materials has to do with both the overall message of the Chuang-Tzu and the correct understanding of the issue of valuation. My selection among the materials that abound both in chapter one of the Chuang-Tzu and the text as a whole is bound to emphasize a certain point of view and to exclude some other points of view. But I believe that the selection fairly represents the most essential or core component of the meaning structure of the Chuang-Tzu.

The central objective of the Chuang-Tzu is self-transformation. In the first two chapters I have alluded to this goal, and in this chapter I will set out the mythical materials that symbolize its attainment. In the following chapters, I will produce textual evidence and logical argumentation to support the claim that the central objective of the Chuang-Tzu is one of self-transformation on the part of the subject reader. In this chapter I will be calling attention to the fact that the Chuang-Tzu begins with a story of transformation in a mythical form, a fact that deserves our special attention.

The Great Fish and the Big Bird

The central and beginning myth of the *Chuang-Tzu* is the story of a great fish that changes and becomes a bird.[2] Like Genesis there are two accounts of the central myth, but the first version is, to my thinking, the most important one. The two versions differ in that the first version makes explicit reference to the theme of transformation. The second version differs significantly in that the fish and the bird are treated as two separate creatures. I cannot account for the discrepancy, and I can only think that the second version is possibly in some way spurious and the result of later editing.[3] While no one, to my knowledge, has drawn attention to the two versions of the myth, I think that the first is preferable in that it embodies the central theme that is at the core of the *Chuang-Tzu*.

In Watson's translation, the *Chuang-Tzu* begins with the mythical story:

> In the Northern Darkness there is a fish and his name is K'un. The K'un is so huge I don't know how many thousand li he measures. He *changes* and becomes a bird whose name is P'eng. The back of P'eng measures I don't know how many thousand li across and, when he rises up and flies off, his wings are like clouds all over the sky. When the sea begins to move, this bird sets off for the southern darkness, which is the lake of Heaven.[4]

That this is a myth is clear from both the name of the habitat of the fish (the Northern Darkness) and the destination of the bird (the Lake of Heaven). It is also clear from the fact that the size of the creatures contradicts known scientific possibility, and even more from the fact that the fish changes into a bird, which is counter to fact.

The *Chuang-Tzu* does not begin by telling us that it is a philosophical treatise which will have as its main theme the subject of transformation. In fact, the message is veiled so subtly in the substance of the story that most commentators have failed to pick it up at all. But the message is there for all that, intertwined within the story so that the reader can at most expect to understand it symbolically. But the myth does not simply function as a symbolic message. It embodies the message so subtly precisely because the author does not intend for us to analytically comprehend the point of the story. The mythical content of the story operates on the preconceptual level so that it can be appropriated by the intuitive function.

The elements of the story tell us that we begin in darkness. The presence of darkness at the beginning is indicative of the epistemological starting point. We do not begin with any preconceptions or conceptions.

If we begin with preconceptions or conceptions we are most likely not going to be able to follow the point of the story in the proper sequence.

In the middle of the story the fish transforms itself into a bird. I do not believe that the animals are casually chosen. The idea of beginning with a fish possesses significance. A fish symbolizes a creature that can be caught. As the fish is introduced at the very beginning, we may easily recognize the fish to stand for the subject reader. The fish, like ourselves, is living in darkness or, epistemologically speaking, in ignorance. The fish, however, possesses the capacity within itself to transform itself into another creature. The creature chosen to stand for the transformed creature is a bird. This, too, is no literary accident. A bird symbolizes a creature that we associate with freedom and transcendence. The thematic message is that a transformation to knowledge is an inner possibility that lies within all of us, and the result of that transformation is the attainment of freedom. It is also the attainment of happiness, as is symbolized by the choice of destination—the Lake of Heaven. So much has already been told to us about the entire message of the *Chuang-Tzu* in just this mythical starting point alone! The idea is to catch the unwary or ignorant reader, to teach us that the capacity for self-transformation lies within us, and that the outcome of this is the attainment of freedom and happiness.

While I may be accused of reading too much into this story, I think it may be well noted that the fish does not require any outside agency to transform itself into the bird. It accomplishes this all on its own. A reader whose cognitive capacities have been both stilled and awakened by the form of the myth will apprehend on some level the message contained in the myth. The myth, of course, is not the whole argument of the *Chuang-Tzu*. Suffice it to say that it is coherent with the central message of the *Chuang-Tzu* as will be elaborated in the following chapter. It is remarkable in that it is a microcosm of the argument structure of the *Chuang-Tzu* as a whole and it is, in my view, no accident that it is offered at the very beginning. The beginning of any book or story is normally a hook to catch the reader's attention. This hook already contains the fish as well!

The Cicada and the Little Bird

I would now like to turn to the reaction to this story, which is the very next set of stories in the *Chuang-Tzu*. The immediate reaction to this story is given by the cicada and the little dove or quail.[5] The reaction of the cicada and the little dove is to laugh at the big bird, P'eng. They do not believe that the big bird can travel so far. (It is said that he can travel for ninety thousand li.)[6] The cicada and the little bird are skeptics. They are the first exemplars of the Philistines or the literal and petty minded of the world. The first reaction of the petty minded is that such a myth as has been presented is a bunch of poppycock. Chuang Tzu knows that the reader's first reaction (of his conceptual mind, which reacts while his intuitive mind has assimilated the content of the myth on a subliminal level) is one of skepticism and disbelief. What is interesting to note is that what the cicada and the little bird are skeptical of is *how* the big bird can make such a journey. They are not skeptical of the putative existence of such creatures *per se*. They are skeptical of the possibility of the journey of transformation. In Watson's translation:

> The cicada and the little dove laugh at this, saying, "When we make an effort and fly up, we can get as far as the elm or the sapanwood tree, but sometimes we don't make it and just fall down on the ground. Now how is anyone going to go ninety thousand li to the south!"[7]

The cicada and the little bird are applying the laws of common sense or scientific truth to the possibility of the myth. This is more evident from the passage that follows:

> If you are going a hundred li, you must grind your grain the night before; and if you are going a thousand li, you must start getting the provisions together three months in advance.[8]

In the world of empirical fact, the story of the big bird P'eng is utter nonsense. If we use the standards of common sense then all of this talk about transformation is utter nonsense.

But what is important is the position that the *Chuang-Tzu* takes with respect to this issue. The *Chuang-Tzu* does not state that both of these viewpoints (that of myth and that of common sense) are of equal value. Early on in the *Chuang-Tzu*, a definite stand is taken with respect to the question of valuation. It is very clear and very explicit that the standpoint of the big bird and the standpoint of the cicada and the dove are not seen as possessing equal value. The immediate reaction of the *Chuang-Tzu* to the objections of the cicada and the little bird is one of disvaluation:

> What do these two creatures understand? Little understanding cannot come up to great understanding; the short-lived cannot come up to the long-lived.[9]

It is important to note not only that Chuang Tzu has stated explicitly that the viewpoint of these two creatures reflects a narrow mind, but that his choice of little creatures in the first place (one of which is an insect) has already told us this.[10] Chuang Tzu does *not* present the viewpoints of the cicada and the small bird as being on the same axiological plane as the viewpoint represented by the big bird P'eng. The cicada and the small bird are plainly portrayed as lacking a scope of vision and are in this respect contrasted with the big bird. They possess little understanding. Retrospectively, then, the big bird has been portrayed as possessing Great Understanding. It is evident that the standpoint of the big bird is a preferential standpoint. This is important to note at the outset of the *Chuang-Tzu*, for early in the first chapter of the book Chuang Tzu is sounding the theme that certain perspectives are of higher value than other perspectives. The perspectives of the big bird and those of the cicada and the small bird are not treated as being of axiological equality.

We may also take note of the fact that a distinction has been introduced between different levels of understanding. If we insist upon relying upon the conventional empirical standards of the world, we will not be able to measure or effectively comprehend the level of understanding at which the *Chuang-Tzu* aims. Chuang Tzu does not, of course, set this out in prose. He is not interested in arguing on a conceptual plane for the superiority of a certain level of understanding. However, he has effectively prepared the mind to acknowledge the possibility, which at this point is only a possibility, that there is a level of understanding that differs from the ordinary level of understanding. We can see the small bird and the insect as the cynics who laugh at the efforts of the enlightened man to transform himself to attain to the Heavenly Tao.

In the first two chapters I have treated the question of why Chuang Tzu does not state his message explicitly. All that is related here is a story about birds and fish and insects. But I have argued that this is not a mere literary convention; it possesses too much indirect content to be only poetic indulgence. As the narrative begins in myth and moves to a more storylike form, it is too fanciful and too fabulous to have a mere historical reference. It seems to me that it most definitely serves an epistemological function.

To abbreviate what we have said about the formal function of myth and story in the previous chapters, a twofold epistemological function is served. First, the conscious mind that applies empirical standards of judgment is lulled into rest by the mythical form. There is a suspension of the critical faculty, as this is plainly a story which need not be tested for its truth value. In the act of suspension, the mind does not become cognitively void. It has switched off its reality testing. After all, fish do not really change into birds and birds cannot really fly ninety thousand li; furthermore, cicadas and doves do not talk. On the other hand, the material presented is taken in, unjudged, and believed in, in a certain, special sense. Does anyone doubt that what is said to happen in a myth really does happen in the myth?

The absence of the application of conventional standards of truth does not imply that the story will be taken as absolute nonsense (except by those who are said to lack the appropriate understanding). There is truth value in the story, but it cannot be measured by convention. How then is it understood? First of all, it is *absorbed*. It is not negated or erased, but is taken in by the mind on some level. Such a preparation by absorption is a propaedeutic for the taking in of materials or insights which from ordinary standards might stretch one's credulity to the breaking point. These materials, which will be introduced later but which have already been presaged by the myth, are insights which will be of such a nature as to be magical. What I mean by calling them magical is that they will appear to defy ordinary truth standards when such standards are applied by plebian minds. They will also be extraordinary because they will be transforming. And finally, to answer to the highest sense of the word 'magic', just as the magic of myth appeals to our deepest hopes and wishes, these insights will in some way answer the highest questions of life and provide a fulfillment to our most secret and important wishes and desires.

If we take this understanding of myth, which here specifically refers to transformation, and couple it with the formal aspect of myth we have introduced earlier, we will have a fairly full picture of the epistemological function of the myth. First, understanding myth as a type of metaphor (which in the last chapter we called the archetypical metaphor), the myth trades on the cognitive intelligibility of metaphor in general. It presents an idea or a set of ideas which can only be grasped by a total act of cognition. What this means is that part of the mind (here in content labeled as the skeptical understanding) cannot stand back and evaluate while the rest of the mind partakes of the idea. If it does so, the mind as a whole cannot partake of the idea. While the idea is apprehended in either mythical form or the form of fable, it is being apprehended in a pictorial representation. A pictorial representation must be grasped as a whole. In addition, the pictorial representation here is in the form of a child's story that must be believed in implicitly: it is taken in completely or not at all. (No one questions whether the Trojan horse could really hold so many Achaeans!) The total absorption of the idea is a mental preparation for the later transmission of philosophical ideas which also will seem to be ludicrous when evaluated from the common standpoint. These ideas, some of which are already embodied in the content of the myth, will be ideas which will be extraordinary, transformatory, and in some sense will answer to our most important hopes and wishes.

If what I have said so far is correct, then the mythical presentation is of enormous cognitive significance. What is being accomplished
is not the mere telling of a story. It is the preparation of the reader's
mind for a mental journey of transformation. If we can accept such a
possibility on the level of myth then, in some sense yet to be understood, the mind is readied to accept as possible some ideas on a higher
plane of philosophy. The mythical origins of the *Chuang-Tzu*, then,
are a cognitive technology which simultaneously gives us a message
and informs us (if we know where to look) how this message is given,
much like a watch the inner springs of which are left open to the eye to
inspect while it also tells us the time.

So far, the examples which I have treated from the first chapter
are examples of the main thesis of the *Chuang-Tzu* and of the position
of the *Chuang-Tzu* on the question of valuation. I would like now to
take up two more examples from the first chapter which also illustrate
the central thesis of the *Chuang-Tzu* and the issue of valuation at the
same time. The first of these contains a reference to *mental* blindness
and deafness:

> We can't expect a blind man to appreciate beautiful patterns or a
> deaf man to listen to bells and drums. And blindness and deafness
> are not confined to the body alone — the understanding has them,
> too, as your words just now have shown.[11]

This example treats both the central thesis, albeit indirectly, and
the question of valuation at once. The indirect reference to the thesis
of transformation is that it is a thesis which cannot be appreciated by
those who lack the necessary cognitive tools. Just as someone may be
physically blind, a victim of mental blindness is also ill equipped to
appreciate beautiful mental patterns. While the explicit reference is
merely to a beautiful mental pattern, indirectly the reference must be
to the central message of the *Chuang-Tzu*. The example is at the same
time a valuation, since it implicitly holds that a mentally blind person
is inferior to someone who possesses the requisite insight. There is a
hidden implication, as well, that if a person could understand, or possessed the necessary cognitive appreciation, he could at once see the
beautiful pattern of thought. This implication is that the capacity for
insight into what is beautiful is a self-capacity of the subject seer. It is
not so much that the message must be made more and more beautiful.
The message already is beautiful. What is lacking is the appropriate
capacity for understanding.

The mentally blind or deaf person can be likened to the cicada or
the small bird. These images of blindness, deafness and narrowness of
understanding are one and all instantiations of the intransigent sub-

THE CONTENT OF THE MYTH 47

ject reader or the inveterate skeptic. What is especially noteworthy in the example of mental blindness is again a hidden reference to self-transformation. If the subject reader could only see, the message would be apprehended at once. The responsibility for not grasping the message is placed on the shoulders of the subject reader. While this may be dismissed as begging the question, it is not designed to be an argument on behalf of the truth of the thesis. It is designed to call attention to the importance of the subject's role in perceiving that truth. At the same time, it is a clear value claim that a subject who can understand with insight is superior to one who is cognitively blind in just the same sense that a subject who can physically see possesses an advantage that the blind subject does not possess. It is evident that the blind is not considered to be the axiological equivalent of the sighted, whether we refer to physical or mental sight.

The Story of the Salve

The final example which I would like to discuss represents the capstone of chapter one. It is the story of the ointment or, as we will understand it, the mental salve.[12] But it is important, before we discuss the story directly, to note its placement. It comes after the reference to mental blindness and deafness. The mind has already been prepared extensively for the proper apprehension of the story of the ointment.

If we try to understand this story or any other story in the *Chuang-Tzu* in an ordinary or habitual way, it will be as if we are mentally incapable of grasping what is to be said. In order to understand, a minimal act of transformation is already required in the sense that one must open one's eyes in order to be able to see. Whether or not what is being said is true is not the point here. All that I am attempting to establish is that Chuang Tzu is indicating that *something of cognitive significance* is being related even though we are in the midst of a mythical and fable-telling form of presentation. This point cannot be overemphasized. There is something intelligible here (according to the intentions of the author) which is not on the level of a pleasant fiction. What is intelligible will require an effort, if you will, on the part of the reader; otherwise, the cognitive content will not be noticed or noticeable. In the middle of the telling of fables, we are given such notice.

The final story in the first chapter concerns the mental ointment which will heal the pain of the mind. Of course, in the story it is not presented as a mental salve but as a physical salve; to present it as a mental salve would be to lift it out of the realm of metaphor into the realm of homily—to alert the mind that this *is* a message or theme—and this would negate its cognitive function. As we have discussed earlier in this chapter, the cognitive function of the storytelling device can only be successful so long as the reader is not too aware that there is a meaning to the message. Of course, on some level the reader is perfectly aware that this is a teaching story with an object lesson, but it would not do to call this to the reader's attention too strongly.

We all know, or at least presume, that the *Chuang-Tzu* is a book of philosophy and not a book of medicine. Obviously, the physical ointment described in the story is not to be understood on the level of a physical medicine. But this is all known intuitively or inexplicitly by the subject reader. The hidden premise in the use of the example of ointment is that at some point the reader will be given some clues the function of which will be to ease mental suffering. The mind of the reader is thus being deftly and subtly prepared for the proper reception of such a message to come, in the same fashion as a photographic plate is first placed in a solution for immersion before the prints which will be taken from it can take.

The story of the salve, in brief, is that a man in the past (in Sung) had known how to prevent hands from chapping and as a result his family could bleach silk in water. (What is being said so far is that there is traditional wisdom and its use in the past was only to earn a small livelihood. This could be likened to a much prettier version of the petty minded man or the cicada of earlier examples.) Now, a man comes on the scene who offers to buy the formula. The family sells it for a sum of money, thus confirming the petty mindedness archetype that the family represents. The buyer, who thus represents a man on the road to greater understanding, sells it to a king, who uses it to win a naval battle and awards the seller with a piece of land.

The moral of the story is that the same formula (or brain) can be used in two different ways: one to bleach silk, the other to gain a piece of property. The point seems to be that we all possess the same basic equipment; the only difference is the use to which it is put. Same brain, different uses.

This story is another preparation device which prepares the mind of the reader for the receiving of the higher message of the *Chuang-Tzu* that is yet to be given. This message, of course, has already been proleptically contained in the story itself. The story of the ointment is especially designed to appeal to the intellectual reader; i.e., one who considers herself or himself to be more intelligent than the average person. It does so by employing an example from the realm of commerce where one of the chief fortes that is required is the ability to outsmart one another. Apart from being an especially pointed example for the intellectual reader, this example adds a new element to the examples that have been adduced so far, the element of reward. In terms of the use of the brain, one can obtain a small benefit or a large benefit in the story of the ointment. With respect to the message of the *Chuang-Tzu*, the reader, depending upon the use he or she wishes to make of the material, can reap a small or a large benefit.

It is up to the willingness and the cleverness of the reader (aided by the incentive of greed) to think in larger terms than the immediate material reward. In a material sense, the smart man in the story sells the prescription to a king. The correspondent message on a higher level is that the brain can be used for a higher purpose. The brain-power is the same; what matters is the purpose to which it is put. Just as on a material plane the secrets of the brain can be offered to a king, on a spiritual plane the secrets of the brain can be used for an elevated purpose, self-actualization on the highest mental level. Or, in another meaning, the subject reader can identify himself with the king, who would know the best use to make of the secret of the making of the ointment.

This last story I have chosen to discuss is a story of the way of transformation since it shows that one can better oneself by the right use of one's understanding, and it also shows how it is by an act of larger understanding that one betters oneself. In other words, it is not a story of transformation *simpliciter* like the story of the fish. It is far more explicit that the transformation is achieved through an act of understanding. It is a story of transformation as a man betters his condition considerably, albeit in a material sense. He has transformed himself through his cognitive capacities. The specific mode in which he has transformed himself by utilizing his cognitive capacities is also made explicit here. He must think in larger terms than the ordinary, near-sighted family who only thought in terms of selling the formula for a simple payment. In this respect, the man on the road to enlightenment here is utilizing the Great Understanding of the big bird. The man who sells the salve to the king is an exemplar of Great Understanding. It is Great Understanding that leads to enlightenment. In an important sense, Great Understanding is already enlightenment.

This is the mental balm. The story of the balm also takes sides: it is clear from the story that the man who sells the prescription to the king is superior to the family who only sells it for an instant reward. The family which gains only a temporary material benefit is not on the same axiological plane as the man who ultimately gains something permanent, symbolized by the gift of land.

With the story of the ointment, we have completed our discussion of both the form and the content of the myth. While the ointment story is not exactly a myth, it is told as a legend, which can be taken as a lesser form of myth. It appeals to the more intellectual reader both because it is more clearly a teaching story and because its content emphasizes the importance of the intellect in advancement. At the same time it appeals to the greed of the subject reader.

The story of the salve bridges the gap between the pure myth (that which could not have happened), and the legend (that which might have happened). This story falls more in the category of legend than myth. For this very reason, it also appeals to the intellectual reader because it falls more within the level of possibility. While the intellectual reader may not believe that such a story ever actually happened, he does know that something like this story could have happened. This leads him to the hidden belief that something like the transformation possibility to which he is being ever so gradually exposed could happen. It is a possibility. And it is a possibility that carries with it a great reward.

4 The Monster as Metaphor

While I have touched upon the use of monsters in the *Chuang-Tzu* from time to time, especially in my second chapter on the art of metaphor, the plethora of monsters in the *Chuang-Tzu* deserve a more extended treatment. It may be objected that my use of the term 'monster' is misleading as some of the associations carried by the term do not fit perfectly well. For example, the term 'monster' normally carries with it the connotation of the frightening. Surely, cripples and hunchbacks, which I use as examples of monsters, are not frightening. I would maintain that they are. They may not be frightening to everyone, but in some way they summon up something that is frightening and to that extent, they are socially avoided. Thus, while they might not be truly monstrous in the sense of the monsters of science fiction movies, they are monstrous in the way in which they function. In a philosophical sense, they are feared. They are monsters in the sense of falling outside of the social norm.

This is not to say that a monster, in the sense in which I am using the term ought to be feared or socially avoided. Quite the contrary. As the arguments in this chapter develop, it should become obvious to the reader that the monster (or the violation of the normal) is both the key to the alteration of consciousness and the embodiment of the principal objective to be achieved, namely, spontaneity. Be that as it may, the fact is that empirically speaking, among the *hoi polloi*, monsters are perceived as frightening. And this perceived fact is exploited here in the use of the term 'monster'. By the use of the term 'monster' a certain shock value is achieved and this is the desired and necessary effect. Our fixities of consciousness require a sudden and sometimes unpleasant shock to become broken down. The higher realization, after the proper understanding is achieved, is that monsters (in our sense) are our greatest blessing and without them, we could neither progress in a spiritual direction nor would we have a constant reminder and embodiment of that progress. For the time being, however, the monster must perforce play its frightening role.

51

Some of the monsters used in the *Chuang-Tzu* can be said to be truly monstrous both in Aristotle's strict sense of the definition of a monster as an abnormal birth and as being so physically deformed to qualify as truly frightening. Consider the lame, hunch-backed man with no lips, for example.[1] Or Master Shu, whose physical description makes him sound like a Yoga contortionist:

> My back sticks up like a hunchback and my vital organs are on top
> of me. My chin is hidden in my navel, my shoulders are up above
> my head, and my pigtail points at the sky.[2]

In any event, whether the monster is a simple monster as in the case of a cripple or a compound monster such that he is a genuine freak, the monster is abnormal. The monsters differ from each other only in degrees of abnormality. If a simple cripple is less fearsome to us, it is only a matter of degree. Perhaps we do not want to be seen in the company of the cripple. In this case, we fear the social opinion of those around us. Fear is present.

In no sense is our behavior justified or justifiable. But to deny our inner feelings (albeit existing, hopefully, only among the unaware) would also be to self deceive, and the monster is certainly not deceived. We must admit that an element of fear is present if only to understand how to understand and transcend that fear. An unwelcome fact of empirical social life must be brought out in the open to be understood and dealt with in order that this prejudice be completely banished from our unconscious and conscious lives.

The complete acceptance of the "monsters" among us will signify the absence of the category of the monstrous on the empirical level and the achievement of a high level of consciousness on the philosophical level. In any event, however much we may dislike the category of the monstrous, it is used to much effect by Chuang Tzu as it is by Plato. To ignore it would be to turn a blind eye to the text.

All types of monsters, then, are monsters in the sense of being social pariahs, that is, of being genuinely abhorred or at least avoided by the general public. If there is any avoidance (in all honesty, how many of us have blind friends?) of the monsters, then one must grant that a certain element of fear must be present, be it the fear of the appearance itself or the social disapproval of the "normals" who will find us associating with the monsters. Whether these figures are monsters or not; they are certainly *treated* as monsters.

What is the philosophical significance of the choice of monsters as philosophical mouthpieces? In fact, the monsters are frequently given the best lines. One is reminded of Plato's use of lesser figures such as shoemakers and horsetrainers to illustrate his arguments. In fact,

Chuang Tzu makes ample use of such lesser monsters himself with choice stories being narrated by butchers and carpenters. While there has been excellent treatment of such figures, there has not been enough investigation of the use of the more monstrous types.[3] In passing, however, I would like to say that the use of figures from the ordinary ways of life is monsterlike in its function. In this respect, and in this use, Chuang Tzu uses everyday laborers in much the same way as Plato. Blue collar laborers function as lesser monsters in the sense that in a dialogue which is philosophical, one expects that the interlocutors will be from the upper, intellectual classes. The use of blue collar laborers such as butchers possesses shock value in just the same sense as does the use of the full fledged physical monster as we will discuss below.[4] The blue collar worker as a social class monster is only a different type of monster and, as such, the same discussion that applies to the more flagrant cases of monsters applies *mutatis mutandis* to the blue collar workers.

The use of the monster serves two philosophical functions. First, the monster is a living counterexample to the norm, whether cultural or biological or both. When given philosophical lines, the monster becomes philosopher. The monster type as philosopher is an embodiment of the philosophical principle which is also feared and avoided by the normal.[5] What is this philosophical principle that is avoided by the multitude?

That which all monsters possess, which is feared and avoided by those who live according to the rule, is spontaneity. In a very subtle way, then, the first philosophical significance of the monster is to make us aware that the value represented by the monster—spontaneity—is a value which is feared and avoided by normal society. It is highly apposite that a monster, which is a biological violation of the rule of nature, should stand for a social violation of a rule of society. If one looks through the various philosophical positions adopted by the monsters one will find that spontaneity is a feature that all of them have in common. Perhaps it is because of the fact that they have no fear that they are spontaneous. If they are already feared for their physical appearance, what do they have to lose by adopting viewpoints that will also be fearsome? Philosophical monsters are a bit like madmen; they are free to say what they like. In fact, the madman is really another form of monster, the mental monster. Just as in Western literature the words of the madman or the fool are respected, so here in the *Chuang-Tzu* the monsters are protected. Because they are different, they can get away with saying things that ordinary mortals cannot. They have the freedom to be spontaneous: and this is the philosophical quality that is feared when they are feared. To put this in the opposite way; when we have the courage to become monsters or to share the monster's point of view we will be able to be spontaneous. In that very act of spontaneity we will have come that much closer to being able to apprehend what is true.

In addition to representing spontaneity, the second philosophical function of the employment of monsters is closely related to the earlier discussion on myth and metaphor. The monster represents a bridge between the purely mythical creature and the historical/legendary character that is also employed by Chuang Tzu for carrying philosophical messages. In fact, in many cases the historical/legendary characters are put to monstrous uses; that is, they are credited with holding doctrines which are very much contrary to their actual, historically known philosophical positions.[6] The monster is a fantasy visual image which is one step closer to life than the fantasy visual image of myth. With the monster, one need not rely upon a literary tradition. One may utilize people around one in daily life: the hunchback, the cripple, the blind man and other deviations from and distortions of what is generally held up to be the standard or the norm to admire.

In terms of the cognitive function of the use of monsters, the monster leads us one step closer to the living embrace of the values represented. In the case of myth, such values as are represented might still be taken as not fully actualized or actualizable. In the case of legend, such values might be taken as actualizable but only by the supernormal. In the case of the monster, such values are represented in daily life examples of the creatures around us. Oddly enough, the values would appear to be overachievable in that they are achieved by the subnormal. This is another way of saying that they are not achieved by the normal—but at the same time if they can be achieved by the subnormal then they are eminently achievable by the normal. With the monster, fiction and reality merge.

Of course, all of this is paradoxical. The use of an unideal type as ideal is paradoxical in itself. Paradox, as we shall observe later on, is a species of verbal monster. The monster shocks. One is shocked by visual monstrosity in the same fashion as one is shocked by the verbal monstrosity of the paradox. The visual paradox is even more powerful than the verbal paradox, because its shock value takes place entirely beneath the plane of conscious evaluation. With the verbal paradox, it is relatively easier to conceive of it as an intellectual play of some kind or another. It may still deaden the analytic mind by cancelling out the logical options (as we noticed in an earlier chapter on the double-headed interrogative), but in the case of the verbal paradox the cancellation is more self-conscious. Hence, its sleight of mind may be more easily spotted. In the case of the visual monster, the paradox presented is more buried. There may be a verbal paradox which the monster presents, which can add to the subtle dimension presented.[7] If there is not, then the paradox is that a view which is to be endorsed is being endorsed by a view-holder whom we normally shun. In a word, we are told both to follow and not to follow what is advocated!

In terms of the verbal statement which the monster makes, we are told (implicitly at least) to follow or endorse what views are being put forth. In other words, in most cases, the viewpoints of the monsters are honorifically held and have the tacit implication all honorifically held viewpoints possess: that we should hold these viewpoints as well, at the very least, that it is good to hold these viewpoints. Characteristic of the monster viewpoints, then, is that we are being implicitly enjoined to embrace them as well.

But the monster image tells us simultaneously to hold back. It requires immense social and philosophical courage to follow the lead of the physically lame, the repugnant, the old and deformed, and the hunchbacked. If we can identify with the monsters, then what will be held back will be our own conventional value judgements. If the monster image "works" we will suspend our consciously learned preconceptions in order to embrace the values that are being imparted in just the same way that we will have to overcome our abhorrence of the misfit and the reject in order to be receptive to what they are saying. The monster image is an immediate shock to the conceptual system. It shocks the conceptual system into paralysis, which enables us to approach and assimilate the ideas being offered for their intrinsic value. Since more often than not the ideas will be shocking in and of themselves, it is better that we are given the monster as novocaine in order to stand the shock value of the ideas that are presented.

From a cognitive standpoint, the cognitive process that is involved in the appropriation of the point of view of the monster is the suspension of conscious evaluation. As one cannot be very effectively (or self-consistently) enjoined explicitly (or consciously) to suspend conscious evaluation, one can only be led to the act of suspension of conscious evaluation through a subliminal, non-conscious or pre-conscious device. The monster is just such a device. In accepting the monster as a bonafide holder of values one must switch off conscious judgement. This is exactly what one does when one treats seriously whatever statement is placed in the mouth of a monster. This is the beauty of the monster's speech: it can be entirely appreciated (and in fact it can only be appreciated) during the at least partial disengagement of the conscious, analytical judgment. The effectiveness of the monster image lies in the opposition between its own ugliness and the beauty or truth of the message which it bears. Its own ugliness, if effective, is so shocking that it turns off the conscious mind. Because of its shock value, it is of all devices the most effective in dulling the dominance of the analytical, conscious function. Because of its oppositional quality, by the same token, it is the most effective in providing an occasion for the emergence of the aesthetic function. In the clear-cut separation between form and content (monster and true speech), there is the greatest chance for the cancellation of the analytical judgment at the same moment as the engagement of the receptive, intuitive function. While the sharpest delineation is present, the successful functioning of this device depends upon the greatest employment of philosophical courage. The acceptance of the monster as a brother takes social and philosophical courage. Such an acceptance, in a philosophical sense, means that one is willing to set aside conventional value judgments. If one is able to do this, the chances of being able to apprehend the truth value of what is being spoken are very great. By the same token, the measure of difficulty in being able to do just that is also very great. As Spinoza says at the end of his *Ethics*, "All noble things are as difficult as they are rare."[8]

It could be objected that this discourse in which I have been engaging requires the analytical function of the mind. And, of course, that is quite correct. But this truth does not detract from what I have been maintaining, which concerns the particularities of the effectiveness of this mode of metaphor. To discourse about this effectiveness involves the work of reflective thought and hence involves the use of concepts and abstract judgment. But that which is being talked about involves a level of cognition where the abstract function has not yet been brought into play. In fact, it cannot be brought into play if the metaphorical element is to function cognitively.

The monster as philosophic voice functions no differently than other devices for the cancellation of the analytic function; it is only that it is a very graphic functioning. Exactly at the moment of apprehending the putative truth of the monster's utterance, the very fact that it is a monster's utterance has required the suspension of conventional value judgments. This suspension of the analytic faculty allows the truth of what is said to be absorbed more directly by the intuitive or aesthetic faculty, inasmuch as the analytic function has at that precise moment been disengaged.

The mind cannot, as it were, do two things at once. To appropriate the monster, its conventional standards must be disrupted. This, in turn, has a twofold implication. On one level, it allows the message or theme unimpeded access for cognition. On another level, it carries with it the hidden stipulation that we must violate conventional standards of judgment if we are to attempt to appropriate such views as are being put forward. The two fold process of cancellation is both oriented toward the present and future paced. We must cancel or suspend conscious evaluation to apprehend the message at the moment of hearing it. At the same time, the mere fact that we have done so also carries with it the implication that in order to apprehend such value messages in the future, we will have to be prepared to cancel or suspend our normal or ordinary standards of judgment.

Let us now discuss the dialectical progession of the monster form and then supply a few examples from the text of that which we have been talking about. What we have noted so far is a movement from the fabulous monster of myth to the everyday monster of the lame, the deformed and the social reject. If we view this progression from a dialectical perspective, we could say that Chuang Tzu begins with the ostensibly real, which is actually a human invention (the myth), and moves to the really real (empirical examples which are, to be sure, selectively chosen). They are really real in the sense that they are presented as historically real people. In the myth, the creatures are not presented as fantasy; they are presented as real. It is only our knowledge of fact that prevents us from taking them as real. But our knowledge of fact does not prevent us from taking the cripples as at least possibly real. His last choice of characters, the historical figures used unhistorically, are a blend or a synthesis of the two previous types. In this third type we have real figures again used in ostensibly real situations. To review, first we have pure fiction parading as fact (myth). Second we have a selected version of reality which portrays an ideal of reality. Third we have historically real figures from the past (a blend of the past quality of myth and the real quality of history which at the same time borrows from legend the larger than life quality of these historical figures) used unhistorically as myth. The process of transformation is from pure fiction to selected reality to quasi-fiction. This seemingly queer progression or, if you like, dialectically progressed casting of characters, will assume a more meaningful dimension below.

As we look at the use of monsters in the Chuang-Tzu, we can also consider another element that the monster as metaphor borrows from the myth: the overlay of magic. The monster carries with it the teaching story quality of the mythical creature and the legendary figure. Just as the deviation from the norm represented by the mythical creature is understood in some tacit sense to be magical, the deviation from the norm represented by the monstrous also possesses this magical quality. The hunchback almost seems to us to be an unreal creature. The stronger the deviation, the more magical the transformation will appear to be. The magical element represented by the physical appearance lends its strength to the authority given to the statements uttered by the monster narrators. This adds a certain paradoxical quality. While before we discussed the reluctance of the mind to take as serious what a monster might be saying, here we are suggesting that the monster borrows from the myth a certain authoritative status.

Both are true. The analytical function is reluctant to consider seriously anything which an un-ideal type might be saying. But the intuitive function of the mind is charmed by the magical function of the monster. The intuitive function of the mind, excited at the prospect of meeting a monster in real life, so to speak, is prepared to grant certain magical properties to the statements spoken by the monsters. There is a certain tacit understanding that just as the physical properties of the monster are indications that the monster is a transformation from the normal, what the monster has to say may also carry a transformational or magical quality.

The monster type is truly complex. At the risk of compounding this complexity, I would like to discuss one further way in which the monster metaphor borrows from the mythical form. In the myth we were led to expect something strange as content and at the same time realized that it would be all right to accept that content within the form of the myth. The teaching medium of the monster borrows this same quality from the more customary teaching medium of the myth. From the lips of a cripple we expect to hear something strange as a message; we are already accustomed, having first been exposed to the form of the myth in the order of cognitive assimilation, to anticipate that the message, however strange sounding it might seem, will be all right within its context. Quite naturally, all of these cognitive lessons take place on a pre-conscious level as nothing concerning the pedigogical technique is stated overtly, but is contained only in the dialectical progression of the forms of presentation.

We move from the form of the myth, which we accept as humanity's teaching story, to the physical and social grotesques around us who will now figure as society's teaching agents. While all of this is a bit unbelievable, it is in turn only a preparation for the ultimate use of the sage as the final carrier of the message, the supreme mythical exemplar. The sage, a figure we will discuss later on, is the ultimate blend of myth, legend, and reality. However, in a sense, the sage is too good to be true, and although the sage is the ultimate teaching principle, it is not necessarily the best one. It may well be that we are more likely to learn from the more unlikely bearer of the message, the monster.

There is no need for a complete catalogue of monsters since a few choice examples should serve as a means for identifying others that the reader will come across in the body of the Chuang-Tzu. We can classify monsters by their deformities, of which there appear to be four major categories:

1. Cripples, who can be subdivided into varieties of the lame such as one-footed or no-toed.
2. Miscellaneous deformities such as hunchbacked, missing lips, and physically contorted.
3. Simple uglies, including those whose only monstrous quality is a deviation from the norm in terms of being unbeautiful.
4. Madmen who are mentally deformed, robbers (who are a species of madmen), and social deviates.

I would exempt from the monster catalogue the fabulous sage of old, who I think fits better into the category of myth, and the sage, who is a blend of myth, legend and reality.

All of the above types represent deviations from the normal course of development, whether biological or social. That the monster as educator is not an accidental literary device should be apparent not only from the dialectical progression of teaching figures that I have indicated earlier, but also from the number of times the strategy is employed and the variety of the types of monsters that are given parts to play. Needless to say, there is an overlap between the above categories as there are many examples of mixed types.

The first appearance of a monster type in the *Chuang-Tzu* is the cripple. The *Chuang-Tzu* begins with the use of cripples, possibly because this type would be the easiest of all types to assimilate. The first example of a cripple in the *Chuang-Tzu* is the simple cripple who is one-footed. Chuang Tzu is quite gentle in his introduction of the monster form as he adds to the natural sympathy we would feel for the simple cripple the fact that this cripple is a former military commander. We are thus led to believe that this distortion may have been the result of a war wound. In addition, the granting of a high military rank to this cripple bestows more authority on what he will have to say.

> "It was Heaven, not man," said the commander. "When Heaven gave me life, it saw to it that I would be one-footed. Men's looks are given to them. So I know this was the work of Heaven and not of man. The swamp pheasant has to walk ten paces for one peck and a hundred paces for one drink, but it doesn't want to be kept in a cage. Though you treat it like a king, its spirit won't be content."[9]

While the text seems to indicate that it is a congenital defect ("When Heaven gave me life . . ."), this is not likely as the speaker probably would not have served in the military and risen to the rank of commander if he had been born with one leg missing. The interpretation of "When Heaven gave me life" probably refers to the destiny that was in store for him.[10]

What is of special interest for us to note is the care with which Chuang Tzu introduces the first cripple in his gallery of monsters. The cripple is first of all a former military commander, which gives his deformity a certain dignity. Second, the deformity is traced to the work of Heaven. This too elevates the deformity and prompts us to look at it with respect. It is as if Chuang Tzu is aware of the natural reluctance to face the deformed. He introduces his first cripple buffered with military and heavenly status. It is to be noted that it is a cripple that is first introduced to us, not a hunchback. The spontaneous sympathy we feel for the cripple is different from the instant repugnance and horror that is inspired in us by the hunchback, who is introduced next, and the madman, who inspires in us the greatest fear and is introduced very late.

In his gentle and buffered introduction to the world of deformity, Chuang Tzu is like a painless dentist, first injecting us with the novocaine of an honorably crippled man so that by the time he drills us with madmen, we are perfectly willing to accept as philosophically valid some message that issues forth from the lips of a madman![11] Notice, also, how subtly the message of the commander is woven into the description of the commander's appearance. It is almost as if there is no break between the self-description and the philosophic point the commander has to make. The story of the swamp pheasant is a *non sequitur* from the description of the man's injury as destined. We can, of course, make the connection in that the need for freedom in the swamp pheasant is also inherent in us. But there is no obvious cleavage between the self-description and the point that is to follow. This is a flawless example of the monster metaphor at work. The conceptual capacity is lulled into silence at nearly the very same moment that the theme is given to the intuitive capacity, whose interest has been aroused by the arresting aesthetic imagery of the crippled commander.

The second appearance of the archetype of the cripple is Shu, whom we described before as having the body of a Yoga contortionist.[12] Chuang Tzu has definitely escalated here as Shu is described as unredeemingly crippled. His crippling has no heavenly sanction and Shu has no earthly status either. In fact, Shu seems to resemble the village idiot who is left alone precisely because of his deformity and even benefits from it:

> When the authorities call out the troops, he [Shu] stands in the crowd waving good-by; when they get up a big work party, they pass him over because he's a chronic invalid. And when they are doling out grain to the ailing, he gets three big measures and ten bundles of firewood. With a crippled body, he's still able to look

after himself and finish out the years Heaven gave him. How much better, then, if he had crippled virtue![13]

It is of some importance to note the context of Shu's appearance in the *Chuang-Tzu*. The story of Shu is given immediately after the fourth appearance of the famous tree story in the *Chuang-Tzu*.[14] The tree archetype has been very much discussed in the literature, though as a story, not as an archetype *per se*.[15] Therefore, there is no need of a prolonged discussion here of such a famous image in the *Chuang-Tzu*. But it is important to connect this story with the use of the monster as metaphor because the tree which is not cut down because it is worthless and useless is worthless and useless precisely because it is monstrous. Consider the first appearance of the useless and monstrous tree, which amazingly enough is also called Shu:

> Hui Tzu said to Chuang Tzu, "I have a big tree of the kind men call SHU. Its trunk is too gnarled and bumpy to apply a measuring line to, its branches too bent and twisty to match up to a compass or square. You could stand by the road and no carpenter would look at it twice."[16]

In the casting of monstrous characters we could have included trees as well as men. But the trees have no lines to read. In the case of Shu, he is very much like a tree in that he, too, is given no lines to speak. What is good about Shu is what is told about him, not what he himself pronounces. Shu's virtues shine through his actions, or more precisely his lack of actions, not his words.

The normal size trees are cut down at their prime of life to be made into coffins in the fourth appearance of the tree archetype.[17] Immediately after this account and directly prior to the introduction of Shu, there is a general comment made about the monstrous which is highly relevant for our discussion of the use of monsters in general. It is the concluding comment made to the short list of creatures unusable for sacrifices. We may examine the entire passage in which it appears:

> In the Chieh sacrifice, oxen with white foreheads, pigs with turned-up snouts, and men with piles cannot be offered to the river. This is something all the shamans know and hence they consider them inauspicious creatures. But the Holy Man for the same reason considers them highly auspicious[18]

Incidentally, we notice here the use of the monstrous in animals which are also for that reason understood as either being disvalued or valued. What is of interest for us is the opposite interpretation that can be placed on the monstrous (disvalued-valued), depending upon the source of the valuation. From the standpoint of the shamans, who are interested in sacrificing creatures (apparently men with piles are considered on the same level here as monstrous animals), creatures possessing these deformities are disvalued because they cannot be sacrificed. From the standpoint of the Holy Man (which, from the appellation we construe as an honorific standpoint), the very same quality renders these creatures (including the unfortunate men with piles) valuable. What is valuable about these creatures according to the Holy Man is precisely that they possess a life-saving quality. Their monstrosity is to be prized because it saves their life. It is plain from this passage that Chuang Tzu sets a very high store on monsters to the extent that he gives them a certain endorsement from a figure of authority and reverence. Oppositely, those with small minds, set only upon immediate gains, disvalue the monstrous because of its inutility. The shamans are another exemplar of the petty minded men that we first met in the persona of the cicada and the dove. While the ordinary man looks down upon the monstrous, those who possess insight know that the monstrous possess a very special value.

The story of Shu functions very well as a disassociative and associative story. Chuang Tzu takes no pains to introduce us to Shu in a gentle or honorific way as he did with the crippled commander. He introduces us to Shu immediately within the context of pigs with turned-up snouts and men with piles. Shu's description is enough for us to know that this is no monster of a minor status. Apparently, by this stage in the text, Chuang Tzu feels confident that he can dispense with the niceties of softening the monstrous blow. The shocking quality of Shu's appearance is designed as a strong shock to our conceptual system, especially when we consider the context in which it is given. From a cognitive standpoint, then, all conceptual barriers are briskly swept away with the somewhat shocking appearance of Shu amidst monstrous pigs and other sacrificial animals and even men. In this numbed state of consciousness, we are given not prescriptive utterances but rather a description of the benefits Shu gains from his chronic invalidism (the English language offers an irresistible pun here in the word for sickness and the word for an illogical argument). This description of benefits can be taken in by the intuitive mode of apprehension so that on a subliminal level we are left with the definite impression that there is something good about being monstrous. It is on the very tails of that impression that the one and only injunction appears:

How much better, then, if he had crippled virtue![19]

After we have been very exhaustively prepared for the acceptance of physical deformity the suggestion is planted that even Shu would be better off if his thinking were askew. The conclusion here, which is the major point of the example, is given at the end in an almost offhand fashion when we least expect it. It is given at a point when the defenses are the most worn down and when they least expect to be faced with a new, positive feature of Shu. It is precisely for this reason that the point that Shu would be even better off with a different way of thinking can have its maximum effect.

With Shu, we have the example of the monster par excellence. Since Shu is a hunchback, he may be taken to be the archetypical form of the human monster (in conformance with conventional models). We may think here of the classic case in the West: the Hunchback of Notre Dame. He does not have to say anything (in the case of Quasimodo, he was a deaf-mute) and in fact is given no lines to speak. His appearance speaks for itself and by the same token so do the rewards that life brings him. While the reader may be left with the impression that these rewards still do not make the life of a hunchback desirable, on the other hand the reader knows that this is not the point of the story. The ultimate point of the story is that we should consider being able to think in a different direction. And the beginning of that way of thinking has to do with distorting our conventional value judgments.

I will confine myself to two further illustrations. Of special interest is a case of a mixed type, a monster who possesses three deformities. This is the case of the man with no lips whom we met at the beginning of this chapter.[20] He is lame, is a hunchback and, most interestingly of all, has no lips. It would seem to follow from the lack of lips that this monster will not be capable of speech, in an ordinary sense, and in fact he is given no lines. I think that we may take it for granted that this monster — and there is no question that there is a monster here — cannot speak in an ordinary sense. Otherwise, I am not at all sure what the absence of lips would signify. The lack of the ability to speak altogether would be better indicated by the example of a man who lacked a tongue, not one who lacked lips. In fact, later on in the text it is said that No-lips talked with Duke Ling. But none of his lines are reported in the Chuang-Tzu. This further strengthens the impression that the speech of No-Lips would be something out of the ordinary. The subliminal impression created, of course, is that the message of the Chuang-Tzu is so extraordinary it can be understood only by a special language, in this case, the language which is unheard. It does occur (unlike the unspoken language of the tongueless man) since he conversed with Duke Ling of Wei, but mysteriously enough, we are not told what he said. This adds to the effect of his having no-lips that what he had to say possessed such a mystique that it was above ordinary reportage. It is not that that which is to be known cannot be found in language at all. In that case we would have the example of the mute and not that of the man who lacked the conventional mechanism for word formation. What we are in fact treated to is the example of a man who, in order to communicate, would have to form words in a very special manner. What better image of the *Chuang-Tzu* could we find than this! If we are to understand the message of the *Chuang-Tzu* we have to realize that language and its forms are not being used in any ordinary fashion but in a very special form which make up in fact a special language of its own. How much is given to us in this image of the man with no lips!

The mystique of the unheard speech of the man with no lips is augmented by the bizarreness of the no lips portion of the triad of deformities possessed by the no-message bearer. While other deformities, such as a hunchback or club foot might be relatively normal abnormalities, the absence of lips carries with it a heightened degree of bizarreness that shocks our sensibilities to a greater degree than the ordinary deformity. This degree of shock and heightened bizarreness is appropriate to the heightened degree of understanding that would have to be reached to comprehend the higher, soundless message not delivered by Mr. No-Lips. It may also seem cruel and crude to the point of unfeelingness to name a deformed man with his deformity or deformities, but this, too, is in keeping with the tactics of the *Chuang-Tzu*. There is no mincing of words here. A club-foot is a club-foot. The very act of labelling via deformity shocks and affronts our sensibilities as indeed it is meant to do so. The act of naming is to a great extent the strategy which carries with it the greatest shock value as to simply refer to the deformities (and to use conventional names for the men who possessed them) would cloak and gloss over the offense and shock we must feel for our conceptual minds to snap and our cosseted scheme of pre-set values to collapse so that the messages transmitted can be truly taken in.

It is fitting, then, that the monster with no lips should be given no lines. If any lines were reported, this would detract from the connotation created that a special language is needed in order to communicate the message of the *Chuang-Tzu*. However, in the course of talking about Mr. Lame-Hunchback-No-Lips, Chuang Tzu does manage to say something about the nature of true forgetting. While it is not a line spoken by No-Lips, it is a statement which appears in such close proximity to No-Lips that it will most certainly be associated with him. The passage about true forgetting appears in a most paradoxical form:

> But when men do not forget what can be forgotten, but forget what cannot be forgotten — that may be called true forgetting.[21]

While it is too early in this work to explain this passage in depth, we can certainly conclude that there is some form of forgetting that is considered valuable. If we think of this statement in relation to Mr. No-Lips, we can understand it in this way. We certainly cannot forget the fact that the monster in question has no lips. But if in a certain sense we do forget this fact we will be forgetting what cannot be forgotten. We can forget this only by the complete suspension of the side of the mind that judges in conformance with rules. When this side of the mind is not operative, we will not see a man with no lips; precisely at this moment we will also be told that there is something called true forgetting and that this true forgetting has something to do with Mr. No-Lips. If we anticipate what we can only explain somewhat later in the text, we can say that it is only our own original nature that cannot be forgotten. It cannot be forgotten because it is not something that we ever learned in the first place. However, when we act naturally, without being conscious that we do so, we may be said to be truly forgetting. Mr. No-Lips who, presumably, was not self-conscious about his own triad of deformities, is an object lesson for us. We can say that he was not self-conscious of (was able to forget) his own deformity because he talked freely with Duke Ling. If he could forget his own deformity (which truly could not be forgotten), then how much easier it would be for us to be able to forget our own real nature. But true forgetting means being able to act out of that nature just as Mr. No-Lips acted out of his deformity. Simple things may be forgotten. But that is not the kind of forgetting that Chuang Tzu is talking about. He is talking about a forgetting of that which is not really forgotten because it is still the mainspring of our action.

A classic case of the simple ugly is introduced rather late, in chapter five of the *Chuang-Tzu*: Ai T'ai-t'o attracted both men and women alike despite or perhaps because of his ugliness. Women in particular were said to be attracted to him by the numbers:

> ... when women saw him, they ran begging to their fathers and mothers, saying, 'I'd rather be this gentleman's concubine than another man's wife!' — there were more than ten such cases and it hasn't stopped yet. . . .
>
> On top of that, he was ugly enough to astound the whole world. . .[22]

It could be easy enough to explain such a case away by arguing that it was on account of some internal quality that one was attracted (as in the case of the notorious physical ugliness of Socrates), but for Chuang Tzu (as for Plato, who makes use of this feature of Socrates'), this is not quite the whole story. Part of the magnetism of the attraction is a direct result of the physical ugliness which acts as a repellance-attraction. The irregularity of the features draws at the same time it repels. Of course, an inner magnetic quality must exist as well. But inner magnetism could exist together with physical attractiveness. Here, it is the combination that is of special importance. The physically repugnant features act as a drawing card. The very fact that they are strikingly incongruous with the norm is part and parcel of their drawing power. While we may be amazed and incredulous that someone so ugly could be considered that attractive to the opposite sex, the entire point of the story is to shock us, to upset our normal scale of values and to permit the child's mind to absorb the inner meaning of the message.

It could be argued that the simple ugly should precede the cripple as the softest form of the monster. This would entail a re-positioning of this fragment in the text. Actually, it appears quite late in dialectical sequence in the text, after the madman. While, in my opinion, the fragment definitely belongs before the story of the madman, it is not so clear that it should be placed before the cripple. On the one hand, as the simplest of the types and the least deviated from the norm, it would appear to belong first. It is on account of its very simplicity that it functions so powerfully as a metaphor. However, its simplicity is deceptive. Actually, it is a fairly advanced form though not so advanced as the madman and belongs, most likely between the simple and the multiple deformity. However, for our purposes, it is less distracting to the main thread of our argument to treat it after the multiplied deformed monster and before the madman. It would not work as the beginning type because it is important, as I have argued above, that Chuang Tzu begin his types with an honorable monster to set the stage for monsters as ideal types. An ugly man, to whom women are attracted, would not be as sympathetic and credible a figure.

The simplicity of the simple ugly as a type is deceptive because this type functions so powerfully for three reasons. First, it is surprising in its simplicity because we are not expecting ugliness as a form of monstrosity, thus, it is capable of breaking our conceptual defenses by virtue of this surprise element. Second, it is, of all types, next to the madman, perhaps the best example of simple polar opposition. Ugliness and beauty seem to be at the extremes of opposition to us, like black and white. And yet here, the extreme opposite of beauty acts as the force of attraction. This powerful reverse of expectancy is a strong assault on our conceptual dividing lines and creates much confusion for the conceptual mode of valuation. Third, when this is coupled with the fact that the content of the example is an aesthetic content (beauty/ugliness), the conceptual/aesthetic criteria of evaluation become confused with each other. This is what is meant to be and what makes for the power of this example. The very objective of replacing a conceptual framework with an aesthetic one is hinted at in the choice of the example and then the traditional aesthetic values are reversed as well. A simple inversion of one normal scale of values where the ugly, on account of its ugliness — mixed with the appropriate inner values — becomes *more* attractive than the beautiful on its own terms (the power to attract the opposite sex), creates a powerful push-pull to our conceptual/aesthetic values and creates the greatest possible confusion by disturbing both spheres of the mind simultaneously. This is why the simplicity of the example is deceptive. It is not enough to replace our conceptualizing with an aesthetic mode of apprehension. Our aesthetics themselves must seek a re-orientation. Wars are waged simultaneously on two fronts. The aesthetic fights the conceptual and wages a civil war with itself. Such is the deceptiveness of the simple ugly which reveals itself as one of the most complex of all the types in the monster gallery.

A very late story in the inner chapters combines the deformed and old (therefore to that extent ugly) with the beautiful in appearance in the example of the unnamed Woman Crookback who has the complexion of a child. This combination, however, is less effective.[23] It does, however, show off the versatility of Chuang Tzu as he combines the beautiful and the ugly in one type. The combination, however, being less strange, is less successful and may be mentioned only in passing.

The last example with which we will deal is that of the madman. From the standpoint of a philosophical catalogue rather than a conventional, visual one, the madman is the ultimate archetypical monster in that it is clear that the distortion is inherently mental. It is clear that whatever is being said by or attributed to the madman is inherently self-contradictory. A man who is by definition mad cannot say something which is sane. This is the most monstrous assault on our intellect. We are being told to value something which is in essence completely outside the range of value.

The madman as mental monster functions in precisely the same way as the physical monster, except that the contradiction that is presented is more accessible to the intellectual reader. The sleight of mind that is required is a sleight of mind that is more obviously required. For that reason, the madman as a device, although it does represent the ultimate form of monster — a mental monster — is used less frequently than the physical monster. It is almost as if we have an example here of a metaphor that is too good to be true. The onslaught on the conceptual mind is so devastating with the case of the madman that it is a case of overkill. It may be that the recognition of this kept Chuang Tzu from employing this device on too grand a scale.

The madman is the most threatening image of all to us. For this reason, perhaps, we tend to hide such figures from the rest of society by secreting them behind the walls of clandestine and removed institutions to which there is virtually no public access. These institutions are removed not for the sake of the inhabitants or the safety of the normal population, but more so from the desire to keep these institutions and their inhabitants out of our consciousness.

The reason why this type is feared is the same as the reason why all monsters are feared. It is only that the property is more obviously inherent in the case of the madman than in the case of any other of the monster types. The property is spontaneity. The madman is feared because she or he has the license to say whatever she or he wants. The freedom of thought available to the madman is what we find most truly fearful. If this were not the case then why would we not use simple physical restraints on the so-called dangerous madmen rather than also cutting off virtually all communication between the world and them and they and the world.

The madman, in a philosophical context, is feared because he is not bound by the rules of logic. The use of the madman, then, carries with it the overlay that the normal rules of logic will not apply in considering the putative truth of the madman's message. While this is no doubt true from the standpoint of the *Chuang-Tzu*, it is also somewhat obvious. The obvious quality of the device is what keeps it from being too effective. On the other hand, when Chuang Tzu does use the madman as metaphor, the lines that he gives to the madman are powerful indeed. Consider the first appearance of the archetype of the madman in the *Chuang-Tzu*, immediately after the story of crippled Shu.

We are very well prepared for this story by its having been preceded by that of Shu. In fact, the last line about Shu anticipates the madman: "How much better, then, if he had crippled virtue!" We are then treated to an example of one who, by definition, has an abnormal frame of reference. The madman is out of his mind, so anything he will say cannot be measured by the standards of normalcy. On the other hand, we have also been excellently prepared by this point. Normal standards have time and time again been found lacking. We are prepared to accept the message of a madman. And what the madman has to say is surprisingly sane.

The madman makes his entrance in the corpus of the *Chuang-Tzu* by assuming the role of a critic of Confucius. This in itself could be taken as a mad act given the esteem and authority in which Confucius was then held. One cannot help but think that Chuang Tzu does this tongue in cheek, knowing that it is his own position that he is putting into the speech of the madman.[24] The madman shouts out (the entire episode reminds one forcibly of Nietzsche's madman in *Zarathustra* shouting out in the marketplace) a criticism of Confucius. I will reproduce but a part of it here:

> When Confucius visited Ch'u, Chieh Yü, the madman of Ch'u, wandered by his gate crying, "Phoenix, phoenix, how his virtue failed! The future you cannot wait for; the past you cannot pursue.... Happiness is as light as a feather, but nobody knows how to bear it. Calamity is as heavy as the earth, but nobody knows how to avoid it. Leave off, leave off—this teaching men virtue!"[25]

The madman criticizes Confucius both for not being virtuous and for attempting to teach virtue. Implicit in his criticism is his own positive view. As he chastizes Confucius for anticipating the future and pursuing the past, it is plain that the remaining option, to experience the present, is the correct one to be taken. In making one of the most memorable remarks in all of the *Chuang-Tzu*: "Happiness is as light as a feather, but nobody knows how to bear it," the madman proves himself full of philosophic wisdom. No one had thought that happiness would be something difficult to bear. But the madman-philosopher notices that no one stays happy for very long. His trenchant remark is so shocking that it does full justice to his mental condition. We are reminded of Dryden's, "Great wits are sure to madness near allied, and thin partitions do their bounds divide."

The madman is spontaneity personified. Even more than the cripple, he can get away with saying what he wants, as he is not mentally responsible. Consequently, he can make the most daring statements and he does. In criticizing Confucius, the madman is daring. Only a crazy person can advise Confucius to stop teaching virtue. Only a crazy person can tell us that nobody really knows how to be happy.

The madman as monster brings us to the end of the types of monsters in the *Chuang-Tzu*. With the madman and the later robber type, Chuang Tzu pulls no punches.[26] We are fully prepared for the madman's statements to be strange, for if they were not he would not be mad. As the madman is a critic of Confucius we are being philosophically prepared for the position that Confucius is to be criticized, and to criticize him successfully we must adopt a position which is akin to madness.

Since the madman has been given some strong truth-bearing lines we know that there is some association between being mad and being able to see and speak the truth. What that association is we have spoken of before. The association of madness is with the ability to be free from conventional standards of judgment. There is a further association of madness with wisdom. The very act of not being confined to conventional standards confers some quality of wisdom upon the madman. Perhaps the wisdom comes from the fact that the freedom from convention allows the real nature of the madman to shine forth. And the real inner nature of all of us is filled with wisdom and goodness. But this is something that we must speak to later on.

5   The Beautiful as Metaphor: The Symbol of Metamorphosis

It would give a false impression of the *Chuang-Tzu* if we were to leave the reader with the idea that Chuang Tzu favored only the ugly as a means of representation. While the ugly and the grotesque certainly abound in terms of the numbers of images, there is a very central image in the *Chuang-Tzu* that is simultaneously an image of the beautiful and an image of transformation: the butterfly. In fact, the butterfly can be taken as the image *par excellence* of transformation. The butterfly story is probably the best known single story in the corpus of the *Chuang-Tzu* and is possibly the most influential in terms of the understanding of the *Chuang-Tzu* that has developed so far. As a result, it is important to study this story and its surrounding context with great care, for the correct understanding of the butterfly story will have profound consequences for the correct understanding of the *Chuang-Tzu* as a whole.

In this chapter, I would simply like to focus on the use of the butterfly image as the symbol of metamorphosis. The choice of the butterfly as the image of transformation is not accidental in my view, and therefore it will be of great use to study the qualities that belong to the butterfly. If what I have been arguing in previous chapters is correct, and the employment of metaphorical form has cognitive implications, then the choice of the metaphorical image is of some consequence. If the butterfly image is the most celebrated image in the whole of the *Chuang-Tzu*, then it may well be that a great deal of thought went into the selection of this particular image.

There are at least four salient characteristics of the butterfly image that I would like to note. Whether or not the author of the *Chuang-Tzu* had any or all of these in mind is a hypothesis that is impossible to verify. In a general sense, I would argue strongly that the choice of the butterfly as a central image is not simply random. That it is not a random choice is indicated by the importance of the qualities of other metaphorical choices that permeate the *Chuang-Tzu*. If the other metaphorical choices (for example, the use of monsters) are not random, then why should the use of the butterfly image be random? In addition, since the function of this metaphor will be to represent such a fundamental point of the text, the importance of its choice must be considered with some care. It would be unlikely that the author of the *Chuang-Tzu* would capriciously choose an image which plays such an important role in his text. Finally, even if we were to grant that the choice was unintentional, it can still be argued that the choice does play a cognitive role in the text. From this perspective, we could argue that Chuang Tzu could not have chosen better. The appositeness of the choice, however, argues strongly that it was intentional.

First, there is no doubt that the butterfly is a symbol of the beautiful. It is difficult if not impossible to imagine a butterfly that is ugly. We can think of an ugly horse, for example, but we would be hard put to think of an ugly butterfly. The image carries with it the idea of beauty. In fact, I cannot think of any other creature which has been captured and preserved simply on account of its beauty alone.

The idea of the beautiful as a metaphor has the same striking quality as the idea of the monstrous as metaphor. The mind is captivated by the idea of the beautiful. In this respect, the use of the butterfly as an image is more like the use of myth than it is like the use of monster. In the use of monster, the striking quality is to repel the mind. Here, the striking quality is used to attract the mind. The use of beauty as a metaphor trades on all of the historical associations that beauty as an ideal possesses. Beauty has a very strong value attached to it. It stands for something that we somehow consider both good and important. In Plato, beauty is considered the highest value of all (if we read *Symposium*). It is an attribute that all of us prize, whether it be in our choice of mates, our standard for works of artistic excellence, or for more utilitarian works such as houses, cars and ships. In any case, the choice of a metaphor of beauty carries a strong historical connotation to the reader of something highly positive. Whatever function the butterfly image is to serve, then, it comes to that function with a highly positive built-in valuation.

Second, the butterfly is the image of metamorphosis. It is, in fact, not only the image of metamorphosis but the archetype of metamorphosis. One reason for the power it carries as an image is that it itself is the archetype and, in this respect, is alone among all the images in the *Chuang-Tzu*. Whenever an archetype is employed as its own image, the effect is uniquely powerful, for the connotation to the aesthetic dimension of the mind is that much more powerful. Like the use of myth, the use of archetype carries with it the history of a civilization's use of an image in all of its forms, for an archetype always carries with it all of its exemplars in terms of secondary associations. For this reason, much of the success of the butterfly image may be attributed to the fact that it is an archetype in addition to being an exemplar.

It is not as strictly correct to call the butterfly the image of metamorphosis as it is an embodiment of metamorphosis. In that respect, the butterfly is the symbol of metamorphosis. But since it is also an image, we can refer to it as such. In any event, it both signifies metamorphosis and is itself an example of metamorphosis. This double relationship to metamorphosis is another reason for the power that this image carries with it.

That metamorphosis is a quality of a butterfly no one would deny. The fact that a butterfly is a result of a metamorphosis is one of its chief defining features. No one can think of a butterfly without thinking that it is the result of a transformation of an earlier version of itself as a caterpillar. Part of the miracle of the butterfly's beauty is the fact that it is a dramatic change from a stage of ugliness.

The choice of the butterfly as an image cannot be without a realization of its functional significance as the archetype of metamorphosis. To say that the butterfly is casually chosen and it is by pure coincidence that it is the image of transformation is to totally ignore the context of its appearance in the story, in the chapter, and in the book in which it figures. Since the surrounding story, the surrounding chapter, and the surrounding book all sound the theme of transformation, to argue that an image of transformation, nay, the archetypical image of transformation was chosen to play a significant role in a story about transformation was a literary coincidence is to attribute entirely too much to the power of chance.

The butterfly is the image incarnate of the transformation. What is a butterfly today was once a caterpillar. That the metamorphosis was from the ugly to the beautiful adds a tremendous element of power to the metamorphosis, for the change is not merely an exchange; it is an elevation. The change from the ugly to the beautiful is the fulfillment of the mythical ideal: the frog that turns into a prince; the ugly duckling that turns into a swan; the begrimed Cinderella who turns into a princess.

The butterfly is the symbol of metamorphosis from the inferior to the superior, from the old to the new, from the lowly to the high, from the crawling to the flying, from the less developed to the more developed. The butterfly is in fact the symbol of birth — the birth of beauty. It is a symbol of the movement from crawling to transcending, from infancy to adulthood, through rising up, through leaving behind what once was and no longer is.

Such power that the image carries makes it unlikely that the author would have employed this image unintentionally. Surely, the author would have been aware of the supreme appositeness of this image to its purpose. The choice of the butterfly as a symbol of transformation actually further strengthens the hypothesis that the *Chuang-Tzu* is about transformation, and, more specifically, transformation of a very special sort.

Third, the mode of the transformation of the butterfly from the chrysalis is of special interest. The transformation to the butterfly takes place by shedding the skin of the chrysalis. This serves to illustrate that transformation can only take place when the old gives way to the new, and what is more, that the giving away of the old and the change to the new is an *internal* change. The transformation to the butterfly requires no outside agency. It is not an external change but a change that happens from within and can only happen from within. Further, it is not a mere exchange or physical change. It is a transformation from the inferior to the superior. It is a transformation, not a change: a very dramatic transformation that reflects a change from the inside of that which is ugly and lowly to that which is beautiful and transcendent. Finally, it is not an endless or cyclical change. It is a one-time change. The butterfly does not change back to the caterpillar. It is a one-way change in a certain direction. It is a final change. Once the transformation is complete, it does not repeat itself. The significance of this will become more evident in subsequent chapters. What is important to note at the present is that the butterfly represents a transformation which is assymetric in that the change is from what is less valued to what is more valued. It is a transformation that occurs only once. In its one change, there is a defined goal. The caterpillar is to turn into the butterfly. The direction is clear. The transformation is one which we all understand to be highly dramatic. And the transformation is one which is entirely internal.

For a moment, we may dwell on the concept of shedding one's own skin. This concept serves to illustrate the importance of the internal element of the change. Transformation can only take place when the old gives way to the new, and the old must give way before the new can emerge. It is not a mere matter of physical change. It is definitely a matter of progression. The progression involves an abandonment of something which was present earlier: an old identity. One must shed one's own skin, as it were, to allow the transcending beauty to emerge. This is a powerful image because it betokens the central message of the *Chuang-Tzu*. One must shed one's old concept of oneself before one can attain to a new identity. In fact, it is the very process of shedding one's old self-identity that is the attainment of the new identity. This is, of course, to anticipate much of that which will be discussed in ensuing chapters. But the metamorphosis of the caterpillar into the butterfly is such a supreme example of self-change that it must be noted here.

The fact that the change is internal, that it happens from within, is a strong reminder that the change of which the *Chuang-Tzu* is ultimately speaking is a self-change. The transformation which the *Chuang-Tzu* refers to is a self-transformation. While this thesis cannot be fully established at this stage of the argument, the employment of the butterfly as a metaphor is a powerful piece of evidence in this thesis.

Fourth, the butterfly is a transient creature. It is transient in a biological sense, as its life span is measured in weeks and sometimes in months. Its emergence from the chrysalis is a birth that occurs and is complete within a very short time frame. We are strongly reminded of the description of the suddenness of the appearance of the Great Sage who will not only understand but will be able to explain everything to us:

> If it happens once in ten thousand ages that a great sage knows its explanation it will have happened as though between morning and evening.[1]

The transience of the biological life span of the butterfly is another testimony to its beauty. It is beautiful and a symbol of transformation despite and perhaps because of its temporality. One thinks of the fabled cherry blossom of Japan, appreciated as much for its brief life span as for its beauty. The transience of the butterfly is not reflected only in its life span. It is perceived as a highly delicate creature, easily injured because of its fragility.[2] This fragile quality is another element in its transience, and is also an intimation that the self-transformation that the butterfly symbolizes is something which is highly delicate and may be injured or broken quite easily.

We could say, of course, that this is simply a story about a butterfly which possesses no significance outside of itself. But such a claim will break down when it must face such an overwhelming array of both logical and textual evidence to the contrary. I think that the choice of the butterfly as the master image of self-alteration is no literary accident. I think that the rest of the text will bear out the claim that the butterfly is strategically chosen precisely because it is beautiful, the symbol of transformation, the symbol of self-transformation, and the symbol of transience.

There is another quality of the butterfly which we ought to consider: its playfulness. The butterfly is a carefree creature. I have set this quality out from the other four because I think that metaphorically it serves a slightly different purpose than the other four qualities.

The playfulness of the butterfly is the attitude of the butterfly; it is not part of the physical description of the butterfly. The playfulness of the butterfly reflects, as it were, the result of the transformation. The result of the transformation is both a certain self-delight on the part of the butterfly and a feeling of freedom. While this may be seen as imaginary conjecture on my part, we do, as readers, associate such qualities with butterflies and that is all that matters. After the transformation, despite its brevity of existence, the butterfly is very playful and seemingly a happy creature. We do think of it as playful or carefree and we associate this carefree playfulness with freedom. The result of the transformation, then, can be said to be happiness, freedom and a certain playfulness.[3] As the story of the butterfly is not, of course, a simple tale about butterflies, these qualities are designed to point to the resultant values of the transformed individual human being. This is not said overtly — at least not at the moment of the telling of the butterfly story — but it is implied in the choice of the metaphorical image. If, as we have said, this image is not chosen by chance, then our child's mind, delighted with the image of a butterfly, is at the same time being given some very powerful intuitive messages. Later on in the course of the *Chuang-Tzu*, such messages may be given explicitly in speeches of sages or other figures. Here, these messages occur only implicitly as part of the meaning structure of the image that is chosen. But that is the very point of the use of the metaphor as a means of cognitive transmission.

I doubt that I have expounded on all of the possible or likely associations that we would make with butterflies.[4] That has not been my intention. But these meanings, at least, seem to be inherently contained in the idea of a butterfly. While it may be argued that there is no proof that Chuang Tzu had any of these meanings in mind, it can nonetheless be argued that it would be difficult to read the *Chuang-Tzu* without taking in these meanings. As for the actual intentions of the author, Chuang Tzu could have chosen a cow as the dream subject in the story instead of a butterfly; are we not justified in considering his choice significant?

Having said all of that, in the story in which the fabled butterfly image appears it is Chuang Chou whose awakening most concerns us, and not the state of mind of the butterfly. But the butterfly image still retains its cognitive function. We will leave it to the next few chapters to analyze the butterfly anecdote in greater detail. Suffice it to say for the moment that the butterfly image presages what Chuang Chou must undergo in order to awaken. In the case of Chuang Chou, the transformation is mental, not physical. But the image is not to be totally discarded on this account. Just as the butterfly is the archetypical symbol of physical transformation, so the change in consciousness which

Chuang Chou undergoes must stand for an archetypical symbol of mental transformation.

The change that is being betokened is a philosophical change, a total change, a metamorphosis. It is a complete change in *being*, a total change of identities. The change is from the ordinary and lowly and earth-bound to the extraordinary and transcendent, from the ugly to the very personification of beauty. The change is an internal one and takes place in the very act of shedding one's skin, one's old identity; and the change, when it happens, takes place all in the course of a single day.

Finally, once the change is made there is a change in attitude as well, and it is this that is truly most important. The change in attitude is one which is connected to the ideas of freedom, carefreeness, and playfulness. The transformation is the necessary condition for the emergence of these values; these values are the trademarks of the fact that a transformation has taken place. We may say that these values are the criteria that enable us to recognize the transformed or the enlightened human individual. The enlightened human being will be free and will be free from cares. The freedom from cares is in fact the mark of the achievement of true freedom. And freedom from cares is manifested in a certain spirit of playfulness.[5]

6 The Butterfly Dream: The Case for Internal Textual Transformation

After having lavished so much praise on the butterfly image in the last chapter, I think it is only fair to say that the entire butterfly dream story, as it stands in its current edited form, is extremely opaque. While the butterfly story is undeniably the most celebrated story in the whole of the *Chuang-Tzu*, it has suffered from the lack of a very compelling interpretation. Part of the problem has been the highly metaphoric and ambiguous presentation of the dream story. But part of the problem, in my opinion, lies in the ordering of the fragments that make up the story. I would like to demonstrate that in order to understand the real meaning of the butterfly dream, we must seriously entertain the possibility of re-ordering at least some of the fragments that make up the dream story within the butterfly dream anecdote and also seriously consider relocating the butterfly dream anecdote vis-à-vis the Great Sage dream anecdote. At the same time that we are considering the arguments supporting these textual transformations, we must also consider that the butterfly dream story itself can only be rendered fully intelligible by reference to the Great Sage dream story.

In order to make this case out fully, we will need two separate chapters. In this chapter I will attempt to show that the currently accepted order of the fragments that make up the butterfly story is logically problematic if not unsound. In the present order of the fragments, the story is logically incoherent. I refer to the present order of the fragments as the raw version of the butterfly dream story. As there is no reason to believe that the present order of the fragments is sacred — and in fact strong reason to doubt the authenticity of the present order — the arguments which I will put forth to recommend a more logically sound order are not at odds with a well established textual order.[1]

The second part of the argument is contained in the following chapter, in which I argue that if we nevertheless wish to retain the present raw version of the dream we can consider that this version is but an awkward, incomplete, and provisional form of the Great Sage dream which properly completes and explains it. In either case, the butterfly dream is in for some textual transformation. We either retain the present order and see the butterfly dream as the precursor to the Great Sage dream which fulfills the intention of the butterfly dream in a more adequate fashion, or we modify the order of the fragments that make up the butterfly dream story. Ideally, we can do both. We can modify the fragments that make up the butterfly dream story and then also relocate the story with respect to the Great Sage dream story which, even with the re-ordering option, presents itself as a superior medium. Or, we can maintain the present order, which does have a long historical tradition behind it, and simply explain the inadequacies of the butterfly dream by seeing it as a preliminary version of the Great Sage dream. This still requires a shift in the sequence of the story such that the butterfly dream story will precede – not succeed – the Great Sage dream story. We could, for sentimental reasons, keep the order of the fragments the same; in this chapter, however, I will put forth as strong a case as possible for the re-ordering of the fragments that make up the butterfly dream story.

Before proceeding immediately to the argument for the internal textual re-ordering of the story with which this chapter will be mainly concerned, I would like to make plain the presuppositions which underlie my thesis. As I have indicated in the previous chapter, I take the butterfly dream story to be an analogy of the enlightenment experience. The enlightenment experience, or the experience of illumination, is the phenomenological correlate of what I take to be the central objective of the *Chuang-Tzu*, that of self-transformation. It is not only the phenomenological correlate; it is the essential precondition for self-transformation. While at this point in the argument this can be but a presupposition, I hope that by the end of these two chapters this presupposition will receive very strong support. The butterfly dream story, under the above presupposition, is a story which is primarily about waking up from a dream. The physical act of awakening from a dream is a metaphor for awakening to a higher level of consciousness, which is the level of correct philosophical understanding. The "transformation of things," the famous statement with which chapter two allegedly ends, refers in my argument to the transformation from ignorance to enlightenment.

In the conventional interpretive treatments of the butterfly dream story, there appear to be two basic schools of thought. The first and most generally pervasive school follows what I term the confusion hypothesis. While this might appear to be a pejorative label, in fact it turns out to be a faithful description of the hypothesis of this school of interpretation. The second and more minor school of interpretation follows what I call the external endless transformation hypothesis, or the endless transformation hypothesis for short. I only call attention to the external quality of the transformation to ensure that this version of transformation is not confused with the self-transformation thesis (the transformation of the subject reader) that I am advancing. The only possible confusion lies in the sameness of the term 'transformation' in both cases. However, in my view, the primary thesis of the *Chuang-Tzu* most certainly relates to the transformation of the self. While the external transformations of things are definitely discussed in a number of places, this discussion is, in my opinion, not to be taken as the central thesis of the *Chuang-Tzu*. The external transformations that are cited are, in my view, further supporting arguments for the self-transformation thesis. But this claim I must leave for later substantiation.

The second school of interpretation which follows the endless transformation thesis can, under analysis, be seen in some instances to collapse into the confusion hypothesis. Some interpreters take portions from each school of interpretation or switch back and forth between the endless transformation and the confusion hypothesis. This may be because the endless transformation thesis, when pushed to its logical conclusion, turns into a version of the confusion hypothesis. There is also a version of both the confusion hypothesis and the endless transformation hypothesis which makes use of the self-transformation hypothesis but to establish a state of realization which is different from the one which I am attributing to the self-realized subject.

In this chapter, I will follow the following basic order of argumentation. First, I will set out what I take to be the positive meaning of the butterfly dream. Second, I will examine the raw version of the butterfly dream so as to point up its inherent illogic. Third, I will set out a modified version of the dream and demonstrate its superior logicality. Fourth, I will try to show how the conventional interpretations of the butterfly dream story take their rise from the raw version of the dream story. I will also try to point to basic weaknesses in the conventional interpretive options. Fifth and finally, I will again refer to my own interpretive option, which arises from a re-ordering of the fragments of the butterfly dream story.

In the modified or new order of the butterfly dream, the meaning of the dream is to be understood as an attempt to signify the objective of achieving an internal transformation. Even in this new order, its argument is somewhat incomplete and cannot be appreciated in its entirety except in conjunction with the Great Sage argument to be discussed in the following chapter. Be that as it may, it still can be taken as an initial attempt to signify the objective of achieving an internal transformation.

Strictly speaking, the butterfly dream does not, of course, constitute an argument of any kind. It is an analogy rather than an argument proper. On the most basic level, it is simply an account of a highly imaginative physical dream. However, in the account of the dream, the experience of waking up is pointed to. The analogy for which I argue is that just as we can and do awaken from a physical dream, so we can mentally awaken to a more real level of awareness. While this is not, of course, explicitly stated to be the case, I take it that the dream does signify something. And the correct signification of the dream is very important to the correct understanding of the central message of the *Chuang-Tzu*.

The butterfly dream, in my interpretation, is an analogy drawn from our own familiar inner life of what *cognitive process* is involved in the process of self-transformation. It serves as a key to understanding what the whole of the *Chuang-Tzu* is about by providing an example of a mental transformation or awakening experience with which we are all highly familiar: the case of waking up from a dream.

There are two points which are involved in the selection of waking up from a dream as a metaphor. First, we are provided with an example of an awakening, albeit on a physical level. Second, we are also being provided with an example of a mode of certification or validation of an awakened state. The experience of awakening from a dream is a self-certifying or self-validating experience. It is an experience which can only be known from the inside out. Regardless of whether one is mistaken or not about the awakening empirically, the corrected understanding of a false awakening is itself only possible from the inside out. The experience of awakening from a dream is self-certifying and self-corrigible. It is important to keep in mind that any and all interpretations of the butterfly dream must make use of this epistemic dimension of the story. While all of the interpretations of the butterfly dream story trade on the epistemic self-discovery nature of cognition that is inherent in the dream-awakening model, none of the interpretations take the implications of this sufficiently into account. Once the uniquely epistemic aspects of this cognitive model are noted, it can be seen that all interpretations are ultimately based on a self-transformation model.

Let us proceed to an investigation of the raw version of the butterfly dream so as to take note of its inherent logical ambiguity. It is this inherent logical ambiguity that has led most interpreters astray:

Once upon a time, Chuang Chou dreamed he was a butterfly;
   flitting and fluttering he darted wherever he wanted;
   he did not know he was Chuang Chou.

Suddenly waking up,
　　the Consequence (of awakening) is,
　　he is Chuang Chou.

But, he doesn't know if he is Chuang Chou who had
　　dreamt he was a butterfly,
　　or a butterfly dreaming he is Chuang Chou.

Between Chuang Chou and a butterfly,
　　there must be some distinction;
　　this is called the Transformation of Things.[2]

In the above ordering of the lines, which is the conventional order, there are two fundamental ambiguities. First, the status of not knowing if he is Chuang Chou or a butterfly is introduced as a post-awakening phenomenon. This is very odd as it does not cohere very well with the consequence of awakening and finding himself to be Chuang Chou. Second, the statement that despite this state of ignorance there must be some distinction, and that this is the transformation, is extremely ill-founded and obscure. If Chuang Chou is in a state of ignorance, how can he be sure that there *must* be any kind of distinction? And what is the referential index of the "this" in the Transformation of Things? Because these fundamental ambiguities prevent a compelling interpretation of the butterfly dream, I refer to this initial order of the lines as the raw version of the dream anecdote.

If we modify the order of the lines to achieve a logically more coherent version, we arrive at the new order:

Once upon a time, Chuang Chou dreamed he was a butterfly;
　　flitting and fluttering he darted wherever he wanted;
　　he did not know he was Chuang Chou.

In fact, he didn't know if he were Chuang Chou dreaming
　　that he was a butterfly or a butterfly dreaming he was
　　Chuang Chou.

Suddenly he awakens.
　　He sees that he is Chuang Chou.

So, there must be a distinction between Chuang Chou and
　　a butterfly;
　　this is transformation!

What are the significant similarities and differences in the modified or amended version and the raw version of the butterfly dream anecdote? With respect to similarities, both versions begin with the subject of the dream (the dreamer), Chuang Chou. There is no doubt about this. This is the unquestioned starting point of all of the versions. It may be questioned later on in the story, but at the start it is accepted as the beginning of the story. *From the standpoint of verbal order, the implicit suggestion that is being made is that Chuang Chou is taken to be the dreamer regardless of what later confusion might be introduced over this point.*

With respect to differences, the only significant difference between the raw version and the amended version is that in the amended version, it is only after becoming unsure of whether he is Chuang Chou or not that the thought arises that he might in fact be a butterfly. It is after he doubts his identity that he considers the possibility of being a butterfly. In the raw version, the thought that he might be a butterfly is introduced after the statement that he is Chuang Chou. This is a *non sequitur*, or at least a very unlikely place in the argument to introduce such a doubt. In both versions, after awakening, Chuang Chou sees that he is definitely Chuang Chou. The butterfly does not awaken to notice that he is a butterfly. The awakening of Chuang Chou, instead of the butterfly, is coherent with the initial statement that it is Chuang Chou who is considered to be doing the dreaming at the beginning of the passage. The logical place for the consideration that the dreamer could be a butterfly would be as part of the dream content prior to awakening. After awakening, and after being sure that he is Chuang Chou, it is unlikely that such a doubt would occur. It could happen, to be sure. But it is a logically less likely place for such an occurrence. In fact, if the doubts were to occur after the awakening, it makes even less sense that the very next thought should be that there is necessarily a distinction between Chuang Chou and a butterfly.[3] But that there must be such a distinction between Chuang Chou and a butterfly follows perfectly logically in the modified version.

If we attempt to follow the logic in the raw version, the argument reads as follows. *After* waking up, he does not know if he is Chuang Chou dreaming he was a butterfly or a butterfly dreaming he is Chuang Chou. But it is clearly stated that it is Chuang Chou who has awakened (and who was having the dream). It is never said that it is the butterfly who is awakening. Thus, to think that he might be a butterfly after all does not make a great deal of sense at this juncture of the story. If he knows that he is Chuang Chou, how *could* he be a dreaming butterfly? To add insult to injury, if after awakening, he does not know if he is Chuang Chou or a butterfly, how can he know that he is Chuang

Chou? This version makes no sense, which is why, I propose, it has lacked a very satisfactory interpretation. If he does not know if he is Chuang Chou or a butterfly, he certainly cannot know that he is Chuang Chou. Finally, *after* waking up he should have no problem. Clearly, according to the raw version, he, Chuang Chou, has awakened. He cannot be a butterfly dreaming he is Chuang Chou. It is not possible to raise this doubt at this point or else it makes no sense to say that he knows that he, Chuang Chou, has awakened.

· In the final, modified version, the dream has a very intelligible and significatory meaning. Before one raises the question of what is reality and what is illusion, one is in a state of ignorance. In such a state (as in a dream) one would not know what is reality and what is illusion. After a sudden awakening, one is able to see a distinction between the real and the irreal. This constitutes a transformation in outlook. *The transformation is a transformation in consciousness from the unaware lack of distinction between reality and fantasy to the aware and definite distinction of being awake.* This is what I take to be the message, however implicit and inchoate, of the butterfly dream anecdote. After all, we know from the viewpoint of common sense that men do not really turn into butterflies and butterflies do not really turn into men. Therefore, it seems that the point of the story can only be an analogy of some kind. And the analogical change that is being pointed to is a change in the *level of consciousness.*

What if we do not perform this act of textual transformation? Without any sort of philosophical interpolation, the dream as it stands in the raw version is decidedly ambiguous. The two major schools of interpretation that have arisen have based their interpretation on the raw version of the butterfly dream story. Both of these schools of interpretation have, as a direct result of tying their interpretations to the raw version of the story, arrived at interpretations which are themselves ambiguous. Let us examine these two schools of interpretation in turn.

First and foremost among interpretations is the version which I label the confusion hypothesis. Simply put, this interpretation is that we do not really awaken and so we are not actually sure of anything. The transformation that is pointed to is one among external things. The transformation that is traded off, however, is a reverse mental transformation. We think we have awakened but we really have not. The confusion hypothesis appears to be the viewpoint expounded by Fung Yu-lan:

> This (the butterfly dream story) shows that, although in ordinary appearance there are differences between things, in delusions or

in dreams one thing can also be another. "The transformation of things" proves that the differences among things are not absolute.[4]

This argument would appear to follow from the conclusion of the raw version of the dream story, and it suffers from two weaknesses. First, because it appears to follow from the conclusion of the raw version, it takes on all of the questionable properties of the raw version. Since it does not question the order of the statements of the raw version, it must accept all the built-in logical ambiguity of the raw version. Second, it leaves us in a state of confusion. Not only is this epistemically unsatisfying, it is inherently non-self-validating. The problem with a state of confusion in which there are no differences or distinctions is that the state of confusion is systematic, absolute and non-correctible. The state of dreamland is a state of illusion. In a state of illusion, we can be wholly mistaken about what we think is the case. In confusion this complete, on what grounds can we even be sure that our interpretation (that we may be dreaming) has any truth to it at all?

The redoubtable A. C. Graham follows Fung in accepting the confusion hypothesis. In an early paper on the subject, Graham takes a point of view which is virtually identical to that of Fung. In discussing the butterfly dream story he tells us that ". . . it reminds us that what we think we know while dreaming contradicts what we think we know while awake, and suggests that like the opposite opinions of philosophers, these have equal status. The last sentence [of the raw version] suggests that the divergence between Chuang-Tzu and the butterfly which he becomes in his dream is no different from the divisions and developments which we think we know about in the waking world."[5]

This type of interpretation coheres with a view of the entirety of chapter two (and by extension for the *Chuang-Tzu* as a whole) that it is a kind of relativism. Such an interpretation of the *Chuang-Tzu* as a type of relativism deserves separate treatment, and I will devote a separate chapter to examining this claim. For the time being, we can see that it certainly does not cohere with the general interpretation of the *Chuang-Tzu* that I have been advancing in the course of this book.

While we could understand the raw version of the butterfly dream to be saying that waking and dreaming are not different from each other, this requires us to gloss over certain logical improbabilities in the story as it currently stands. In addition, the confusion hypothesis points us in the direction of relativism. As I will point out in the next chapter, it is extremely difficult to interpret chapter two of the *Chuang-Tzu* as a relativistic tract, especially when we take into account the Great Sage dream anecdote. One could argue (as Graham does) that the Great Sage anecdote makes one point while the butterfly dream makes another, and this would be of no great harm if the two points were not contradictory to each other. But, if the butterfly dream anecdote makes the point that Graham claims that it does, it negates the point of the Great Sage dream anecdote. Such a negation renders the Great Sage dream anecdote totally meaningless. Likewise, the point of the Great Sage dream anecdote contradicts and negates the point of the butterfly dream anecdote. On the interpretation that I am bringing forward, both dream anecdotes can retain their meaning and, in fact, are mutually reinforcing.

If we examine a more recent work of Graham's, we can see that he is still adhering to the confusion hypothesis. He compares the Great Sage dream and the butterfly dream and comes up with the conclusion that they are making different points:

> Our illusory picture of a multiple world is compared with a dream from which the sage awakens. The famous story of Chuang-tzu's dream of being a butterfly seems, however, to make a different point, that the distinction between waking and dreaming is another false dichotomy. If I can distinguish them, how can I tell whether I am now dreaming or awake?[6]

While we must save a detailed analysis and comparison of the two dream anecdotes for the next chapter, it is sufficient to note here that Graham's recent interpretation of the butterfly dream is still the confusion hypothesis: we are unsure if we are awake or dreaming. In this case, the whole concept of awakening makes no sense at all. At the very least, it loses all of its force. At most, it entails that anything we think that we know will lack all veracity and all possibility of verification. This impossibility of knowledge in principle applies equally well to the confusion hypothesis itself. If we are existing in a state of irremediable confusion, then we may well be deluded about the very validity of the confusion hypothesis.

There is some indication that Graham himself is not totally satisfied with the confusion hypothesis, as later in the same book he makes a comment in passing which identifies his interpretation more with the endless transformation hypothesis. That these views are not wholly consistent with each other is not a point he takes into consideration. However, in a footnote to his actual translation of the story, he seems to imply that the identities of man and butterfly are actually changing, that it is not simply an epistemological confusion but an actual ontological transformation that is occurring. What is more, man, in attunement with this transformation, can validly signify himself as either man or butterfly. The endless transformation thesis implies cognitive veracity. While I will explore the endless transformation hypothesis below, it is of interest to note that Graham is flirting with it here. The problem with it for Graham is that if we are in a state of confusion, how can we know that we are really changing from one to another? How can we validly apply the appropriate name to the appropriate state? Graham does not seem to be aware of these difficulties, for in his footnote he interprets the butterfly dream anecdote he has just finished translating as as example of a sort of continuous transformation which requires a constant shifting of appropriate labels:

> The point is that the Taoist does not permanently deem himself a man or a butterfly but moves spontaneously from fitting one name to fitting another.[7]

While it is not completely clear from this quotation that this is an ontological change, it would appear from the context that this is what Graham has in mind. Otherwise, the "Taoist" (who is neither man nor butterfly?) arbitrarily selects a name regardless of the appropriate state of being. This would not seem to be likely, as there never would have been any butterfly problem unless there had been some puzzle concerning identity. And if the endless transformation hypothesis is true, as Graham seems to suggest here, how can one know either which state man is in or which name to apply? This type of knowledge would appear to be denied to man if the confusion hypothesis were correct. In fact, if the confusion hypothesis were correct, it is difficult to know how one could be aware of a transformation in the first place. If one can be aware of a distinct phase of one's existence, one is not in a state of confusion. One could argue, on behalf of the confusionist, that the state of change might only be apparent (and the naming therefore a kind of meaningless game), but it is not even clear how one could be capable of knowing *this* with any degree of certainty or veracity. The confusion hypothesis does not permit valid cognition, and this fact effectively rules out both the confusion hypothesis itself and its attendant ontological endless transformation appendage.

The endless transformation thesis proper finds its highest expression in the writings of Mark Elvin. Elvin himself refers to the famous anecdote of the butterfly as an example of the self in what he terms continual transformation. I have supplied the concept of endless transformation since it seems to be implied in the viewpoint taken. Elvin also supplies his own translation of the butterfly dream anecdote:

> Once Juang dreamt he was a butterfly, a butterfly delighted with itself, doing whatever it felt like doing, and unaware it was Juang Jou. Suddenly, he woke up and realized with a shock that he *was* Juang Jou. He had no idea if he was the Juang Jou who had dreamt

he was a butterfly or the butterfly dreaming he was Juang Jou. There was assuredly a difference between Juang and the butterfly. This is what is meant by 'the transformation of things'.[8]

Elvin describes the endless transformation thesis most concisely and clearly in the following passage:

Dreams [in the Chuang-Tzu] provided evidence that things were constantly turning into other things, a process that he [Chuang Tzu] compared to molten bronze taking first one shape then another in the hands of a master smith. His vision of the self in this flux of continual transformation can be found in the famous anecdote of the butterfly.[9]

While Graham, strictly speaking, is not an adherent of the transformation thesis, it would be constructive to counterpose his translation in analyzing the concept of endless transformation:

Last night Chuang Chou dreamed he was a butterfly, spirits soaring he was a butterfly (is it that in showing what he was he suited his own fancy?), and did not know about Chou. When all of a sudden he awoke, he was Chou with all his wits about him. He does not know whether he is Chou who dreams he is a butterfly or a butterfly who dreams he is Chou. Between Chou and the butterfly there was necessarily a dividing; just this is what is meant by the transformation of things.[10]

In all of the translations as in the Chinese original, there is no clear referential index for the "this" in the final statement. That this "this" is ambiguous is one of the sources of the variant interpretations. In my own version, which is no less linguistically ambiguous on this point, the *this* refers to the change in consciousness *from* the seeming butterfly awareness *to* the awareness of Chuang Chou. My argument is based on the superior logic in this interpretation. The difference that is noted between Chuang Chou and the butterfly is what is seen after the transformation. The transformation in its noetic and epistemic aspect consists of the *certitude* of the realization of the difference between the two. The transformation in its noematic aspect consists of the realization of the difference between irreality and reality. If we examine the choice of words, I believe that there is more logic supporting the modified interpretation. For example, in Elvin's translation, there is a very astute choice of the word "assuredly" when referring to the difference. In my interpretation, this "assuredly" must come from an inward state of realization (betokened by the waking up) which is the self-certifying evidence which can only result from an *internal* awareness of the difference. The awareness on the noetic side is the change or *transformation* of consciousness foreshadowed and also clarified by the analogy of awakening. Elvin's choice of words neatly captures the noetic aspect of the transformation which, in my view, is the transformation from the world of dream-confusion to the world of reality-distinction making.

Elvin's use of the word "transformation" instead of Graham's "transformations" also is supportive of my view that the transformation is a transformation of consciousness for which the butterfly dream story is but a metaphor. "Transformations" can only refer to the external changes of things. In this regard, Graham's translation is more suited to the external transformation hypothesis than Elvin's. There is only one consciousness (in the self-transformation thesis which I am expounding), but clearly there can be a plurality of things. In this respect, Elvin's translation is to be favored. Since, as we shall see later, Elvin supplies a concept of transcendence in addition to that of external endless transformation, it is not surprising that his translation is more congruent with some form of self-transformation.

What of the external endless transformation thesis proper? At the risk of appearing scholastic, I find five major objections to the endless transformation thesis. While these certainly overlap, there are sufficient unique features of each that make a separate consideration worthwhile. All five objections are tied together by a common thread. The common thread is that in one form or another, the endless transformation hypothesis does not take the unique features of the dream metaphor sufficiently into account.

The first objection to the endless transformation thesis is that the conclusions to be drawn from the butterfly dream story are too weak. We do not need to have recourse to a dream metaphor to arrive at the awareness that things are constantly changing from one to another. If our only concern is transience, we do not need any sort of awakening to become aware of this transience. We would not first have to go through some puzzle involving a confusion of reality with illusion. We would only have a philosopher's lament about the brevity of existence. We would not mistake what is for what is not. The butterfly dream would serve as an inapposite metaphor for a complaint about the constant succession of things in the world—a complaint that is lodged later on in the *Chuang-Tzu* in a much better form in the famous description in which life is likened to a galloping horse glimpsed through a crack in the window.[11]

If the meaning of the butterfly dream were to be taken as merely representing the ephemeralness of life, then this would appear to be a very weak conclusion for which, it would seem, the metaphor of representation is ill chosen. In my opinion, the butterfly dream is not a symbol of external transformation at all. If in this metaphor Chuang Tzu were pointing to the fact that everything in the world is impermanent and is transformed into something else, why would the question be posed as to which is which? This type of question only makes sense if there is a puzzle concerning levels of reality and illusion. This type of question does not make sense if the only concern is the evanescence of what is. If all the awakening from the dream establishes is this, then the butterfly dream metaphor is a maladroit metaphor for establishing a prosaic conclusion.

This same objection applies even if we take the interpretation that there is no waking up from the dream. If there is no waking up from the dream and the conclusion is that everyting is in flux, then this is a conclusion one could reach without falling asleep. In fact, many able philosophers have arrived at this conclusion without relying upon a dream metaphor. Whether one remains in the dream or wakes up from the dream, if all that is established is that things are constantly changing, this would appear to be a rather weak conclusion to have reached from the butterfly dream story. If there is some waking up from the dream and what we learn upon awakening is that things are constantly changing into other things and what we were confused about (during the dream) had been the distinction between one thing and another, then there does not seem to be very much that will have been gained from the awakening. If there is not much difference between the results of dreaming and awakening, then what is the force behind the concept of a necessary division (in Graham's language) that exists post-awakening? To make use of the dream metaphor to establish transience is, I think, to achieve too pedestrian an end. If upon waking up from the dream we arrive at the same conclusion as in the dream, then there was not much use in falling asleep in the first place. If we never wake up from the dream at all, and we reach a conclusion we can reach while awake, again we make very little use of the dream metaphor.

The second objection is that the endless transformation hypothesis, when pressed to its logical implications, transforms itself into the confusion hypothesis. The same problems that affected the confusion hypothesis, thus, apply here as well. If all things ultimately are changing into all other things, then there is no stability at all. A constantly changing world is one that cannot be known. Endless transformations apply to distinctions as well. Whatever is to be known also changes. What we claim to know has no permanence to it. There is but a short distance from this to the full-fledged confusion hypothesis where nothing at all can be known with any degree of certainty.

The third objection to the endless transformation thesis is that it is not well supported by the evidence of the dream metaphor. The external endless transformation thesis makes no distinction between worldly transformations which we can consider both intra-worldly (from one external thing in the world to another external thing) and inter-worldly (between the level of the world and another level of interpretation). If one takes the dream argument as an illustration of intra-worldly change, this is counterfactual. The change that takes place within a dream is a special kind of non-physical change which is that of consciousness as over against a world and not simply as part of a physical world. Indeed, to take the dream argument as an illustration of intra-worldly change could provide a further confusion since the dream interrupts the orderly change processes of the world and even throws them open to question. The reason that the endless transformation thesis is not well supported by the evidence of the dream metaphor is that the endless transformation of the physical world does not take the mental world sufficiently into account.

The fourth objection to the endless transformation thesis is that not only is it not well indicated by a dream argument but it may well be contraindicated by a dream argument, since one of the chief characteristics of a dream is that its cognitive contents are not reliable. If one learns in whatever fashion from a dream that the world is in a state of constant succession, then this learning might well be part of the illusion of the dream. The endless succession of things is not a privileged position within a dream cognition. Indeed, in a dream, the endless transformations cannot have any veridical status. If all is but a dream, there is no way of knowing that the endless recyclings are but a moment's passage in the world of reality.

My fifth and last objection to the endless succession thesis is that it does not take sufficiently into account the one-way direction of awakening from a dream that is part of the modified version of the butterfly dream story. The dream story, in my view, carries with it the inherent implication of the eventual possibility of waking up from the dream. It is not only the story of a dream, but also the story of waking up from a dream. If, as in my view, the result of awakening is the achievement of a different level of insight, this would seem to imply that there is some level of cognitive veridicality achieved which is the difference between the pre-awakened and the post-awakened consciousness.

As best as I can make out the external transformation hypothesis, it comes to this. During the dream, one has confused man with butterfly. The result of the awakening is to see the difference and to note that all things, while different, do eventually change into each other. This interpolation of the dream narrative makes use of the two differing levels or layers of cognition that I claim must be there. In the layer of cognitive corrigibility (the realm of dream), one could not tell

Chuang Chou from the butterfly. In the layer of cognitive veridicality, one can both tell them from each other and see that they endlessly transform from one to the other. Alternatively, one could also argue that one cannot tell one from the other because they transform back and forth into each other, as I have suggested in the second objection. But this too requires a level of knowledge or insight that presumably differs from the dream level and thus is also dependent upon a bi-level of corrigibility/veridicality. The only difference is that we know that we cannot know in the state of knowledge, whereas in the dream state we simply did not know. In this latter case, the endless transformation thesis collapses into the confusion hypothesis. In the former case, the endless transformation thesis becomes a sophisticated version of the confusion hypothesis which we will examine below.

To summarize my five objections. The first objection is that the conclusion reached by the endless transformation hypothesis seems too weak. If it is a conclusion that is reached because one does not wake up from a dream then this is also a conclusion that one can reach while awake. If it is a conclusion that is a result of awakened knowledge and it turns out to be more or less the same as what one knows while dreaming, then the conclusion which one reaches in the higher level of awakened knowledge is both the same as the conclusion one can reach while dreaming and while normally awake. The second objection is that a state of endless change is tantamount to a state of endless confusion, in which case one cannot claim to have any assurance concerning the truth of the endless transformation hypothesis itself. The third objection is that the thesis of an endless external succession of things is not well supported by the evidence of a dream, which is an internal, mental transformation. The fourth objection is that if dream evidence is used to adduce a thesis of endless transformation then this evidence is itself suspect since all contents of a dream are liable to the charge of illusion. The fifth objection is that the endless transformation thesis does not take into account the portion of the story that involves awakening from the dream. Awakening from the dream involves some higher level of cognitive veridicality. If the consequences post-awakening are the same as pre-awakening, this would appear to blur the distinction between dreaming and awakening. Whatever transformation is involved cannot be endless. The transformation has to be one-way (from butterfly to man) if the realization of even the endlessness is to be considered as veridical; otherwise, this realization would occupy no privileged status. The transformation of consciousness as one-way awakening would appear to be necessary even to be able to recognize the endlessness of cosmic change.

Even in the endless transformation hypothesis of Elvin, there is nonetheless a concept of transcendence included which signifies that

we must rise above the transformation of physical things.[12] By including this element in addition to the pure physical transformation theme,
Elvin's view more closely approximates the transformation of consciousness view that I have been presenting. There is one difference, of a
minor nature, which involves the nature of the transcendence which is
included. For Elvin, this transcendence is comprised of indifference,
since the transcendent consciousness is impervious to change. To establish his conclusion that, "The ultimate aim was an all-encompassing
indifference,"[13] he points to a passage which well supports his conclusion and which he presents in an intriguing translation from the seventeenth chapter of the Chuang-Tzu:

> The long enduring causes it [great knowledge] no dull stupor, nor
> does the transitory make it flustered, since it knows that there are
> no terminal points to duration.[14]

This view makes Chuang Tzu out to be a sophisticated sort of Stoic,
who is aware of both Parmenidean and Heraclitean standpoints but
sees both (including the Parmenidean) from a higher and presumably
changeless standpoint.

While this conclusion certainly follows from the evidence and is
extremely well captured in the phrase "all-encompassing indifference,"
it is at odds with the value hierarchy that is built up in the early, inner
chapters of the Chuang-Tzu. For this reason, I regard the evidence
taken from the famous and influential seventeenth chapter as contradictory to the point of view of the inner chapters. From my own point
of view, one of the problems with the seventeenth chapter is that its
transcendence hypothesis is not based upon the concept of an awakening. In fact, if the transformation itself refers to the endless transformation of things, then there is no sense of a transformation from an
immanent to a transcendent consciousness. But it is my view that some
type of self-transformation must take place if one is to change from
one level of consciousness to another, and this is the value of the butterfly dream story. Nevertheless, if one's version of transcendence is
tied to the seventeenth chapter, then Elvin's interpolation is both faithful and astute. It is, in my opinion, the best one can do with Chuang
Tzu if one insists upon retaining the seventeenth chapter. Elvin's conclusions follow impeccably from the evidence taken from the seventeenth chapter, and if we were to exclude evidence taken from the
seventeenth chapter the difference between Elvin's and my view of
transcendence would be likely to vanish.[15]

There is one more version of the confusion hypothesis I would
like to examine separately because it is argued for in such sophisticated terms. In his book, Chuang-Tzu: World Philosopher at Play, Kuang-

ming Wu understands the butterfly story in terms of waking up from ignorance to knowledge.[16] Thus he sees the butterfly dream story as a metaphor for a higher kind of knowledge. But what he wakes up to is the confusion hypothesis all over again, the not knowing if he is Chuang Chou or the butterfly.[17] While Wu, in my opinion, captures perfectly the concept of the dream as representing the higher level of knowledge that one obtains upon awakening, the notion that one awakens to puzzlement does not satisfy. It follows very faithfully from the raw version of the dream, but this raw version is, as I have argued, logically untenable.

In a more recent article, Wu states the sophisticated confusion hypothesis in a remarkable passage:

> What Chuang Tzu attained by reflecting on his dream is the awakened knowledge that we cannot know our fixed identity. It is this knowledge that releases the dreamer (ourselves) from the tyranny of obsession with objective realism. This is a meta-knowledge, an awakening to self-ignorance. This awakened ignorance issues in a care-free meandering in the flux of ontological transformation.[18]

Here the confusion hypothesis in a sophisticated knowledge of ignorance form is coupled with the ontological transformation thesis.

I believe that this is the best that one can do with the butterfly dream if it is maintained in its raw form. I think, however, when we bring the butterfly dream together with the Great Sage dream that we will analyze in the subsequent chapter, that we can reach an even more powerful conclusion. If we are truly able to wake up, which both the modified version of the butterfly anecdote and the Great Sage dream anecdote maintain, then we can leave the dream and its attendant confusion behind. While we must save further comment on this for the next chapter, we must take note of the fact that Wu attributes cognitive veridicality to the dreamer of the story; and if the butterfly dream is seen as a dream from which we can awaken, then there is no *prima facie* reason why our knowledge must be restricted to an awareness of ignorance. If, on the other hand, we are still not sure if we are awake, then it is not at all clear how we can trust even this insight, namely, that all we know is that we cannot know. The problem with the raw version of the dream is that at the end of the dream we still do not know if we are dreaming. And in a dream no insight is privileged; all insights are corrigible. If we are still within the dream, then it is not clear how even Wu's brilliant analysis is justified. But given the raw version of the butterfly dream, one would be hard put to come up with a better interpretation.

The basic meaning of a dream requires that that which takes place within the dream is not real. The only way to make sense of a dream is to awaken from it. The butterfly is the token which represents what was once thought to be real and is now known to have been a figment of Chuang Chou's imagination. There is no literal physical change from butterfly into Chuang Chou; butterflies do not change into men and men do not change into butterflies. If one can wake up from a dream—and this is the point of the revised version—then, as one wakes up, the dream contents disintegrate. This is what is transformed: what was thought to be (and no longer is) was really something else. It was Chuang Chou all along. The dream image was after all, his image. This is the "transformation of things" of which Chuang Tzu speaks and with which he ends his story. Although the referential index is unclear, the correct understanding of the dream story requires that what is altered is not one real thing into another real thing but one illusion that is changed into reality. Or, since this is but a metaphor, the transformation proper is a change from a dreaming consciousness to a consciousness aware of reality.

One last point. If what is truly signified by the butterfly story is the change in internal consciousness—from a dreamer with a dreamy consciousness to a waking subject with an enlightened consciousness— what of the fact that the final statement, in most renditions, reads, "this is the transformation of things"?[19] If it is the consciousness itself that is transformed, this should be singular, not plural.

I think that the usage of the plural here is explained by the fact that when one awakens from the dream, one's vision is transformed. In the transformation of one's inner vision, of course, one's vision of reality is also transformed. Everything in the world will be transformed at the sudden moment of awakening. In the moment of awakening, one will see clearly the distinction between the unreal (the butterfly) and the real (Chuang Chou). This very cognitive act also extends to one's vision of the outer world. The world, being a world of plurality, will be seen in the plural. The awakening process is the key to seeing all things as they really are. Such is the real transformation of things, transformed in our proper understanding of them.

7 The Butterfly Dream: The Case for Ex̦ternal Textual Transformation

In this chapter I should like to review the option of retaining the existing order of the fragments that make up the butterfly dream story. If one accepts the raw version of the butterfly dream story, is there any way to make sense of the story as it stands? It is my contention that if one accepts the raw version of the butterfly dream story as authentic, then the only way to make sense out of the story as it stands is to see it as an earlier, provisional, and imperfect attempt to make a point which is made more completely and perfectly in the Great Sage or the Great Awakening dream anecdote. This requires an external textual relocation of the butterfly dream story so that it precedes rather than follows the Great Sage dream anecdote. The Great Sage dream anecdote will then end chapter two of the *Chuang-Tzu* and will be seen as the conclusion to the chapter. The most cohesive and coherent rendition of chapter two of the *Chuang-Tzu* would be to incorporate both internal and external changes. However, if for sentimental reasons there is a strong resistance to the alteration of the butterfly dream story itself, one can nonetheless keep the present order intact and still retain a logical coherence within chapter two by understanding the butterfly dream story to be a provisional statement of the point to be made in the Great Sage dream anecdote.

If we prefer the option of retaining the raw version of the butterfly dream, we can make sense out of the story by understanding it as an incomplete and preliminary attempt to put forth an argument that is more completely and satisfactorily put forth in the Great Sage dream anecdote. Before proceeding to my argument proper, one important qualification is to be noted. The overall strategy of comparing the two anecdotes for parallel elements makes sense only if we grant the premise that the two anecdotes are designed to make a similar point. If they are designed with different intentions in mind, the case to compare them becomes weaker. It is my contention, however, that they are designed to make a similar point.

If we were to decide that the butterfly and the Great Sage dream anecdotes were designed to make different points, it would be important to make certain that the two anecdotes were not making contradictory points. To know whether or not the two anecdotes are making similar or different points, we first need to know the point made by each anecdote. The point made by the Great Sage dream anecdote is fairly straightforward and, as we shall see below, there is no question about its meaning. The butterfly dream anecdote, as I have indicated in the previous chapter, is, on the other hand, decidedly ambiguous and difficult to interpret in its present form and present textual placement.

In the previous chapter, I explored two major types of interpretation that are possible for the butterfly dream in its raw version (by possible, I mean that are in accord with the internal logic of the butterfly dream anecdote): (a) that it has as its primary intention the conclusion that we are never sure whether we are dreaming or awake (the confusion hypothesis); (b) that it has as its primary intention the conclusion that everything is in a state of endless physical transformation. Since (b) to a large extent collapses into (a), for reasons which I explored in the previous chapter, I will simply refer to the confusion hypothesis as the only legitimate alternative to my hypothesis: (c) that the primary intention of the butterfly dream is to make the same point as is made in the more complete and satisfactory Great Sage dream anecdote. Simply put, the reasons for this were that endless transformation without an ultimate awakening would also mean that we would never be sure if we were awake or dreaming. If we were never certain if we were awake or dreaming, any hypothesis that we could frame as an interpretation would be just as suspect as the contents of any dream.

If we take (a) as the meaning of the butterfly dream anecdote, then this meaning directly contradicts the meaning of the Great Sage dream anecdote. Even if we insist upon the possible legitimacy of (b), this is also contradicted by the Great Sage dream anecdote as (b) does not provide for an ultimate awakening. If the butterfly dream anecdote contradicts the Great Sage dream anecdote, then even the butterfly dream loses its value because we do not then know which to believe of the two stories. At this point, the text loses its integrity. We either assume it is a self-contradictory text, or we are forced to construe one of the two stories as being either unimportant and/or spurious. It is my contention that by understanding the two anecdotes as making a similar if not identical point we can save both of the anecdotes and thus maintain both the integrity and the value of the text.

It is not enough, as I have argued in the previous chapter, to say with Graham that the two anecdotes are making different points and simply leave it at that.[1] We must make certain that the points that they make are not contradictory to each other. If the only possible interpretation of the butterfly dream is the confusion hypothesis, then this is directly contradicted by the Great Sage dream anecdote. As we shall see below, the Great Sage dream anecdote states explicitly that there will be a Great Awakening and after this awakening it will be possible to distinguish between the state of dreaming and the state of waking. What is more, it will be possible to distinguish the one as real (the waking state) and the other as illusion (the dream state).[2] This conclusion is in direct contradiction with the conclusion of the confusion hypothesis. If the confusion hypothesis is correct, then the meaning of the Great Sage dream anecdote is contradicted. If we are in a state of endless confusion as to whether we are awake or dreaming, then we can never rise out of this state. If the Great Sage dream anecdote is taken as meaningful, then the confusion hypothesis cannot be correct except as a preliminary attempt to put the point which is much better put in the Great Sage dream anecdote. What is more, if the confusion hypothesis is correct, then even the butterfly dream story by itself becomes unintelligible since we can never be certain of the validity of the conclusions to be reached in a state of potential illusion. It seems, then, that the only interpretation of the butterfly dream that is possible under that hypothesis would make a different point than the Great Sage dream anecdote and in fact contradicts the Great Sage dream anecdote, leaving us with a truncated or self-contradictory and unintelligible text.

I will proceed to offer a basis for my belief that the butterfly dream is an earlier version or an earlier attempt to articulate what is more fully articulated in the Great Sage dream. If we take the raw version of the butterfly dream as final, then it is my judgment that the butterfly dream in this version is a lisping version of the Great Sage dream, attempting to say what the Great Sage dream is saying but saying it less completely and less perfectly. My argument shall compare the two anecdotes textually so as to demonstrate that they both reveal a similar line of development; in so doing I hope to demonstrate how the Great Sage dream achieves more of what the butterfly dream is ostensibly attempting to achieve. This approach possesses the virtue of making sense out of both dream anecdotes and also of eliminating any possibility of a contradiction arising between the two. The elimination of the possibility of contradiction goes far toward preserving the integrity and thus the value of the chapter in which both of the anecdotes are to be found, and thus ultimately of the *Chuang-Tzu* as a whole. In what follows, whenever I employ the expression 'butterfly dream', I will always intend the raw version of the dream story. This will enable the arguments of this chapter to stand on their own without reference to the arguments put forth in the previous chapter.

My argument has two sides: (i) from the order of exposition; (ii) from the order of explanation. While these two arguments overlap, they nonetheless possess some important distinctions and thus benefit from separate consideration. Taken together, the arguments from the order of exposition and explanation make up the total argument for the preliminary or provisional status of the butterfly dream anecdote.

(i) The argument from the order of exposition or composition is based upon the assumption that the earlier an argument is formulated, the less complete it is. As an argument unfolds, it becomes more and more complete. The less complete argument therefore belongs earlier in the text based upon its having been formulated earlier. If, therefore, an arguably earlier argument is found later in the text and there are reasons to believe that the textual arrangement of arguments is a moot one,[3] then this will constitute an argument for the misplacement or the incorrect editing of an argument. The argument from the order of composition is that the less complete an argument is the earlier it has been formulated; therefore it rightfully belongs in an earlier textual sequence. This argument is based upon the psychology of exposition being such that an argument evolves as it is being formulated and its later formulations represent a truer state of the argument than its earlier attempts (as, for instance in the B and A versions of the *Critique*). The more evolved the version of the argument the more mature it is. If, therefore, we can show that the Great Sage dream anecdote is a more sophisticated, complete, self-conscious, explicit, and coherent version of the butterfly dream anecdote, this will constitute the argument for its having been composed later and therefore belonging later in the text.

(ii) The argument from the order of explanation is very similar to (i) in that it assumes that the more sophisticated version of an argument is later than a less sophisticated version. It adds to the argument from composition the feature that if an argument explains both itself and another version then it is logically posterior and should be placed later in the text on logical grounds. It makes less logical sense for a less full account to succeed a more full account in terms of the proper order of explanation. The *explanans* should succeed the *explanandum*. That argument which is less explicatory and requires an additional argument for its being fully or adequately explained is logically anterior to the more complete argument and should be placed prior to it.

The Argument from the Order of Composition

The argument from the order of composition is more difficult to make than the argument from the order of explanation, but it nonetheless is worthwhile to consider it. In composing an argument from the psychology of composition, the inexplicit precedes the explicit in time. As one develops an argument, more clarity is reached as to the conclusions one is attempting to establish. Anyone who has tried his hand at first order philosophy is familiar with this phenomenon. Therefore, the more complete and comprehensive the argument, the later stage it must occupy in terms of the temporal and therefore the spatial order of composition. The butterfly dream anecdote is a more incomplete and inexplicit stage of the argument than the Great Sage anecdote and therefore in all likelihood was put forth earlier in the stage of composition and belongs earlier in the text than the Great Sage anecdote.

We may regard the Great Sage dream anecdote first. It is clearly more complete and sophisticated than its butterfly counterpart. There are no logical contradictions within the narrative and there are no steps left out of the narrative. The basic structure of the Great Sage anecdote is as follows. First, it is stated that all men are existing on the level of the dream. Second, it is stated that even philosophers are dreaming when they expound their theories. Third, the author includes himself as a philosopher who is therefore also dreaming as he expounds his own theory. These three steps are put forth with complete self-consistency and without any ellipses in the argument.

Table 1: The Great Sage Dream Narrative

My Condensation of the Argument	The Text[4]
1. All men exist on the level of the dream	Yet all the while the fools think they are awake
2. Even philosophers are dreaming as they expound their theories	Confucius and you are both in a dream
3. I am also dreaming as I expound my philosophy (which in this case is the philosophy that you are dreaming)	And when I say that you are in a dream, this is also a dream
4. In principle it is possible that we can arrive at a state of knowledge whereby we can distinguish between what is a dream and what is not a dream	And someday there will be a great awakening when we know that this is all a great dream[5]
	By and by comes the great awakening and then we shall know that it has all been a great dream[6]

The author of the *Chuang-Tzu* also includes a new premise that one day there will be a great awakening in which we will be able to become aware that all that has so far progressed is in fact part of a dream. Such an expectation, if we may anticipate our conclusion here, would appear awkward if it were to appear prior to the butterfly dream anecdote, where we are apparently left at the end not knowing whether we are awake or dreaming.

If, on the other hand, we were to inspect the butterfly dream, we would find it (at least in its present version) to reach a far more tentative conclusion of a much narrower scope. It is not at all logically contiguous or logically sequential if in fact it were to have been composed later in time or if it were meant to appear after the Great Sage anecdote. Consider:

> Once upon a time, Chuang Chou [i.e., Chuang Tzu] dreamed that he was a butterfly, a butterfly fluttering about, enjoying itself. It did not know that it was Chuang Chou. Suddenly he awoke with a start and he was Chuang Chou again. But he did not know whether he was Chuang Chou who had dreamed that he was a butterfly, or whether he was a butterfly dreaming that he was Chuang Chou. Between Chuang Chou and the butterfly there must be some distinction. This is what is called the transformation of things.[7]

If we compare the Great Sage dream with the butterfly story in its present form, the butterfly story will in contrast appear to be radically incomplete. In the butterfly dream anecdote, we are told that we are not sure if Chuang Chou is dreaming or if it is the butterfly who is doing the dreaming. In the very next sentence, there is a tentative attempt made to claim that there must be some distinction between the two. (In the fragment I am arguing is later, the Great Sage is put forth as one who could possibly be aware of such a distinction.) However, in the butterfly anecdote, while the necessity of there being such a distinction is recognized, it is not at all clear who could possibly be aware of such a distinction. It clearly cannot be Chuang Chou, who might well be dreaming this possibility and therefore might be mistaken. I will not speculate upon the possibilities of this distinction being made by the butterfly. A distinction is markedly called for but the condition for the possibility of the distinction is not given within the limits of the butterfly anecdote.

Finally, in the butterfly anecdote we are told that such a distinction may be called the transformation of things. In the context of the butterfly anecdote this makes very little sense. The transformation of all things would be witnessed by a subject knower who would not occupy a veridical standpoint. The conclusion reached (such as the transformation of things) is not at all justified or justifiable. That there is a transformation of things does not appear to be a well warranted conclusion if it is a conclusion which is to be reached from the butterfly dream anecdote taken by itself. The conclusion that this is the transformation of things clearly does not follow as a logical consequence of the butterfly dream anecdote. It stands by itself as a logically unwarranted conclusion without any textual justification.

However, if we consider the butterfly dream anecdote to be an earlier attempt at stating an argument which anticipates or adumbrates the argument which is stated in its fuller form in the Great Sage dream anecdote, the conclusion of the butterfly dream makes perfect logical sense. First, we are told that Chuang Chou might well be dreaming (this is more or less the point of the butterfly appearing in the story in the first place). This fits in very well if it were to precede the Great Sage dream. For example, in the Great Sage dream in its entirety, the story commences with a story of those who are dreaming of drinking wine. In this context, just as the people in the dream are dreaming of drinking wine (and are therefore inebriated in their dream and their dream judgment impaired), they do not know if they are dreaming or not. *What* the transformation of things is, they are not quite sure, although they realize upon awakening from their winy slumbers that they have not been drinking wine at all. This now places the butterfly dream on the same level of dreaming of drinking wine and hunting. The only difference is that an enthymeme is present. In the Great Sage dream the mock wine imbibers know that there is a transformation, but what is left out is how they could know this. This information is supplied by the appearance of the Great Sage, who can appear later and explain everything to them. (I have conflated the two stories for the moment in order to put my point most plainly.) Chuang Chou, or the butterfly, is Chuang Chou dreaming. He needs to wake up in order to understand this properly. The distinction between Chuang Chou and the butterfly can only be made with clarity and certainty after an *ultimate awakening*. The distinction between Chuang Chou and the butterfly that is said to exist (within the butterfly anecdote) must be as the result of a small or non-final awakening. I say this not only because there is no mention made of a great awakening here but also because as soon as he recognizes that he is Chuang Chou, he does not know if he is Chuang Chou or not. The awakening that he experiences is not a full or real or final awakening because as soon as it occurs he is not sure if it is not part of a dream. The conclusion which follows, that there must be some distinction between Chuang Chou and the butterfly, is illegitimate if it is based upon the internal logic of the butterfly dream anecdote taken as a complete argument in itself. It makes sense only if we understand the butterfly dream anecdote as a precursor to the Great Sage dream anecdote in which the conditions for the possibility of the truth of the butterfly dream anecdote's knowledge claims are given. As an anticipation of a more complete argument, it makes a certain amount of sense. If it stands alone as a conclusion to an argument, the conclusion offered by the butterfly dream anecdote taken by itself — that we can know that there must be a distinction between Chuang Chou and the butterfly — is an illicit conclusion.

The butterfly dream anecdote makes sense if it precedes the Great Sage dream. A final and lasting distinction between Chuang Chou and the butterfly can only be made after the Great Awakening. The distinction between Chuang Chou and the butterfly that is available inside of the butterfly dream anecdote is premature and uncertain. Such a tentative and corrigible distinction can only be the result of a temporary and non-ultimate awakening.

In the butterfly dream anecdote, an attempt is made to make the same point as the Great Sage dream anecdote (that we can see reality only after awakening), by having Chuang Chou awake with a start prior to making a distinction. The problem with this is that after awakening he is not certain if he is even Chuang Chou. Thus, the concept of awakening is not yet used to full effect. After awakening, he is confused as to his self-identity just as if he were still in a dream. To make matters worse, he becomes aware that there must be a distinction between Chuang Chou and the butterfly while still within this state of confusion. It seems clear from this analysis that the butterfly dream anecdote must be a primitive or rudimentary version of the Great Sage anecdote and was probably first in the order of composition.

The Argument from the Order of Explanation

The argument from the order of explanation is very much like the argument from the order of composition; however, unlike the argument from the order of composition, the argument from the order of explanation does not argue as to which argument must have been designed first in time. The argument from the order of explanation argues from the standpoint of a complete (consistent, cohesive, and coherent) explanation that it makes more logical sense that the argument which is the more comprehensive and self-conscious (that can explain both the other argument and itself) should follow the less comprehensive, less consistent, and less self-conscious argument as the *explanans* should follow the *explanandum* and not the reverse. This argument is based on the grounds of what constitutes the most satisfactory explanation and is independent from the actual intention of the author. Therefore, it is not necessary to subscribe to subsequent false and misleading misarrangement by later editing for the argument from the order of explanation to be valid.

As an aid to the reader, I have reproduced below the full version of the Great Sage dream anecdote which in our present version of the text is placed in near proximity to the butterfly dream anecdote preceding it by some three arguments.

> He who dreams of drinking wine may weep when morning comes; he who dreams of weeping may in the morning go off to hunt. While he is dreaming he does not know it is a dream, and in his dream he may even try to interpret a dream. Only after he wakes does he know it was a dream. And someday there will be a great awakening when we know that this is all a great dream. Yet the stupid believe they are awake, busily and brightly assuming they understand things, calling this man ruler, that one herdsman—how dense! Confucius and you are both dreaming! And when I say you are dreaming, I am dreaming, too. Words like these will be labeled the Supreme Swindle. Yet, after ten thousand generations, a great sage may appear who will know their meaning, and it will still be as though he appeared with astonishing speed.[8]

It could be argued, of course, that the Great Sage dream anecdote is of little significance and should be ignored in deference to the insight offered by the butterfly dream anecdote. I would find this solution unpalatable given the sophistication and subtlety of the Great Sage dream anecdote and the comparative primitiveness, incompleteness, illogic, and non-selfconscious paradoxicality of the butterfly dream anecdote.

I think that a close examination of the two fragments reveals that there is a similarity of intent and that the Great Sage dream does what the butterfly dream attempts but is not able to do. The condensation of philosophical elements which follows is an attempt to demonstrate this point. While in my opinion the arguments from the order of composition and the order of explanation are mutually reinforcing, it is possible to argue that on explanatory grounds alone there is a greater coherency to the argument if the Great Sage dream anecdote were to follow the butterfly dream anecdote and indeed to conclude the chapter.

If we take the Great Sage dream anecdote as the later argument logically speaking, it has the power of explaining the butterfly dream; but the reverse is not the case. Once fully awakened, one may distinguish between what is a dream and what is reality. Before one has fully awakened, such a distinction is not even possible to draw empirically.

If we take the butterfly dream as following the Great Sage dream, it would appear as if there is a regressus in the argument. We have already fully awakened; however, we are once again in the situation of not being able to tell if we are awake or dreaming. This makes no sense at all. It could be taken as a refutation of the Great Sage Argument except that it is claimed in the butterfly argument that there must be some distinction between Chuang Chou and the butterfly. Thus, it cannot be taken to be saying something different from the Great Sage dream. On the other hand, if after awakening we can no longer make the distinction even though there must be such a distinction, this would nullify the insight of the Great Sage dream that such a distinction is possible after a great awakening. If we can no longer make such a distinction after a great awakening, this either makes nonsense of the Great Sage dream (which is not likely intended since it is stated that there must be some distinction), or it constitutes an effective *reductio ad absurdum* of placing the butterfly dream after the Great Sage dream. That the intent of the butterfly dream is the same as that of the Great Sage dream is indicated in its assertion that there must be a distinction, but the internal logic of the butterfly dream has not yet developed to the point where it would be possible to make such a distinction. It wants to make the distinction but it cannot. This constitutes the lisp of the butterfly.

If, however, we place the butterfly dream before the Great Sage dream, all the pieces in the puzzle fit together. The butterfly dream cannot explain the Great Sage dream (indeed, it is not even self-explicatory), but the Great Sage dream can and in fact does explain the butterfly dream. The butterfly dream is clearly a case of attempting to put forth the difficulties encountered if one is in a dreaming state. Chuang Chou possessed the insight that there must be a distinction between waking and dreaming (between Chuang Chou and the butterfly) before he had developed the logical tools to explain his possessing the insight. He then elaborated these very carefully in the Great Sage dream anecdote. After saying that there was a distinction between waking and dream and that this was the transformation, he proceeded to explain how this was possible. The transformation was the condition of the possibility. The transformation was the awakening, the transformation of the subject knower. If we take what amounts to his now-earlier statement that it is the transformation of things, we are in a quandary. This is an inexplicit or enythmemic statement of what in a fuller form would read: this is the transformation of things due to the transforming insight of the awakened mind. There is not an endless repetition of the cycle of Chuang Chou and butterfly. He is quite clear that there can be an end to this cycle. In fact, even the recognition of the difference between Chuang Chou and the butterfly cannot be made within the state of a dream or it would be a suspect distinction as the contents of any dream are fictitious. The awareness that there must be a distinction between Chuang Chou and the butterfly must logically follow a moment of awakening. The possibility of seeing the transformation of things (which is another way of saying the correct understanding of reality) is only possible in the fully awakened state.

The explanatory power of placing the Great Sage dream anecdote after the butterfly dream anecdote is great, for it would then explain both the butterfly dream and itself. If we insist upon placing the butterfly dream after the Great Sage dream, we are taking a step backwards and then drawing an unwarranted conclusion that we can know (or that someone can know) there must be a distinction between Chuang Chou and the butterfly while there was a possibility that the subject knower was still in a dream. This makes no logical sense. By placing the Great Sage dream later in the chapter, we are presented with a well formed argument. I rest my case on this.

As an aid to the reader, if we place the Great Sage dream side by side with the butterfly dream, we can take note of the superior self-consistency, comprehensiveness, and scope of the Great Sage dream. All are earmarks of its belonging to a later stage of composition. The greater self-reflectiveness, greater subtlety and in general all-encompassing qualities are also indications of its bringing a more complete and elegant explanation to the problems posed if it is placed later. For purposes of simplicity and for the ease of exposition, I have charted what I refer to as the elements of each dream anecdote.

Table 2: A Comparison of Dream Elements

Elements of the Great Sage Dream	*Elements of the Butterfly Dream*
A. Transformation between dreaming and waking	Transformation between dreaming and waking
wine → weeping; weeping → hunting	Chuang Chou to butterfly; butterfly to Chuang Chou
[This takes place with clearly marked divisions between dreaming and waking so that it would be possible to make the distinction]	[This by retrogressive argument takes place within a realm of not knowing whether one is dreaming or awake, making the argument logically suspect and convoluted]
B. While dreaming, we are not conscious that we are dreaming	While dreaming, we are not conscious that we are dreaming (but this is only implicitly put)

Table 2: A Comparison of Dream Elements—Cont'd.

Elements of the Great Sage Dream	*Elements of the Butterfly Dream*
C. During the dream, we may attempt to interpret our dream	This is omitted altogether [I take this to be the act of the philosopher]
D. When awake, they *knew* it was a dream [N.B., the claim to knowledge is stronger here]	Realizes he is Chuang Chou but in the same breath is not really sure if he is not in fact the butterfly dreaming (therefore, confused knowledge at best)
E. Great Awakening where all life is explained as on the dream level in some sense, thus revealing the metaphorical dimension of the Great Sage anecdote	Omitted altogether—again the interpretive work of the philosopher
F. Confucius and you are both dreaming—even philosophers are dreaming	Omitted and only a lower level reference is made to Chuang Chou and the butterfly
G. Even I am dreaming when I say you are dreaming	Omitted—but implicitly contained in the idea that if it is the butterfly's dream, then what is said has no reality—which constitutes a more oblique and less developed reference to "I am dreaming" in that in content it is different and in fact opposite, but in logical consequence it is the same
H. These words appear paradoxical	Omitted—no acknowledgement is made of the paradoxical character of the anecdote—thus illustrating a less reflective, less explicit, and less sophisticated formulation
I. These words are explicable and will be explained [The coming of the Great Sage]	Omitted—we are left only with the realization that there must *be* some difference between illusion and reality, but we do not know the condition for the possibility of knowing the difference—leaves the possible impression that a fuller or more definitive explication is not possible

The hint of a link between the two anecdotes is given in the phrase, "This is the transformation of things." In the context of the butterfly narrative, the "this" is the understanding of the distinction between Chuang Chou and the butterfly. This *understanding* is the true transformation. When we possess this understanding (as in the case of the Great Sage), then the world becomes transformed to the level of intelligibility. Things are transformed in the sense that they are finally seen to be things; that is, they are understood. In the butterfly dream, the reason is not explicit for why this is possible. All that we can know is that there is a distinction and that the understanding of this distinction is the transformation — whatever this means. In the Great Sage anecdote, the missing links to the argument are supplied: there is a distinction between illusion and reality and the Greatly Awakened Sage will explain what is in principle explicable to us. In the meantime, it might appear paradoxical and dreamlike in the words of the philosophers. Since philosophers speak out of the dream state, such seemingness or interim paradoxicality goes with the territory. Not only is the Great Sage dream self-explicative, it explains or makes sense out of the butterfly dream as well. In the order of composition and in the order of explanation, it belongs later. It reflects both upon itself and the butterfly dream and is therefore clearly more sophisticated. It explains the possibility of its own occurrence and the possibility of the occurrence of the butterfly dream. It states that these dual occurrences are explicable and suggests the condition for the possibility of the explication while at the same time reflecting shrewdly upon the limitations of language involved in these reflections. Its greater self-consistency, comprehensiveness, scope of application, and self-reflectiveness all argue for its being placed later than the butterfly dream in the chapter in order that its greater power of explanation be accorded a more logical sequence in the exposition.

I think that there are some far reaching consequences to the argument that the butterfly dream is best understood as a provisional version of the Great Sage dream. Such consequences lie outside the scope of the present chapter. I will content myself with the following brief observations.

With the placement of the butterfly dream in its raw form at the end of chapter two and with no attempt to see a connection between the butterfly dream and the Great Sage dream, we are left with the conclusion that the awakening consists of a knowing that there must be a distinction between Chuang Chou and the butterfly; but since the awakening is not final (it is a corrigible awakening since even after the awakening he is not sure if he is a figment of a butterfly's dream), we are left with the possibility that the transformation spoken of is an endless cycle of dreams and awakenings with no respite. It is not possible (given the internal logic of the butterfly dream anecdote) to conceive of the transformation as a final awakening or a full awakening unless we regard the corrigibility of the judgment of the awakened subject as reflecting a spurious fragment in the text. If we regard the corrigibility of judgment as part of a genuine textual fragment then it would be very difficult to regard the transformation or any subsequent insight deriving from the transformation as veridical, since it might be another figment of the butterfly's imagination. If we regard the corrigibility of judgment as an integral portion of the butterfly dream anecdote, it does not seem that on the strength of the butterfly dream anecdote alone we could regard the transformation referred to as part of an ultimate or final awakening.

It would appear, if we take the butterfly dream anecdote as a whole and do not excise that fragment that refers to the incapacity to distinguish between reality and dream, that we cannot regard the transformation as taking us out of the butterfly's dream as this change too might be part of the dream. Our only other alternative, it seems, is to interpret the transformation as referring to the endless cycle of wakings and dreamings which casts doubt upon the validity of any knowledge claim. It is difficult to know how one might reach any other conclusion justifiably without taking into account the Great Sage anecdote. The butterfly dream anecdote, taken by itself in its raw form as a complete argument, leaves us with an unsatisfactory statement about reality where we are forever left in a state of unknowingness. How we, in a state of unknowingness, can know that there is a distinction between reality and illusion is left unexplained; given the possibility that the transformation is an endless cycle of alternation between dream and awakening, it may be inexplicable as well.

Understanding the butterfly dream as a provisional attempt to state what is better stated in the Great Sage dream leaves us in a more logically satisfactory position and also in a more optimistic mood. There is a possibility of distinguishing between what is and what is not, and the condition for the realization of that possibility is given. Once we achieve the Great Awakening, we can know what really is and we can explain how our knowledge of this is possible.

If one is forced to choose between an interpretation of the butterfly dream anecdote as betokening an inescapable unknowingness and the Great Sage dream anecdote as being a harbinger of potential explicability, then I would choose the Great Sage dream anecdote. Under these interpretations of the dream anecdotes, both of the dream anecdotes cannot be true at the same time. If the butterfly dream anecdote is true, then the Great Sage dream anecdote is false. If the Great

Sage dream anecdote is true, then the butterfly dream anecdote is false. However, we need not make such a choice.

If we take the interpretation that the butterfly dream anecdote is a foreshadowing and a premature version which is better rendered in the Great Sage dream anecdote, then both dream anecdotes can be seen as consistent with each other and both can be taken as true. The Great Sage dream anecdote will be seen as a fuller and more complete version of what is stated as true. The butterfly dream anecdote will be seen as a partial and anticipatory version of what will be stated to be true. The Great Sage dream anecdote simply fulfills and makes more complete what had been tentatively and awkwardly set out in the butterfly dream anecdote; it states articulately what the butterfly dream anecdote lisps. Since this interpretation possesses the merit of preserving more of the text and of granting a greater self-consistency and integrity to the text, I conclude that the butterfly dream anecdote should be accorded a provisional status in the Chuang-Tzu.

8 *The Question of Relativism*

By this time a reader might well object that I have gone to considerable trouble — even to the point of recommending that key arguments be relocated in the text — simply to rescue the text from being interpreted as an exercise in relativistic ethics. Why not take the simpler route of adopting the standpoint that Chuang Tzu was a relativist and have it done with? As I have stated in the introduction, I believe that such an option trivializes the text. But what is more important, I believe that if we construe Chuang Tzu as some sort of relativist we will have to accept that the text is either self-contradictory or ultimately unintelligible. If one takes the thesis of thoroughgoing relativism seriously, one must be a skeptic. One is therefore not even in a position to advocate one's relativism. As Spinoza has put it, the consistent skeptic must remain dumb.

I have been arguing in the foregoing chapters that there is a definite strategy in the arrangement of arguments in the text and that the strategic outcome is the attainment of a certain enlightened viewpoint as symbolized by the concept of the Authentic Man or the sage. However, if one believes that all viewpoints are to be considered on the same axiological plane, then there is nothing to commend the achievement of the state of sagehood. I think, therefore, that we must carefully avoid the conclusion that Chuang Tzu is arguing that relativism is an ultimate viewpoint.

However, it is commonplace among commentators to take Chuang Tzu to be some sort of relativist. In this chapter, I would like to show more specifically what is problematic with interpreting the *Chuang-Tzu* as an exposition in relativism. To this end, I have classified some of the attempts to interpret the *Chuang-Tzu* as a relativistic tract into four main types. I would like to show that each of these types of interpretation suffers from serious pitfalls. Finally, I will put forth a fifth model of relativism which proposes that the relativism that one finds in the *Chuang-Tzu* is of a penultimate nature and that this model possesses the virtue of saving the text from triviality, self-contradictoriness and unintelligibility and allows Chuang Tzu some posture of valuation.

For the sake of convenience, I have grouped the differing stands interpreters have taken on the question of relativism in the *Chuang-*

Tzu into four separate categories. These divisions are somewhat arbitrary and in some cases are overlapping; they are not meant to be wholly faithful to each interpreter. They do, however, represent the different possibilities of relativistic styles and in this respect enable the reader to more specifically see what is problematic in trying to understand the text as relativistic in an ultimate sense. Since I have utilized some traditional interpretations to represent these different classifications, I would like both to beg these interpreters' indulgence and at the same time to remind the reader that the interpreters do not always adhere to the rubrics under which I have classified them. The use of these classifications is meant primarily as a model for the possibilities of relativistic interpretation and is not designed as a strictly accurate representation of the interpreters' own positions. Otherwise, these commentators, who in many instances do not identify themselves directly as relativists, might justifiably complain that I am setting up a straw man and then knocking it down. My main point is to illustrate the difficulties which attend logically possible options for interpreting the *Chuang-Tzu* in relativistic terms, not to present an exhaustive critique of the authors in question. I am, in fact, much indebted to them for displaying how rich and manifold is the way of interpreting the *Chuang-Tzu.*

The five models (including my own), which I shall set out here are: Hard Relativism (HR); Soft Relativism (SR); Neither Relativism nor Non-Relativism (N/N); Both Relativism and Non-Relativism (B/A); Asymmetrical Relativism (AR) which I also refer to as Either Relativism and Non-Relativism (E/A).

Hard Relativism (HR)

Hard Relativism is a position which makes Chuang Tzu out to be a skeptic in the strongest possible sense: all values are to be taken as equivalent to all other values. The virtue of this position is its univocity. The interpretative outlook of this stance is clear and unmistakable. Hard Relativists include among their number such figures as H.G. Creel, professors Chad Hansen and Lars Hansen, Livia Knaul, and to some extent even Wing-tsit Chan. Of all of these, Creel's view is perhaps the most extreme because he seems to fully recognize the logical implications of a thoroughly consistent relativism. For Creel, the relativist cannot stand for any values as superior to any other values. The logical consequence of this is that the relativist may turn into a kind of moral monster:

> The enlightened Taoist is beyond good and evil; for him these are merely words used by the ignorant and foolish. If it suits his whim,

he may destroy a city and massacre its inhabitants with the concentrated fury of a typhoon, and feel no more qualms of conscience than the majestic sun that shines upon the scene of desolations after the storm.[1]

It is evident to me that this cannot be what Chuang Tzu had in mind. To me, this is a travesty of the concept of enlightenment. But the important thing to remember is that if we understand Chuang Tzu to be a Hard Relativist, we seem to be ineluctably drawn to Creel's conclusions.

In the more academically removed language of Lars Hansen, we can find a similar endorsement of the viewpoint of Hard Relativism as illustrating the outcome of following the *Chuang-Tzu* to its logical conclusions:

> The conduct of the wise man is actively neither good nor bad but eludes approbation or disapprobation in relation to a specifically chosen set of values. His supreme knowledge consists in the recognition of the impossibility of distinguishing right (*shi*) and wrong (*fei*). . . . There exists no standard accessible to our minds, at least of great and small, of what is valuable and what valueless.[2]

Again, if Chuang Tzu is a Hard Relativist, then he cannot consistently embrace any values. Thus, there is no difference between right and wrong. While this is certainly an inevitable conclusion if one accepts that Chuang Tzu is a Hard Relativist, to me this virtually constitutes a *reductio ad absurdum* of the viability of construing Chuang Tzu as a Hard Relativist.

In a more recent essay by Professor Chad Hansen, we can find the following HR statements re-echoed:

> For Chuang Tzu . . . all ways are equally valid — none has any special status or warrant from the point of view of the universe.[3]

And in the conclusion to his essay,, "A Tao of Tao in Chuang Tzu," Professor Hansen states:

> The *Inner Chapters*, in particular the "Ch'i/equalize Wu/thing-kind Lun/discourse," can be more coherently understood as a whole if we regard Chuang Tzu as a relativist and a skeptic.[4]

Hansen's view has the merit of clarity and consistency. However, one cannot simultaneously argue, as I would like to, that the reader of the *Chuang-Tzu* is being led in a higher or more positive direction.

That this viewpoint of HR is still being argued as typifying the thought of Chuang Tzu can be seen from an even more recent essay by Livia Knaul, "Kuo Hsiang and the *Chuang-Tzu*," in which she argues that "Chuang Tzu pleads for a much more radical sweep, for a 'chaotification' of all."[5] Indeed, if the logical consequence of HR is chaotification, it is not at all clear what direction, if any, the reader is given. In any case, "chaotification" can be seen as a form of relativism in the following way. If there is total chaos, then no position can be compared with any other position. All positions are incommensurable. If all positions are incommensurable then there are no grounds to argue that any one position is better than another. Relativism is a logical consequence of incommensurability.

Even the august commentator Wing-tsit Chan seems to commit himself, at least partially, to the uncompromising HR interpretation:

> In this unceasing transfiguration, things appear and disappear. . . .
> They seem to be different, some large and some small, some beautiful and some ugly, but Tao equalizes them as one. This is Chuang-tzu's famous doctrine of the "equality of all things". According to it, reality and unreality, right and wrong, life and death, beauty and ugliness, and all conceivable opposites are reduced to an underlying unity.[6]

In all fairness, Chan does also seem to want to maintain that there is an objective in the *Chuang-Tzu* of spiritual freedom and peace. But to attempt to maintain the existence of such an objective is to lack in logical rigor. If all values are truly equivalent to all other values, then why should one pursue the objective of spiritual freedom and peace?

The strength of the HR interpretation is that it takes ample recognition of the relativistic statements that one finds in the *Chuang-Tzu*. It is, for most of its adherents, an inescapable conclusion to which one is forced if one accepts that the relativistic statements that one finds in the *Chuang-Tzu* are meant to be understood in some ultimate sense.

The weakness of HR is that it does not allow for any valued direction to be taken as an objective of reading the *Chuang-Tzu*. In addition, the non-relativistic statements or implications that are to be found within the *Chuang-Tzu* are left unaccounted for. The text, in my opinion, when viewed from the standpoint of HR, becomes self-contradictory at many points and ultimately unintelligible. What sense, after all, can we make out of a total relativism? We are left without any justification for turning to a higher state of mind if the relativization of all values is complete. What is the point of reading the text in the first place? It cannot even be for the sake of finding out that all inquiry is useless, for this is to grant some legitimacy to argument. But a thoroughgoing relativist cannot even aver that his position possesses any legitimacy.

Soft Relativism (SR)

Soft Relativism (SR) is a view which has found favor with such scholars as Antonio Cua, the later Angus Graham, and David Wong. When scholars of this high distinction are found to be advocating SR, one must take this possibility very seriously. None of these scholars, needless to say, labels his positions in this fashion, and I trust that they will forgive me for employing their words as exemplifying this model of interpretation. But I think that doing so will help to illustrate to the reader the rich possibilities in trying to understand Chuang Tzu as some kind of relativist.

As I define it, SR consists in understanding Chuang Tzu to be a relativist but not a thoroughgoing one. When it comes down to the point of taking ethical action, the relativistic side of Chuang Tzu becomes de-emphasized. SR possesses the advantage of taking some account of relativism while at the same time attempting to make some sense out of Chuang Tzu's exhortations to act in ways in which we would normally consider to be good or wise. The problem with SR is that it leaves us without a sharp understanding of the meaning of relativism if it is to be disregarded in certain special circumstances. While it saves Chuang Tzu from the bizarre conclusions one is left with if one embraces HR, it is not at all clear upon what justification one can soften the boundaries of a relativist viewpoint without dropping relativism altogether. In order to grant some positive values to Chuang Tzu, one takes the risk of making it very difficult to understand what is meant by relativism in the first place. Professor Cua, if I understand him correctly, intimates that one can care in a valuing sense while at the same time being unmindful of distinctions:

> Ceasing to care for distinctions in certain ways is to be construed
> as being free from certain ways of caring and this freedom from
> care is not a denial of care in the sense of not caring or indifference.[7]

One is very much drawn to the effect of attempting to save Chuang Tzu from amoralism while at the same time attempting to preserve his disdain for distinctions. The problem with this attempt, however brilliant, is that it leaves us without a very clear idea of what is meant by Chuang Tzu's relativism.

David Wong states the thesis of SR in very similar terms at the end of his book, *Moral Relativity*. However, in his account of SR we are left without any clear justification as to why we should leave the relativistic posture at certain crucial junctures:

> In evaluating my use of Taoism here, it is essential for the reader
> to remember that I am not advocating that we simply forsake

evaluative categories. To "forget" morality is not to lose the ability to see self and others in terms of these categories, but it is to acquire the ability to suspend the use of these categories at the appropriate times.[8]

While one sympathizes with Professor Wong for his desire to attribute some form of valuation to Chuang Tzu, it is not clear to me why a relativist should have the ability to become a non-relativist at certain times and not at others. SR seems to cut into the concept of relativism too much and leaves it in too ambiguous a state.

In his recent work, A. C. Graham seems to add his considerable weight as a scholar to the cause of SR. In so doing, Graham has departed from his early adherence to N/N, which I will discuss below. In his latest writings on the subject, Graham most clearly belongs to the SR school of interpretation. As best as I can understand Graham's interpretation, he appears to be saying that while the sage needs no moral rules (and in fact is not obliged to follow any), he does follow a general standard which Graham refers to as "Respond with awareness." Now, to choose this standard when all other standards have been waved away is inconsistent with a standpoint of relativism but consistent with the standpoint of SR:

> If like Chuang Tzu we sweep away all moral and prudential standards, certainly "Respond with awareness" will remain in force. Nothing is involved after all but preferring intelligence to stupidity, reality to illusion; of the traditional Western values, Truth, Good, and Beauty, only the first is assumed.[9]

But why should the injunction "Respond with awareness" stay in force? It seems that if we are to be enjoined to follow some rule, however general, that we have left the path of relativism behind. And if we can leave the path of relativism in some instances, then on what grounds should we be relativistic in others? Why should we have preferential grounds for Truth if we have swept away all moral standards? The Soft Relativist wants to have his cake and eat it, too. But if he does so, it seems it is at the price of calling his relativism very much into question.

If we follow Graham's argument further, it becomes more and more difficult to know what could be meant by relativism when one is permitted, as it were, to deviate from it in a seemingly arbitrary way. For example:

> One can pronounce absolutely that a particular man in a particular situation did or did not accord with the Way. There is no contradiction here; as stock examples of the good ruler or the bad,

Yao would be conceived as Taoist as responding in awareness of the conditions of his time, Chieh as not.[10]

But how does one pronounce absolutely in a situation if one has already dispensed with all standards? On what grounds can we argue that it is good or right to respond in awareness? And further, how can we interpret that Yao (who was noble) responded in awareness and Chieh (who was base) did not? Goodness is not referred to as a standard, and yet a ruler is referred to as good. The problem with Graham's Soft Relativism is that it is not really a relativism at all. Unlike Hard Relativism, it does make sense out of there being a moral hierarchy in *Chuang-Tzu*, but in so doing it removes from itself the privilege of calling itself relativism. The term relativism, it seems to me, loses its meaning when it is so diluted as to allow certain grounds of valuation to enter — even very general ones such as preferring aware responses to unaware ones.

Neither Relativism nor Non-Relativism (NN)

Neither Relativism nor Non-Relativism (N/N) is one of the most intriguing of interpretative standpoints to adopt. The position taken in N/N is an attempt to avoid the dilemma of classifying Chuang Tzu as a relativist or an absolutist by arguing that he is neither one nor the other. The problem with this position is that we do find a great number of statements which are relativistic in tenor and a number of statements which are not, and this position takes account of neither group of statements. The basic problem with N/N applied in a blanket sense to Chuang Tzu is that it leaves us with a very high unintelligibility quotient. The seeming advantage of N/N is that it rescues us from the difficulty of having to identify Chuang Tzu as a relativist or an absolutist of sorts. While it succeeds in rescuing us from this dilemma, it leaves us without knowing what Chuang Tzu is at all.

The N/N posture can be represented both by Graham Parkes and the early A. C. Graham. Of course, neither party makes any explicit avowal of an N/N approach as this classification system is, as far as I know, of my own invention and possesses only heuristic value.

Parkes' position can be found in an essay he has written comparing Chuang Tzu and Nietzsche, entitled, "The Wandering Dance: Chuang Tzu and Nietzsche." He does not label his approach one of N/N, of course, but describes it as radical perspectivism. While this at first glance might appear to be another case of HR, the view is more subtle than it first appears. Parkes does allow for some kind of awakening that would appear to run counter to HR. On the other hand, the awakening that is possible is to the realization that we are always bound by some perspective. If we are to awaken, then this cannot be a case of HR. HR would not allow that a higher or better state of mind could exist, as all values, according to HR, must be on the same axiological plane. On the other hand, if we awaken to perspectivalism, this is also relativism all over again. It is an awakened relativism however, and a different form from those we have called HR and SR; at the risk of appearing perverse, I have chosen to refer to this as Neither Relativism nor Non-Relativism. In Parkes' own words:

> Like Nietzsche, who emphasizes that experience is always neces-
> sarily perspectival, Chuang Tzu does not believe that we could
> ever attain a kind of "perspectiveless seeing". What we wake up to
> is the realization that we are always bound by *some* perspective:
> this awakening is itself a perspective.[11]

Parkes does not want to say that there is no awakening at all — which would be the standpoint the Hard Relativist would be committed to. An awakening implies a higher set of values to which one awakens. But the type of awakening he has in mind is to the ultimacy of perspectivism. By granting the possibility of an awakening of some kind, Parkes escapes from the relativistic thesis. On the other hand, by limiting the awakening to the realization that one cannot go beyond relativism, Parkes calls relativism back into being. Since relativism is at first transcended and then called back into being, it appears as if it has cancelled itself out. I have therefore chosen to call this Neither Relativism nor Non-Relativism, as I am not sure how we have transcended if we are bound by some limitation.

As best as I can understand what Parkes is saying, one only becomes aware of one's being bound after one has transcended, but it is difficult to see how this constitutes some kind of transcendence. If one is bound in a state of transcendence, it is difficult to understand how this constitutes freedom. Parkes goes on to explain what he means by transcendence:

> The story of the dream [the butterfly dream] makes the further
> point, relevant to Nietzsche's perspectivism, that when one is in a
> certain perspective it is impossible to see it *as a perspective*. Only
> when we are placed in a different perspective can we appreciate
> the limitations of our former standpoint.[12]

But if we are similarly bound in our transcendent perspective, in what sense can we appreciate our limitations? If this is freedom, it is the freedom of the turnspit. We are bound and yet we are aware of our bonds. This is not relativism, as we have risen above relativism so that we see it from some higher viewpont; but the higher viewpoint is none other than relativism itself. I cannot make this out to be relativism *simpliciter* since it allows for a higher standpoint; on the other hand, the higher standpoint does not really seem to be any higher, so it seems to be relativism all over again.

The case of the early A. C. Graham appears to be of a very similar kind. One may well raise the question why one should consider the early position of Graham when he himself seems to have abandoned it in his most recent writings. I think that, given Graham's stature as an interpreter of Chuang Tzu, his early position has value if for no other reason than to show how difficult it is to settle upon an interpretive stance for the *Chuang-Tzu*—so much so that even such a renowned interpreter as Graham finds himself changing positions. He seems to wish to avoid classifying Chuang Tzu as either a relativist or not a relativist. In an early essay of his, entitled "Chuang Tzu's Essay on Seeing Things as Equal," he points out:

> Throughout the chapter we frequently find Chuang Tzu formulating an idea and then revising it or attacking it. Sometimes perhaps he is criticizing a provisional formulation of his own, often certainly he is attacking an idea already current.[13]

By seeing Chuang Tzu as not taking up any clear position at all, Graham relieves himself of the obligation to classify Chuang Tzu as a relativist or as a non-relativist: it appears as if Chuang Tzu has no position of his own. The problem with refusing the classification altogether is that we are left without any clear notion of what Chuang Tzu is.[14]

If we examine A. C. Graham's version of the dream metaphor to be found in chapter two of the *Chuang-Tzu*, it seems that he comes round to adopting a position which is very much like that of Parkes. I am not suggesting that this is the source of the concept since Graham's argument appears much earlier than Parkes', but only that there is a similarity in the leap beyond relativism which turns out to be a leap to relativism:

> Another metaphor rounds off the chapter, the dream in which we suppose ourselves to be awake. (18, 20). This is not, as a Western reader easily supposes, an intimation that life is an illusion from which we wake to the reality behind it, but an illustration of the relativity of all knowledge; it reminds us that what we think we know while dreaming contradicts that we think we know while awake, and suggests that like the opposite opinions of philosophers, these have equal status.[15]

Here is a relativism that is the result of awakening—just as in Parkes' account. It seems like a form of relativism, but if we are bound to relativism then we can know nothing for certain, not even that we have awakened to a kind of relativism. The later Graham has moved away from this understanding of Chuang Tzu, but it is important to note his view in passing as it does possess historical interest as one possibility of interpretation among others. We have here a view of awakening which would appear to entail that there is the possibility of attaining a higher form of knowledge. This would seem to transcend simple relativism. But the knowledge we obtain is a purely relativistic knowledge. It is not relativism because it provides for a transcendence. On the other hand, it is not non-relativism since it introduces us to a relativism all over again. It is not at all clear what great advantage is gained in learning that all is relative. It is also highly problematic how one could attain to even this knowledge since within a relativistic viewpoint all viewpoints would be suspect, including the viewpoint that all viewpoints are relativistic. It is not clear how one could even enjoy the limited satisfaction of knowing that all knowledge is corrigible, since even this act of knowledge is in turn corrigible and therefore uncertain.

Both Relativism and Non-Relativism (BA)

The fourth possible viewpoint that one can maintain within the relativistic standpoint is that of Both Relativism and Non-Relativism (B/A). Both/And possesses the advantage of being the most fully developed position articulated so far, as it is the most faithful to the text. It takes full account of both the relativizing statements and the non-relativizing statements and does not attempt to reduce one of the sets of statements to the other. It possesses the advantage of doing the most justice to the text by not attempting to minimize or discount either type of statement. By the very same token, however, it provides us with the most paradoxical interpretation, as it makes abundantly clear the self-contradictory nature of maintaining both positions simultaneously without attempting to ameliorate the ensuing paradox.

I have only been able to discover one representative of this viewpoint, Russell Goodman, but he presents his case very ably. While he does not label his position B/A, I think that B/A nicely captures his depiction of Chuang Tzu. Goodman states:

> I turn to the supremely balanced position set out in the *Chuang-Tzu*, which, as Chan notes and I shall show in some detail, embraces both a thoroughgoing skepticism and a carefully measured response to the commonsense world.[16]

And again:

> Chuang Tzu is not just provisionally interested in the world
> revealed by his senses, as many skeptics maintain themselves to
> be, he relishes that world.[17]

However, as I have suggested, B/A is not a problem-free standpoint.
Even Goodman, to his credit, seems to recognize the difficulties this
position poses:

> In trying to form a complete picture of Chuang Tzu's position, it is
> difficult to reconcile this lively interest in the world's operations
> with his mocking and skeptical flights.[18]

Goodman has put his finger on the prime difficulty with the B/A
interpretation. While it is refreshing in its acknowledgement of both
the relativism and the non-relativism that is to be found in the text, it
suffers, as it were, from leaving the text too much the way it is. By
forcing no interpretation on the text at all, it leaves the text too much
alone. As a consequence, the apparent self-contradictions between
advocating relativism on the one hand and demonstrating a positive
attitude towards life on the other are left to rankle and disturb the
reader. In a brief moment, as if aware of this quandary, Goodman slips
into N/N when he says of Chuang Tzu:

> Note that he does not say "this" and "that" have no opposities, but
> rather that they do not find them. To some this will seem an avoid-
> ance of an answer, to others a wink in the direction of an answer
> that cannot be stated definitively in any one formulation.[19]

But this is not in keeping with the bolder spirit of his generally
B/A approach, which has the merit of not hiding what Chuang Tzu
has to say and thus creates no distortion of interpretation. However, its
very lack of interpretation is also its downfall. It does not go far enough.
An interpretation cannot simply repeat the text; it must suggest how
we can solve or in some way reconcile apparent contradictions that
arise in the text.

Hard Relativism suffers from making the claim of relativism too
hard and thus leading us to the most perverse possible inferences. Soft
Relativism suffers from making the claim of relativism too soft and thus
not accounting for its status at all. The third view, N/N, leaves us with
no concrete idea at all of what Chuang Tzu's message might be. As an
alternative to these, B/A leaves us with a clear idea of Chuang Tzu's
message, but it suffers from creating the most paradoxical interpretation: it allows apparent contradictions to stand just the way they are! A
clear but self-contradictory message is no better than no message at all.

Asymmetrical Relativism (AR)

It is time to attempt to portray what I take to be the most satisfactory model of explanation of the *Chuang-Tzu*, which I call Asymmetrical Relativism (AR). I also entitle this standpoint Either Relativism and Non-Relativism (E/A). To the best of my knowledge, I am the sole proponent of this point of view. While I believe that it is the most comprehensive model of explanation of the *Chuang-Tzu*, its limitation lies in the complexity of its explanation form.

The seemingly strange appellation of E/A stems from the attempt to take advantage of the faithfulness of B/A, while making one very important distinction. Like B/A, this interpretation is committed to doing as little violence to the text as possible, admitting that both relativistic and non-relativistic statements and non-relativistic implications are to be found within the text. But this is where the similarity with B/A ends. Unlike B/A, E/A proposes that the relativistic and the non-relativistic statements are not axiologically equivalent. The E/A model takes the view that the class of non-relativistic statements and implications referring honorifically to the awakened state or to the possessor of the awakened state, the sage, exist on a higher axiological plane. There is a difference in the two states of consciousness to which the different classes of statements make reference. The class of relativistic statements refers to the unawakened or dreaming consciousness. On this level of consciousness, all values are equivalent because this is the level of unawakened opinion and argument. The relativity of all values holds (and thus we save the truth of the many statements showing the relativity of all values), but it applies only to the dreaming or unawakened consciousness. It would be an egregious blunder to apply the relativity of all values to the state of the awakened consciousness, for then the sage would be no better than the ignorant man and we would have no justification for endorsing the pursuit of the ideals of the sage. It must be the case, then, that the relativity of all values applies only within the world of opinions and arguments of the unenlightened mind, or, as Plato would put it, within the realm of *doxa* or opinion. The relativity of values exists, but only on one side of consciousness: through the veil of ignorance. This accounts for the validity of such adjectives as the perfect man or the true man or the sage (one who possesses knowledge) when applied to the realm of wakefulness. This also accounts for the seemingly perverse label, E/A. In the realm of ignorance, all values are on the same axiological plane. The Either cuts a line between the realms of ignorance and knowledge. Within the realm of ignorance, Chuang Tzu can be said to be a relativist.

What then of the And? The And refers to the state of knowledge where Chuang Tzu is not a relativist. It is better to be a sage than an ignorant man. But it is not the case that Chuang Tzu is both a Relativist and a Non-Relativist. He is only a relativist within the realm of ignorance, and what is most important, both of these states cannot exist at the same time within the same individual. There is a transition between ignorance and knowledge; this transition is what we refer to when we speak of awakening: what we awaken to is the state of knowledge; what we awaken from is the state of ignorance.

The And makes reference to the fact that the concept of relativism makes sense when we refer to the state of ignorance. The Either makes sense when we refer to the state of knowledge. The paradoxical aspect is that even this designation of the Either makes sense only when there is a dialogue from the state of knowledge to the state of ignorance. Once awakened, the awakened mind does not refer to itself as awakened; it does not even refer to itself as non-relativist. This mode of classification is purely for pedagogical purposes. In the state of enlightenment, the Either does not refer to itself at all. Even the concept of awakening is not its own self-designation. While this might appear to be paradoxical, the concept of awakening is designed as an explanatory concept for the one who is in a state of ignorance. It is thus a pedagogical and not a descriptive concept.

One might well ask, how can one speak in terms of value if value language, *per se*, is designed for exclusively pedagogical purposes? The point is that, for the one who exists in a state of ignorance, value language possesses a certain level of legitimacy. When one achieves a state of enlightenment, one understands the limitations of such a language. It is not that such value language is totally illegitimate; it possesses a certain pedagogical legitimacy in that it is necessary to communicate between levels. This is the sense of the concept of Asymmetrical Relativism. Relativism exists only in the dialogical situation of the sage speaking to the aspirant. Once one has achieved the understanding of the sage, the concept of relativism can be understood as having had only a heuristic value.

The one who claims that the awakened state possesses a higher value than the unawakened state is not the sage *per se*; it is the sage speaking as the philosopher. The philosopher is the one who exists in the twilight zone between ignorance and knowledge; he has a foot in each realm. The philosopher is also dreaming, but his dreaming is a higher form of dreaming than the dream *simpliciter*; it is the interpretation of the dream. We may recall in the Great Awakening dream how the philosopher may be taken as the one who interprets the dream while he is dreaming: "While he is dreaming he does not know it is a dream, and in his dream he may even try to interpret a dream. . . . Confucius and you are both dreaming! And when I say you are dreaming, I am dreaming, too."[20] We may take the use of Confucius in this anecdote to stand for the philosopher. In fact, the author himself also suggests that he is playing the role of the philosopher when he includes himself on the dreaming level. The point of all this is that philosophy is the art of interpreting the dream. It must perforce take place within the dream, but it is not therefore identical to the dream *simpliciter*. It is the dream as interpreted; therefore, it is at a higher state of consciousness, as it were, than the uninterpreted dream. This is not to say that it is indicative of reality: the interpreting, too, is a dream. But it is a higher form of the dream. The words of Chuang Tzu, indeed of the text as a whole, are the words of a philosopher. When he speaks, as a philosopher, of the realm of ignorance, "And when I say you are dreaming, . . ." he is also existing within the realm of ignorance: "I am dreaming, too." But his level of awareness, though still within the dream, is higher than the realm of the dream upon which it reflects, because it is aware of the dream while being in the dream.

At the level of the pure sage, however, there is no longer a state of ignorance or a state of knowledge. If the sage is spoken of as one who possesses knowledge then this is the language of the philosopher. This philosophical language has a dialogical and a pedagogical function only. It serves as a bridge to take us from ignorance to knowledge, but it is still the language of a dream. At the level of the awakened mind there is no relativism and there is no absolutism either. The concepts of relativism and absolutism are philosophical concepts. They exist only on one side of the relationship. This is what is meant by Asymmetrical Relativism. There is a relativism, but it pertains only to the side of ignorance. From the side of knowledge, however, we cannot talk of absolutism. While the philosopher may speak in terms of the sage as being above relativism, this is only the language of the dream, *albeit* the interpreted dream. The Either of the Either/And is an Either that exists from the one side only. But this is true of the And as well. From the other side— the side of the sage—there is neither Either nor And. But Either/And perfectly describes the vantage point of the philosopher who, in order to communicate with the subject learner, refers to the relative state as one side and to the other side as the other that exists as well. This is the And. But both sides exist only from the relative standpoint.

If we utilized the designation Either/Or, this might lead one into thinking that one or the other or possibly both states existed. But Either/And is an indication that both sides exist only from the perspective of one standpoint. AR grants that there is a relativist standpoint, but it is not committed to the position that this standpoint is the ultimate position of Chuang Tzu. This is the standpoint, in fact, which is to be transcended. If the relativistic statements to be found within the *Chuang-Tzu* are designed to have only a provisional validity, then they do not contradict the absolutist statements or implications, or the value laden directions that are endorsed within the text. Understanding the relativistic perspective as being only of a provisional value enables the text to retain its logical consistency and the statements to retain their intelligibility. In fact, if the relativistic statements are understood as having only a restricted scope of application, we can also better understand the possibility of positive valuation as being legitimately expressed in the *Chuang-Tzu*. If we are not committed to a totally relativistic plane of values, then there is no harm in endorsing some values as being higher than other values. We may, in the end, recognize even this sense of 'higher' as also provisional, but at least in respect to total relativism we can say that there is a perspective of greater value than this.[21]

Both E/A and AR are philosophical constructions. One cannot both be unawakened and awakened at the same time. One can only be one or the other; this is the sense of the Either. (We are still within the pedagogical speech of the philosopher.) Retrospectively and prospectively, however, both states do exist. They exist as the state of slumber from which one awakens and the state of wakefulness to which one awakens: this is the sense of the And.

But whether we speak in terms of E/A or AR, we are still within the standpoint of the philosopher. The advantage of E/A is that it allows us to keep both the relativistic and the non-relativistic statements, but *they no longer exist simply alongside each other on the same axiological plane*. This philosophical distinction is itself also provisional. The awakened state does not refer to itself as awakened. If there is to be any chatter at all, it must be the philosopher speaking.

I have attempted to lay out in some detail a philosophical construction which enables us to make sense out of some of the seeming paradoxes that occur within the text when we face both highly relativizing statements and statements which seem to imply that there does exist a higher state of values. E/A exists only asymmetrically with respect to the awakened state. From the philosopher's twilight zone, which is one step higher than the level of pure ignorance, there does exist a stage beyond the Either: this is the And. From the direction of the And, however, there is no Either and no And. From the Direction of the And, there is neither Either nor And; neither is there neither nor nor. This is Asymmetrical Relativism, and it is, in my opinion, the most accurate descriptive designation for the complex set of statements known collectively as the *Chuang-Tzu*. The only difficulty with this

classification, as I indicated at the outset of discussing AR, lies in the complexity of its form of explanation. But that is not so much the fault of AR as it is the nature of the *explanandum*; the mode of explanation must suit itself to the complexity of that which it attempts to explain.

Despite everything, philosophers must speak. I have attempted to argue that while relativism proper, in its different forms, is not an adequate interpretation of the text in that it does not allow for any posture of valuation and makes the text self-contradictory and hence unintelligible, Asymmetrical Relativism is free from these defects.

Asymmetrical Relativism is the most adequate mode of explicating the *Chuang-Tzu* while still retaining its sense. After all, Chuang Tzu was not silent. Since his speech took on such a complex subtlety, its interpretive model must be equally subtle. The merit of AR is that it allows the various statements of both relativism and non-relativism to stand. What is more, they do not stand in a relationship of contradiction to each other; they refer to different realms of consciousness. The philosopher, the lover of knowledge, is partially ignorant and partially wise. He exists to take us from the level of ignorance to the level of knowledge. It is in this sense that the words of the *Chuang-Tzu* exist: they exist as philosophy.

9 *The Origin of the Relativistic Thesis*

The reader may well wonder at this juncture how it is that the interpretation of Chuang Tzu as a relativist has come into being. If, as we have been alleging, to understand Chuang Tzu as a relativist negates the value of the text, why has this viewpoint gained so many adherents? To some extent, I have proposed an answer to this question in presenting a case for the relocation of the butterfly dream and the re-ordering of its internal argument fragments. If one keeps the internal order of the butterfly dream intact and maintains its chapter location as the conclusion to chapter two of the *Chuang-Tzu*, it is not difficult to see why Chuang Tzu has been taken to be an out and out relativist.

I think, however, that we may search beyond this fact alone to discover the bases for interpreting Chuang Tzu as a relativist. This search is fruitful in that if we can show what misunderstandings have been involved and how they have come to be, we can become more and more free of the influences of the relativistic thesis.

To this end, I will propose four major reasons which can account for the pervasiveness of the relativistic outlook that has so characterized interpretations of the *Chuang-Tzu*. The first reason has been the comparative isolation of chapter two as the central source of the message of the *Chuang-Tzu*. If one considers chapter two by itself, without understanding it to be a development of the ideas introduced in chapter one, it may be easily mistaken as an exercise in pure skepticism. The second reason has been an inadequate understanding of the cognitive function of the dream metaphor as it is introduced in chapter two of the *Chuang-Tzu*. While I have already discussed this to some extent, it will be helpful to expand the discussion of the cognitive function of dreams. The third reason has to do with the influence of the titling of chapter two of the *Chuang-Tzu*, which has had much to do with the understanding of this chapter as putting forth a relativistic thesis. The fourth and last reason has been the custom of not making a strong enough distinction between the inner and genuine chapters and the outer, mixed, and spurious chapters of the *Chuang-Tzu*.[1] In particular, the custom of treating chapter seventeen on the same level of significance as chapter two has influenced lines of interpretation in the direction of relativism.

It is my opinion that if we understand chapter two as a development from chapter one we will not be so inclined to take it as simply an exercise in relativism. If, further, we come to a fuller understanding of the cognitive function of the dream argument, we will also be far less inclined to a relativistic interpretation. Moreover, if we come to a better understanding of the issues involved in the choice of a translation of the title of chapter two, we will also be much less inclined to view it as relativistic. Finally, if we can come to appreciate the dangers of blurring the distinction between the inner and outer and miscellaneous chapters, in particular blurring the distinction between two and seventeen, we will be less and less influenced by a relativistic reading of chapter two.

The Connection Between Chapters One and Two of the Chuang Tzu

While it would seem to be natural to look at chapter two of the *Chuang-Tzu* as a continuation from chapter one, such has not always been the case among commentators. Part of the problem may have been the strongly mythical and storytelling quality of chapter one and its child like title translations, e.g., Happy Wandering, which may have led many to dismiss it as unimportant. Part of the problem may have been the necessity of selecting themes involving historical comparisons when writing up historical commentaries, which may have had the inadvertent effect of leaving chapter one comparatively unattended.[2] Whatever the reason, chapter one has been relatively ignored and the result has been the lack of a seen connection between the first two chapters.

Chapter two of the *Chuang-Tzu* has been given elaborate attention by all commentators as being perhaps the most central chapter in the whole *Chuang-Tzu* corpus. But chapter two is not an isolated entity to be analyzed by itself; it is a development of the direction already set in motion by chapter one. I have made no effort to suggest a rearrangement of the order of these two chapters as it seems clear to me that the present order (as arranged by Kuo Hsiang) of the two chapters is the correct one. Chapter one must be the rightful first chapter because, as I have argued in the early chapters of this book, the mind must be predisposed at the start by assuming the child's mind at play.

Chapter one establishes the end-goal of transformation as I have argued extensively above.[3] In chapter one, the goal of transformation is set forth as a valued goal in terms of its embodiment in the story materials. Chapter two, at least from the commonly selected titles, *ostensibly* sets out to be an equation of all values. Chapter one, while appearing to be a myth by framing itself in the form of a myth, actually sets forth the valued end-goal of transformation as a project for the whole of the *Chuang-Tzu* to develop. The outer form of chapter two, in contrast, appears to be a logical argument for the equation of all values—at least up until the introduction of the dream anecdotes. If, however, we understand the two chapters to be working towards the same goal, an understanding which is abetted by the relocation of the Great Awakening Dream anecdote as the proper conclusion to the chapter, we can understand the relativistic arguments of chapter two in a different sense than simply an endorsement of relativism as an ultimate point of view. The arguments which appear to be in favour of relativism become better understood as modes of breaking down traditional conceptual modes of valuation so as to render the conscious, evaluating mind helpless and confused. The antinomical presentation of ideas in chapter two puts the conscious mind, as it were, in the state of the dream—where it is no longer sure of what it is valuing, or of the value of what it had been valuing—until the transformative part (the implicit part of the first chapter) is made explicit in the Great Awakening Dream anecdote.

The dream anecdotes introduced near and at the end of chapter two are not extraneous anecdotes but are in fact the explicit culmination of the arguments of the entire chapter. Whereas in chapter one the concepts of transformation are veiled, as it were, in the stories of fish, birds and material inventions, in the second chapter the concepts of transformation are introduced directly and explicitly in philosophical discussions of dreams and awakenings.

Chapter two is an inverse of chapter one. While chapter one had the form of the myth, thus gaining access to the original mind or the child's mind, in fact it actually carried out an implicit conscious argument all the while. Chapter two has the form of a logical argument carried out on the conscious plane, while its inner work operates directly upon the primary, intuitive process of consciousness. It seduces the conscious mind into thinking that it is being addressed so that it can possess an unhindered access to the unsuspecting intuitive mind. In this fashion, when the conscious mind is worn down by the seemingly antinomical result of argument, the dream/reality distinction can be introduced so that a direct internal transformation can be produced.

While chapter one appears to appeal to the intuitive or aesthetic mind through its overt reliance upon myth, in reality it provides arguments for the conscious mind to evaluate while the defenses of the conscious mind are down. While chapter two appears to be offering arguments for the conscious mind to evaluate, in fact it is breaking down the resistance of the conscious mind so that it can gain direct access to the intuitive, aesthetic mental process. In actuality, both chapters are doing both at once; what is the form of the one is the content of the other. Chapters one and two are thus mirror images of each other. In chapter two, as the logical mind becomes weighted down and immobilized by paradox and the seeming dead-end of logic, then and only then is the mind truly vulnerable to the *realization* (not merely the logical possibility), that all may be a dream. To read chapter two rightly, we must view it retrospectively from the end. The *reason* why our former opinions and values are to be questioned is that they all have arisen from an unawakened or dreamlike state of *consciousness*. This is the central point of the chapter, *not* that all values are to be understood to be on the same plane of valuation. But all values are to be questioned in the sense that the meaning of life is contained on another level of consciousness. Values are not to be questioned as an epistemological parlor trick or as a proof of skepticism, but as a questioning of the mind, as a wearing down of our conceptual defenses so that we can become ready for change.

To take the discussion of values as an end in itself is to miss the development of chapter two from chapter one and also to miss the internal development of chapter two. It is of course difficult to sense the internal development of chapter two with the present ordering of the butterfly dream as the conclusion to that chapter. However, even with the present order, if one pays careful attention to the beginning of chapter two, one can see that it echoes, on a higher level, the beginning of chapter one.

Chapter two of the *Chuang-Tzu* also begins with a story of transformation; in fact, it is a highly developed story of a man who has transformed himself:

> Tzu-ch'i of South Wall sat leaning on his armrest, staring up at the sky and breathing—vacant and far away, as though he'd lost his companion. Yen Ch'eng Tzu-yu, who was standing by his side in attendance, said, "What is this? Can you really make the body like a withered tree and the mind like dead ashes? The man leaning on the armrest now is not the one who leaned on it before!"[4]

This is a clue to the point of the whole chapter. One must keep this story in mind through the various argument forms that follow. If one does not, one misses the point of the argument forms, such as the chirping of birds passage with which I started this book. Just as chapter one begins with a tale of transformation, of a fish which transforms itself into a bird, here a man transforms himself into something else. The something else is not stated, but it is clear that it is the transformation of the mind that is pointed at.

The transformation which is indicated at the very beginning of chapter two sets the tone for the rest of the chapter. At first we are given a real experience, one that has happened to Tzu-ch'i (whether historical or legendary, it is an experience which has been recounted). That which follows seems to leave this account behind. Ostensibly we are treated to a dialectic of opposing ideas and philosophical views. But the point of all that follows has already been indicated from the very outset.

In chapter one, the outer form is a myth or story form. The conscious mind relaxes: after all, this is *only* a story. The conscious mind is not being called upon to exercise its evaluative judgement. What really happens is that arguments and value judgements are introduced while the conscious mind is off its guard. Chapter one has the form of a story while it deals in truth; chapter two has the form of a theoretical argument while it deals in experiential change and the provision of a philosophical framework for the understanding of the conditions of the possibility of that change.

If we understand chapter two as a continuation of chapter one we cannot understand it as an argument for relativism. Its relativistic sub-arguments are part of an overall program for producing an experiential change on the part of the reader. In the first few chapters of this book I concentrated on the special use of linguistic forms which were designed to effect this change. In my first chapter, "On the Chirping of the Birds," the entire passage examined was taken from chapter two of the *Chuang-Tzu*. It is only in the context of producing a change in consciousness that such paradoxical word play makes sense. Except for such an overall goal, it would be easy to mistake such word play for the parlor trickery of an idle rhetor.

The Cognitive Function of the Dream

The second main reason for the ascendancy of the relativistic interpretation of the *Chuang-Tzu* is, I believe, due to an inadequate understanding of the cognitive function of the employment of the dream analogies in the *Chuang-Tzu*. Most if not all of the commentaries on the *Chuang-Tzu* have not focused strongly enough on the use of the dream analogy with its concomitant awakening as an analogue of our philosophical awakening and coming to knowledge. The customary treatments of the dream anecdotes, even including awakening from the dreams, have the subject dreamers awakening to a state in which they are unaware of their identities.[5] If this is to be construed as a type of awakening or knowledge, it is not a significant improvement over what they know (or thought they knew) either before or during their dream state. As a consequence, this treatment of the dream metaphor takes no special advantage of the dream as a mode of movement to a higher cognitive level.

In the account of the use of the dream which I have put forth, the dream allows for tentative philosophical explorations and interpretations.[6] The dream, as a level of consciousness between sleep (ignorance) and wakefulness (enlightenment), suggests a degree of knowledge and an accessing mode which transits between the two states. The dream, as a cognitive level, is both an accessing mode for the actual process of transformation and a necessary condition for the possibilities of philosophical explanation.

As I have argued above, I do not think that it makes a great deal of sense to understand Chuang Tzu's concept of awakening as a mere realization that one is above all transient worldly processes.[7] If this is all that was meant by the choice of a dream/awakening model we could account for the veracity of neither the awakened subject's vision of the world as in flux nor even of the security of the sanctity of the observer's post as a safe house from the too quickly vanishing world. These two visions might also turn out to be part of the dream.

In the concept of the dream/awakening model which I put forth as the correct one, what one awakens to is a state of knowledge; what one awakens from is a state of illusion. This is exactly what seems to be indicated in the text.[8] In this understanding of the dream/awakening model, the cognitive benefit afforded by awakening is the movement into a state of knowledge. What one knows as the result of awakening is on a higher level — a level of truth — than what one thought one knew while in a state of illusion. Thus, there is a definite difference in the level obtained as a result of awakening.

Statements to be found within the text that are relativistic in tone are to be taken as statements made within the dream. This is especially so if the statements are explicitly identified as arguments put forth by philosophers. Since, in the Great Awakening anecdote, philosophers are identified as speaking within a dream, then plainly all philosophical arguments are to be understood as corrigible. However, as the philosophical subject may also awaken, then the sage, speaking as a philosopher, may speak with a higher degree of truth after awakening than before. Thus not all statements to be found within chapter two of the Chuang-Tzu can be taken as being on the same level of truth.

The Influence of The Translation of the Title of Chapter Two

The third reason for the common understanding of the famous second chapter of the *Chuang-Tzu* as a relativistic tract is the title of the chapter. While the original work was written without titles, the titles supplied by a later editor have, I believe, exercised an influence upon subsequent interpretations.[9] In the original Chinese, there are two ways in which one can understand the meaning of the title, "*Ch'i Wu Lun.*" One can emphasize the *Ch'i* (even) or one can emphasize the *Lun* (discourse). There is no linguistic basis for a preferential choice. *Wu* can stand indifferently for 'thing' or 'kind'. If one emphasizes the *Ch'i*, one tends to underline the idea of evening things out, or equalization, as the prime meaning of the title. If one emphasizes the *Lun*, one tends to underline the idea that this is a discourse on one topic among others—but there is no clue as to the bias of the author's stance on the question. It is much the same thing in oral English. If one says that he is writing on "The *Equalization* of Things," the hearer would obtain the probable impression that the author thought that all things tended to be equal to all other things, in other words, relativism. If one says that he is writing a "*Discourse* on relativism," or, to put it into up-to-date philosophical colloquialism, "Notes on Relativism," we are not given any probable direction of the slant of the author's point of view. In such an act of titling as "Notes on Relativism," we are provided with a completely neutral description of the forthcoming contents of the chapter. In such an act of titling as "Ontological Equalization," we are led to believe that the author, most probably, will come out in favor of the equalization of all levels of being.

What I would like to point out is that nearly all of the translators of and commentators on the second chapter of the *Chuang-Tzu* have come out in favor of selecting the concept of 'equalization' as the dominant concept to be emphasized in the title. The result of this has been that there is some predetermination in the eyes of the reader of the following contents of the chapter. Linguistically, however, the Chinese is susceptible to either emphasis. Philosophically, in terms of the varying arguments put forth in this book, there are definite and strong grounds for preferring the emphasis on the concept of 'discourse' rather than on the concept of 'equalization'. Despite this, the predominant choice of an English translation for the title of chapter two has given precedence to the concept of 'equalization'.

To put my point more plainly, I will give a limited list of translation choices for chapter two of the *Chuang-Tzu* in order to better display the probable influence upon interpretation of the choice of titles.

From the literal, "*Ch'i* (even) *Wu* (thing-kind) *Lun* (discourse)" and the knowledge that in Chinese the noun is frequently placed at the end of the sentence, we can literally extract something like, "Discourse on the Equalization of Things." This is, in fact, something like the choice of Burton Watson and the choice (if I were to choose among available choices) that I would personally favor. However, the august A. C. Graham, whom I have classified among relativist interpreters of the *Chuang-Tzu*, has chosen to render the title, "The Sorting Which Evens Things Out."[10] This choice of titles, obviously strongly influenced by Graham's own philosophical preferences, clearly influences the reader in the direction of anticipating that the chapter will concern itself with styles of discourse or distinction makings which will have as their ultimate result an evening out or a relativization of all things. And this from the choice of title alone! One can only imagine the influence of such a title choice (from such a figure as A. C. Graham) on subsequent interpretations of the second chapter of the *Chuang-Tzu*.

One translation that most likely has played a large role in influencing both general readers of the *Chuang-Tzu* and scholars alike is the one chosen by Wing-tsit Chan for the section on Chuang Tzu in his *Sources of Chinese Tradition*. Chan renders "*Ch'i Wu Lun*" as, "The Equality of Things and Opinions."[11] This choice of emphasis clearly favors the *Ch'i* at the expense of the *Lun* and predisposes the reader to expect that the chapter has as its objective the demonstration that all things and opinions are of equal value. As this sourcebook has been widely relied upon by non-Chinese and Chinese alike for its translations of classical passages, it is difficult to overestimate the influence of Chan's translation choice. His choice is aided and abetted by his table of contents, where he classifies Chuang Tzu's thought under the general heading of "Skepticism and Mysticism in Chuang Tzu," which further assists the reader in forming his impression that Chuang Tzu is a relativist.[12] In Chan's case, as in the case of A. C. Graham, the choice of titles (being linguistically undecidable) is based upon philosophical interpretation. It is not surprising to find that Chan (whom we have earlier classified as a relativist) has chosen a translation which encourages the reader to construe Chuang Tzu as a relativist.

Another highly influential source of the choice of emphasis in translating the title of the *Ch'i Wu Lun* chapter is to be found in Fung Yu Lan's classic, *History of Chinese Philosophy*, where he clearly comes out in favor of *Ch'i* over *Lun* in his rendering, "The Equality of Things and Opinions." Here, I take it, *Wu* is either left out altogether or is taken as referring to kinds or distinctions and hence opinions. There is no mistaking the meaning of Fung's choice, as the chapter is plainly concerned with either asserting or proving that things and opinions are of equal worth relative to each other. The title here is unambiguous and states the relativist thesis as a given fact.

In more recent writings of commentators on the *Chuang-Tzu*, we can find examples of translation choices for the title of chapter two which run in the relativist vein, thus showing the continuing influence of these earlier translation choices. Professor Chad Hansen (whom we have grouped among the Hard Relativists above), takes an uncompromising stance with his choice of, "On Harmonizing Discussions of Things," implying, I take it, that all discussions will turn out to be of equal value.[14] By adding the philosophical preposition, "On," Professor Hansen does provide us with a certain level of philosophical neutrality which I find refreshing.

Professor Kuang-ming Wu also seems to favor the *Ch'i* with his choice, "Equalizing Things and Theories," although he offsets this impression by calling this chapter a philosophical joke.[15] Nonetheless, the titling choice may carry an influence of its own despite Professor Wu's most intriguing thesis.

The habit of translating the title of chapter two of the *Chuang-Tzu* so as to favor the relativist thesis is not confined to English language translations. One French translation by Liou Kia-hway renders the title, "*La Reduction Ontologique*," leaving no question as to the translator's (and hence the reader's) view that the chapter sets out not merely to discuss but to carry out the equalization of things.[16] The choice of the technical philosophical vocabulary of, "The Ontological Reduction", is a strong statement that the chapter sets out to level out all being and in fact carries with it the connotation that this is a *fait accompli*.

Without multiplying examples needlessly, the reader can now understand how one's philosophical predilections can influence one's translation choices.

On the side of those translators who have chosen to emphasize the *Lun* or the 'discourse' side of the title, one can find far fewer examples, the most prominent being that of Watson. He has chosen the felicitous, "Discussion on Making All Things Equal," which leaves us with a perfectly neutral expectation as to what position the author will take in the ensuing chapter. By placing the word "discourse" at the beginning, Watson has, in my opinion, taken the right road. Legge's choice, "The Adjustment of Controversies,"[17] appears at first glance to favor the relativist thesis but upon reflection may also possess a certain air of neutrality. It is not clear from the title exactly how controversies are to be adjusted, and it is left open as to whether controversies would have to be solved by choosing a relativist position. After all, controversies could be adjusted by choosing a position such as the one which I have been attempting to put forth in this volume. I am grateful to find at least a small number of translators who have chosen neutral to semi-neutral titles vis-à-vis the question of relativism.

If I were to improve somewhat on the exact choice of words of Watson, I would omit the "All," as this carries with it the very subtle implication that the discussion might perhaps have as its outcome that *all* things would turn out to be equalized. Thus in my own rendition, I would recommend a slightly amended choice, "Discourse on the Equality of Things," which is a bit more colloquial and less misleading than Watson's. If one wished to make this even more philosophically colloquial one could come up with "Notes on Relativism," or, "On the Question of Relativism."

I would like to suggest, however briefly, why I come out in favour of the neutralization of the title choice for chapter two of the *Chuang-Tzu*. Obviously, it should be clear to the reader that since I do not consider that Chuang Tzu is a relativist I would consider it highly misleading to make a translation choice that biased the reader in favor of expecting that chapter two of the *Chuang-Tzu* would be an endorsement or proof of relativism. But in keeping with the line of proof that I am suggesting is characteristic of the *Chuang-Tzu*, I believe that there are stronger philosophical reasons for keeping the title within the realms of philosophic neutrality.

If we make a choice of a title type that is philosophically neutral — and is faithful to the original meaning of the language — then the neutral titling will be in keeping with the philosophical methodology that I have been suggesting is characteristic of the *Chuang-Tzu*. If the title is purely neutral, even to the point of philosophical innocuousness, the consciousness is lulled into a state of unsuspecting vulnerability. With such a title choice as, "On the Question of Relativism," or, "Discourse on the Equality of Things," one's critical, evaluating mind anticipates that it will be evaluating a logical argument. It is in no way ready for any kind of transformative experience. If the title of the chapter implied that some subjective transformation was the goal, it would prepare itself so as to ward off such an anti-intellectual gambit. In contrast, it prepares itself for intellectual battles and thus is quite unprepared for the stunning dream anecdotes to which it will be introduced.

A neutral titling choice is best both from the point of view of not being misleading in any direction and from the point of view of planting the suggestion that what will follow is a dispassionate and detached intellectual discussion. The planting of the suggestion that what follows will be a theoretical discussion allows for the shock value of the experiential change that may be effected by the reading of the dream anecdotes. This strategy, strictly speaking, is not justified or justifiable in terms of occupying a neutral standpoint; it is neutral only as far as the actual meaning of the words chosen go. It is not neutral in its effect, for it tends to lull the possible experiential expectations of the subject reader.

From all points of view, then, it is most appropriate to select a neutral title (on the level of intentionality), since the outcome of the chapter is not to remain neutral, but in fact to be logic-shattering. On the level of logic the title should be portrayed as neutral (as in fact it is). However, the widespread custom has been to choose title translations which imply that the content of the chapter will be to establish the conclusion: that all things will be of equal value to all other things. Such an expectation influences the conscious mind to interpret any and all arguments as having this as their ultimate conclusion. Whatever possible experiential change might occur runs the danger of being cancelled out by this powerful expectation set by the title. A neutral title choice possesses the advantage of allowing whatever may happen within the chapter to happen, without the danger of being interpreted out of existence. A neutral title choice allows the chapter to speak for itself. A title choice which disposes the mind to expect that it will be led in the direction of relativism may well undo the work of the contents of the chapter.

The Problem of Blurring the Distinction Between the Genuine and the Non-Genuine Chapters of the Chuang-Tzu: Chapter Seventeen as an Example

The fourth and last tendency I will put forth as historically influencing a relativistic interpretation of the *Chuang-Tzu* has been the habit of introducing certain sections from the admittedly inauthentic chapters into selections and commentaries upon the *Chuang-Tzu*. While this habit is widespread and by no means limited to the example I will select, the practice of including chapter seventeen either as a selected reading or in terms of influencing commentary has had a particularly deleterious influence. In order to avoid undue prolixity, I will mention only two books that have had some influence upon Western readers. Wing-tsit Chan's masterly *Sources of Chinese Tradition*, includes translations from the inauthentic chapters seventeen and thirty-three alongside the authentic chapters one, two, and three.[18] Since there is no attempt to distinguish genuine from possibly spurious chapters, the reader is led to the conclusion that chapters two and seventeen (for example), which superficially bear resemblance, are saying the same thing. Since chapter seventeen is plainly a relativistic tract, its inclusion alongside chapter two enhances the possibility of influencing the interpretation of chapter two as a relativistic tract. Another influential source has been Waley's *Three Ways of Thought in Ancient China*, in which this gifted translator simply combines passages from all of the chapters willy-nilly without indicating which passages come from authentic and which from inauthentic chapters.[19] Statements from chapter two are again mingled with statements from chapter seventeen, which lends itself to a relativistic reading of the *Chuang-Tzu* as a whole.

In order to make my point more convincing, I would like to enter upon a demonstration as to why, in my opinion, chapter seventeen is not an authentic chapter and thus should not be grouped together with chapter two (where it would add its considerable weight to the impression that the *Chuang-Tzu* is propounding a relativistic doctrine). We could simply rely upon the accepted convention that chapter seventeen is not one of the authentic chapters and thus rule it out as unworthy of being ranked along with chapter two. I think, however, that definite arguments can be produced which go far toward establishing why chapter seventeen is not authentic, and that these philosophically grounded arguments need not rely upon the evidence of philology or literary style.

I would like to focus on one such argument which, in my opinion, is a strong indicator that chapter seventeen is not an authentic chapter and thus should not be taken as characterizing the essential theme of the *Chuang-Tzu*. I would like to propose that the serious weakness of chapter seventeen lies in the fact that the chapter includes no dream analogy in its contents. The implication of the absence of a dream analogy is that there is no indication of the possibility of an awakening from a perspective of illusion to a perspective of veridical knowledge. Indeed, the absence of a dream analogy also indicates that the author(s) of chapter seventeen did not make a distinction between different levels of knowledge.

The absence of any dream analogy is to me a serious flaw in chapter seventeen, normally translated as "Autumn Floods." Such a lacuna is evidence that the author(s) of chapter seventeen did not clearly understand the intention of chapter two. "Autumn Floods" is not simply spurious in the sense of not being written by the same author(s) as "Discourse"; it is spurious in the far stronger sense of violating the sense of chapter two and the rest of the inner chapters.

The reason that the absence of any dream analogy in "Autumn Floods" gives rise to the interpretation that the *Chuang-Tzu* is essentially a relativistic work is that there is no antidote to the relativism that is expressed in "Autumn Floods." This implies that the author(s) of "Autumn Floods" did not sense the development of the text as a whole, beginning with chapter one, "Happy Wandering," and continuing through "Discourse." The developmental aspect that is absent in "Autumn Floods" is the notion that one can rise from a petty outlook to a great outlook. Take, for example, this passage of Jo of the North Sea:

> There is no end to the weighing of things, no stop to time, no constancy to the division of lots, no fixed rule to beginning and end. Therefore great wisdom observes both far and near, and for that reason recognizes small without considering it paltry, recognizes large without considering it unwieldy, for it knows that there is no end to the weighing of things.[20]

But this appears to be in conflict with the views of both of the first two chapters of the *Chuang-Tzu*, where it is clearly indicated that the big bird, for instance, is on a higher level than the cricket. And again:

> Jo of the North Sea said, "From the point of view of the Way, what is noble or what is mean? These are merely what are called endless changes. Do not hobble your will, or you will be departing from the Way! What is few, or what is many? These are merely what are called boundless turnings."[21]

If what is noble and what is mean are simply endless changes, then how can there be an outline of a progression from what is mean to what is noble? If there is an endless recycling of changes, then how can one attain to a higher point of view? While great wisdom is referred to in the earlier passage above, what meaning can there be in the concept of a hierarchy of value if as soon as one obtains wisdom, one becomes ignorant? What value is there, then, in pursuing a path towards wisdom?

It seems to me that chapter seventeen takes an uncompromising stance of hard core relativism (HR). But such a stance seems to be incompatible with the view that the main import of the *Chuang-Tzu* is to point the reader in the direction of self-alteration or self-transformation. If all change is endless and in a cycle of endlessness, then any movement in the direction of transformation would seem to be futile. For this reason, in the main, I consider that chapter seventeen seems to be at odds with the central theme of the *Chuang-Tzu*. Since, moreover, it is considered as one of the outer and hence inauthentic chapters, there is no *prima facie* reason to accept the course of its argument as reflective of the stance of the *Chuang-Tzu* as a whole.[22] Of additional value is the discovery of some solid basis for the inauthenticity of chapter seventeen in addition to historical and literary bases.[23] The discovery that the blanket relativism of chapter seventeen is at odds with the main tenor of the inner chapters is, in my opinion, sufficient reason to pay less attention to its arguments for relativism.

Let us take one final image of comparison between chapter seventeen and the authentic first and second chapters of the *Chuang-Tzu*. This can be found in the conclusion of "Autumn Floods," which, again, has played all too important a role in the secondary literature about the *Chuang-Tzu*.[24] At the end of "Autumn Floods" there is the story of the fish above the Hao river. It begins with Chuang Tzu and Hui Tzu strolling along the banks of the Hao. Chuang Tzu then makes a knowledge claim about the fish in the river: "See how the minnows come out and dart around where they please! That's what fish really enjoy." Hui Tzu replies, "You're not a fish—how do you know what fish enjoy?" After some further exchange Chuang Tzu finally answers:

> Let's go back to your original question, please. You asked me *how* I know what fish enjoy—so you already knew I knew it when you asked the question. I know it by standing here beside the Hao.[25]

The final answer of Chuang Tzu here seems to be a form of naive, perceptual realism. He knows what fish enjoy by simple observation. He uses the testimony of others to buttress his knowing what fish enjoy (Hui Tzu had assumed that Chuang Tzu knew what fish enjoyed by asking him *how* he knew rather than *if* he knew).

The problem with this story is that it is hardly worthy of the stature of Chuang Tzu. First of all, Hui Tzu may not have really thought that Chuang Tzu did know what fish enjoyed. He simply may have left an ellipsis in his argument. What he may have meant to have said was, "If you know what fish enjoyed, how would you come to that knowledge?" Or, "Suppose, for the sake of discussion, you did know what fish enjoyed, how would you possess that knowledge?" The ellipsis in Hui Tzu's statement is not sufficient to prove that he believed that Chuang Tzu did in fact know what fish enjoyed. To make this claim is to be guilty of a sophism which is not worthy of a philosopher of the caliber of Chuang Tzu. Hence, I cannot find this to be a genuine example of the reasoning of Chuang Tzu.

Second and more important, the point of it all rests on a belief in the evidence of direct or, if you like, simple realism. Chuang Tzu knows what fish enjoy by standing next to the river. The point is that the testimony of the senses is taken to be a reliable source of knowledge. The evidence of the senses is taken to be trustworthy. Uncritical realism is put forth as the ultimate source of appeal by Chuang Tzu to defeat the arguments put forth by Hui Tzu. But surely such simple realism cannot be taken as an accurate representation of the thought of the genuine Chuang Tzu.

If we could resolve epistemological disputes by reference to the testimony of the senses, then what would be the point of the dream arguments introduced in the inner chapters of the *Chuang-Tzu*, especially in the "Discourse on the Equality of Things"? In the dream arguments, especially in the all important Great Awakening dream argument, it is evident that observations made in the state of a dream are subject to correction upon awakening.[26] If the author(s) of "Autumn Floods" had been aware of the cognitive function of the earlier dream arguments, then why would the dream argument not be introduced at the end of "Autumn Floods"? If what is taking place in the discussion between Hui Tzu and Chuang Tzu could be part of a dream, then on what grounds could we accept either self-testimony (of Chuang Tzu) or the testimony of others (the supposed verification by Hui Tzu, who has assumed that Chuang Tzu knew when he asks him *how* he knows) as definitive of a reliable source of knowledge that Chuang Tzu knows what fish are enjoying? To indicate that simple observation is a sufficient ground for asserting a claim to truth is to ignore or discount the omnipossibility of the existence of a dream. If Chuang Tzu is dreaming, then his witness (Hui Tzu) may be a figment of a dream and his own testimony may also be a dream illusion. By not introducing this possibility, the author(s) of chapter seventeen would seem to be philosophizing on a less advanced epistemological plane than the author(s) of chapter two of the *Chuang-Tzu*. This is sufficient evidence to me to support the conclusion that the author(s) of chapter seventeen cannot be the same as the author(s) of chapter two and, what is more important, cannot really have understood the implications of the arguments developed in the earlier, authentic chapters. Chapter seventeen seems to be more primitive in its philosophical argumentation and philosophical conclusion. Its primitiveness is due to its lack of understanding of the earlier dream arguments and their cognitive significance. Again, the absence of the dream analogies is a serious weakness in "Autumn Floods" and results in a position of common sense being attributed to Chuang Tzu which is pre-critical in its outlook. The higher criticism of the dream argument is not considered, and as a result a position is attributed to Chuang Tzu which is not only less developed than the position which is developed in the inner chapters but is at odds with that position. For these reasons it is, in my opinion, misleading to group "Discourse of the Equality of Things" with "Autumn Floods" as if they were saying the same thing. The real Chuang Tzu would not be satisfied with the outlook of common sense observation as an ultimate source of appeal to settle epistemological disputes.

The grouping of chapters two and seventeen together gives rise to the misleading impression that both chapters are saying the same thing. There is a danger in this since, according to the foregoing arguments, chapter seventeen is not only saying something different from chapter two, but saying something which is philosophically less developed and contradictory to the message of chapter two. If we view chapters two and seventeen as pieces of the same cloth, we are in danger of misunderstanding the genuine message of the *Chuang-Tzu*; therefore, it is important to consider chapter seventeen as an inauthentic chapter in order to more properly appreciate the true significance of the *Chuang-Tzu*. The consideration of chapter seventeen as inauthentic will go far toward making it possible to understand chapter two as a development from chapter one and not as an argument put forward on behalf of wholesale relativism.

The preceding four basic causes may be taken as a rationale for why the relativistic interpretation of the *Chuang-Tzu* has gained such a widespread acceptance. If we can understand the historical influence of these factors, we can be better prepared to read the text of the *Chuang-Tzu* with a new eye. We can read chapter two of the *Chuang-Tzu* in the context of following upon chapter one and thus as a further development of the progression of argument which has already been prefigured in the first chapter. The dream arguments, as they are advanced in the course of chapter two of the *Chuang-Tzu*, have to be appreciated in their entirety for the implications which they contain for the proper understanding of the *Chuang-Tzu* as a whole. The importance of understanding the philosophical predisposition in the choice of translations for the title of chapter two must be understood in order not to be misled into thinking that chapter two is setting forth a view which it is not. A sharp distinction must be drawn between genuine and spurious chapters of the *Chuang-Tzu* so that a spurious chapter is not accorded an undue importance in constructing an overall interpretation of the *Chuang-Tzu*.[27] In particular, there should be less reliance upon the arguments of chapter seventeen in forming an interpretation of the *Chuang-Tzu*.

It is not surprising that the relativistic interpretation of the *Chuang-Tzu* has had such a heyday in light of the four causes advanced above. When these are coupled with the conventional placement and internal ordering of the butterfly dream fragments, a case for the relativistic interpretation of the *Chuang-Tzu* becomes difficult to break. I think, however, when these historical influences can be understood, that one has progressed far in the direction of being able to read the *Chuang-Tzu* open to the possibility that something other than pure relativism is being intended.

10 The Paradox of Self-Transformation

In the course of this book I have returned time and again to the thesis that the main project of the *Chuang-Tzu* is the direction of the subject reader toward self-transformation. It would be a disservice to the reader, however, not to reveal that such a project as self-transformation contains a highly paradoxical element which seems truly hyperparadoxical. What I would like to accomplish in this chapter is first of all to set out the paradox inherent in the very task of self-transformation. Second, I would like to remove the hyperparadoxical quality of the paradox through an analysis of the temporal context of the description of the stages of self-transformation. Even after this temporal analysis, however, there will remain some paradoxicality which cannot be removed. I will try to explain this paradoxical residuum through the re-introduction of the form of the myth as a communication device.

The project of self-transformation appears in the *Chuang-Tzu* under various labels, most frequently as entering into Heaven or obtaining the Tao or the Way. The master key to the attainment of the Tao or the entrance into Heaven is the employment of the strategy of forgetting the mind.[1] While the English translation for the Chinese is normally 'forgetting', in Chinese it literally means the losing of the mind.[2] In order to retain English colloquialism, I think it is best (and most accurate) to conceive of this as forgetting the mind. As one does not literally (naturally) forget one's mind, all that this can really mean is that the project is to forget (or not operate through) one's conscious mind. One does not therefore become a kind of vegetable; rather, one becomes capable of acting spontaneously from one's intuitive or non-evaluative mental center. If one is successful in mental forgetfulness, one can be said to have achieved the state of unity with the Tao. At one juncture of the text, one is enjoined to forget one's self in order to achieve entrance into Heaven. The mark of achievement of the entrance into Heaven is the success that one has had in forgetting one's self:

> Forget things, forget Heaven, and be called a forgetter of self. The
> man who has forgotten self may be said to have entered Heaven.[3]

If we can take as the mark of attaining heavenliness the success that
one has had in forgetting one's self, I think it is fair to say that mental
forgetting is the master key to attaining the Tao. If we keep in mind
that mental forgetting is the same as learning how not to operate
through one's conscious mental functions, I believe that we will have
found an explicit textual reference which identifies the project of self-
transformation as the central project of the *Chuang-Tzu*. Since it cannot be a literal forgetting of the self but a change in the conception of
the self, this is truly the art of self-transformation.

Two strategies which are described in the *Chuang-Tzu* as means
for self-forgetting or self-transformation are the understanding of the
dream analogy and the argument from the relativity of all values. We
have already discussed the dream analogy at some length in previous
chapters. We have not yet discussed the argument from the relativity
of all values. If we briefly discuss the dream analogy and at the same
time discuss the argument from the relativity of values, we can obtain
a clear understanding of how both these strategies function as means
of losing the conscious mind. To understand these strategies from this
standpoint also makes it more clear how they are not simple manifes-
tations of wholesale skepticism, but how they function specifically as
devices for mental transformation.

The Dream Argument

The dream analogy when coupled with its concommitant awakening analogy may be referred to as the dream argument. While it is
not an argument proper, it functions as a kind of argument in that in
understanding its thematic content the mind is persuaded, as it were,
to alter itself. As we have already discussed, the dream argument is
probably the most dramatic illustration of the analogy for mental transformation. It shares with the argument from the relativity of all values
(which we shall discuss below), a high order of sophistication in its
order of abstractness. It differs from the argument from the relativity
of all values in that the dream argument operates more directly upon
the intuitive or unconscious mental center, while the argument from
the relativity of all values addresses the conscious mental center more
directly. The argument from the relativity of all values has a different
causal direction: it argues from the breakdown of logic to the ultimate
need for a standpoint which transcends logic. It uses logic, as it were,
to show a need to transcend itself in something of the manner of Kant's

antinomies of Pure Reason. The dream argument argues from the standpoint of the unconscious experience as an analogy for the movement to a higher level of consciousness, of superconsciousness if you will. The dream argument may be said to be a higher level of argument than the argument from the relativity of all values in that it focuses more attention on the nature of the 'I' which is to be forgotten than on the values held by the 'I'.

The dream argument, as we have discussed in previous chapters, is an argument by analogy.[4] Just as we awaken from a physical state of sleep and realize that that of which we dreamt was not real, so we can awaken from a mental state of slumber and realize that what we thought was real was not real. Consciousness itself is transformed so that the transformed state of consciousness can call into question the reality concept of its previous stage. The dream/awakening example is an example of an inner transformation that is a change in the nature of consciousness itself. The relationship between dreaming and waking is a relationship between two phases of the same consciousness, the waking phase of which is a more reality-attuned phase. What we awaken from in the state of the obtainment of the highest level of mental transformation is the illusory concept of the 'I'. For example, in what we have termed the raw form of the butterfly dream argument, Chuang Tzu asks, "Did Chuang Tzu dream he was a butterfly, or did the butterfly dream he was Chuang Tzu?"[5] The 'I' might simply be part of the dream illusion. This question shakes our certainty in the reality of the existence of the 'I' that we thought existed.

There are other dream "arguments" that occur throughout the text that suggest that the 'I' that we think of as real is part of a dreamlike illusion. For example, in the sixth of the inner chapters of the *Chuang-Tzu*, a dream argument is introduced that directly questions the existence of the 'I', or, more accurately, the reality of the existence of the 'I' as we imagine it to be:

> What's more, we go around telling each other, I do this, I do that—
> but how do we know that this 'I' we talk about has any 'I' to it?
> You dream you're a bird and soar up into the sky; you dream
> you're a fish and dive down in the pool. But now when you tell
> me about it, I don't know whether you are awake or whether you
> are dreaming.[6]

The connection of the concept of the illusory nature of the 'I' with the attainment of a transformed stage of consciousness is implicit in the Great Awakening dream argument if one includes the dream subject as an object of the dream just as much as the other subjects in a dream are dream objects. Just as when one awakens to the illusory nature of the objects of one's dream, one also awakens to the illusory nature of the dream subjects:

> He who dreams of drinking wine may weep when morning comes;
> he who dreams of weeping may in the morning go off to hunt. . . .
> Only after he wakes does he know it was a dream. And someday
> there will be a great awakening when we know that this is *all* a
> great dream. . . . Confucius and you are both dreaming! And when
> I say you are dreaming, I am dreaming, too.[7]

The dream subject who was drinking wine does not exist in the morning. (I am using the term 'subject' to stand for the one who is in the dream not the dreamer). The one who claims that the other is dreaming is also dreaming; consequently, his existence is just as questionable as the existence of the dream subject who was drinking wine. If everything as we know it is all a great dream, this manifestly includes the dreamer as well as the dream subject. The illusory nature of the dream subject is utilized as an analogy for the illusory nature of the dreamer.[8]

A state of knowledge is pointed to which is located in time future and which pinpoints the concept of knowledge as belonging to a transformed stage of consciousness or a Great Awakening. Knowledge is only possible from the standpoint of a changed consciousness which has been transformed from a consciousness which operates at the level of illusion. One of the discoveries—and I would argue the chief discovery—of the transformed consciousness is the illusory character of the 'I'. The concept of the 'I', just like everything else in the world, is only tenable as a part of an illusory phase of consciousness, and when we attain to a more real phase of consciousness we will discover that the 'I', just like everything else, is an illusory concept.

The content of the Great Awakening is the disgorgement of the previous illusion. The problem of the self is not so much solved or resolved as it is dissolved. Waking, by definition, involves the dissolution of the dream. The 'I' as part of the dream content is dissolved. What is not stated in the text is that Heaven or the Tao or, if you like, the *experience* of self-transformation as an ontological reality is only possible and consists noematically of the *realization of the illusoriness of the 'I'*. Without these noematic contents there can be no awakening or enlightenment. Unless the 'I' is dissolved, there is no awakening, as part of the experience of awakening is the dissolution of the 'I'. Otherwise, philosophically speaking, one has not yet awakened.

The use of the dream model is an indication that the concept of veridical cognition that is to be employed is directly related to a personal experience. The personal experience of the change in consciousness that we undergo when we realize the Tao, or attain heavenly illumination, is very much like the change of consciousness that we undergo when we awaken from a dream. When we physically awaken from a dream, there is a physical, *experienced* change. Our attainment of the stage of veridical knowledge involves an experienced state of transformation.

The experienced state of transformation is the noetic element of the transformation or enlightenment experience. It is not a mere intellectual observation of a winning point in a debate. It is a deep and moving personal experience, and this is part of the reason for the use of the dream/awakening analogy; otherwise, many other corrigible observation-states could be used to question the reliability of cognition. When one awakens from a dream, one's concept of reality changes dramatically. And the noematic element of the experienced change is only made possible by the dissolution of the elements in the dream. One does not simply wake up from the dream; one wakes up *to* the realization that what one took as real was not real. This *understanding* is the transformation of consciousness. What we wake up to as having been unreal (and this is the main point) is the previous seeming reality of the identity of the characters in the dream.

When we wake up from a dream, the dream subjects (the hunters, the wine imbibers) no longer exist. But the dream story is, after all, only a metaphor. It is a metaphor which on a physical level stands for a mental awakening on a higher level. Just as the dream subjects disappear and dissolve into waking consciousness when the dreamer awakens, likewise, when the philosopher awakens, he too will realize that his philosophies were all philosophical dream fictions. The Great Awakening, as opposed to the physical awakening from any particular dream, is the awakening to the irreality of the subject knower.

If we put all of this back into the concept of mind forgetting, what we would liken the forgetting of the mind to is the forgetting of the dream mind (the dream subject) in the dream. Just as we can and in fact do forget the dream mind when awakening from the dream, we can and in fact will forget the waking concept of the 'I' upon entering into a different level of consciousness which is the experience of Tao attainment.

The Argument from the Relativity of All Values

The argument from the relativity of all values is the other major strategy for mind forgetting. It, like the dream argument, also is explicitly tied to the attainment of a transformed and higher stage of consciousness. It differs from the dream argument in that it concentrates on the opinions or values held by the 'I' more than on the nature of the 'I' itself. For this reason, we can say that the argument from the relativity of all values is epistemically inferior to the dream argument as it involves one further step to complete itself. Its occurrence in the text as earlier than the dream argument is an additional indication that it is the inferior of the two arguments. The dream argument, which includes both the values of the dreamer and the dreamer as well, can be seen to be a more inclusive argument because it includes the argument from the relativity of all values within itself. Nonetheless, the argument from the relativity of all values possesses an importance of its own, and it is most effective when it is employed against the resisting conscious centers of the mind to illustrate the futility of the use of logic. It also explicitly points to the need to transcend logic and seek some form of illumination in order to answer the questions that logic and value judgments seem powerless to answer. Its weakness lies in the fact that it can point to no personal experience (as the dream argument does) which can be used as a model for seeking and finding such illumination.

In the argument from the relativity of all values it appears at first that there is no means of settling conflicts between philosophers:

> Suppose you and I have an argument. If you have beaten me instead of my beating you, then are you necessarily right and am I necessarily wrong? If I have beaten you instead of your beating me, then am I necessarily right and are you necessarily wrong? Is one of us right and the other wrong? If you and I don't know the answer, then other people are bound to be even more in the dark. Whom shall we get to decide what is right? Shall we get someone who agrees with you to decide? But if he already agrees with you, how can he decide fairly? Shall we get someone who agrees with me? But if he already agrees with me, how can he decide? Shall we get someone who disagrees with both of us. But if he already disagrees with both of us, how can he decide? Shall we get someone who agrees with both of us? But if he already agrees with both of us, how can he decide? Obviously, then, neither you nor I nor anyone else can decide for each other. Shall we wait for still another person?[9]

The solution which is posed by Chuang Tzu is to look beyond any particular standpoint to a standpoint which is illumined in some way:

> Right is infinite; wrong is also infinite. Therefore, it is said, "Behold the light beyond right and wrong."[10]

And again:

> There is right because of wrong, and wrong because of right. Thus, the sage does not bother with these distinctions but seeks enlightenment from Heaven.[11]

And, once more:

> If the one is right while the other is wrong, and the other is right
> while the one is wrong, then the best thing to do is to look beyond
> right and wrong.[12]

While Chuang Tzu does not say that the standpoint beyond
competing values is the standpoint beyond the self, if we look to an
earlier part of the same chapter we can discover a clue to the connection between the enlightened standpoint and the abandonment of
the self:

> If there is no other, there is no I. If there is no I, there is no one to
> perceive. This is close to the truth, but we do not know why.[13]

It would seem from this passage that the way to the elimination
of value conflicts is the elimination of the subject 'I', which would be
the perceiver or the holder of values. I take it that this is a fair conclusion to reach, as the standpoint of the absence of the 'I' is described as
close to the truth.[14] While this passage is not closely connected textually
with the previously quoted passages relating to the passage beyond
right and wrong, it does occur in the same chapter. In addition, since it
is described as a state which is close to the truth, it can be taken as the
state in which there is an absence of conflict. The absence of conflict, if
we unpack the passage, would appear to be due to the absence of
competing view-holders or arguers who disagree with each other. While
there is not the same clear passage here to a state beyond the 'I' as is
embodied in the notion of waking up from a dream, the end result of a
state of the absence of the 'I', which is indicated as being close to the
truth, is much the same.

A further similarity between the argument from the relativity of
all values and the dream argument is that the recognition of the illusory nature of the evaluator is an internal recognition. The change of
consciousness that takes place is a change that occurs from within. It is
not a change that occurs from a debate that takes place with another,
but an internal experience of a transmutation of consciousness.

The essence of both the dream argument and the argument from
the relativity of all values is the loss of the concept of the 'I'. In the
relativity of all values, there is more emphasis on the need for transcending the viewpoints of I/other; in the dream argument, there is
more emphasis on the need for transcending the concept of the self.
What is common to both is the need to transcend the subject-object
dichotomy. Chuang Tzu describes the Tao as the state which is the
absence of subject/object distinctions:

> When the self and the other (or the this and the that) lose their
> contraeity, there we have the very essence of the Tao.[15]

If the mind is forgotten, as is directly indicated in the dream argument
and indirectly indicated in the argument from the relativity of all values to the need for transcendence or illumination, one may be said to
have entered Heaven or to have attained a unity with the Tao. Mind
forgetting is the gateway to self-transformation. As in the above quotation, when there is no more otherness/selfness, there is the Tao. The
Tao is that state that exists in the absence of the 'I'.

Paradox and Temporality

There is, however, a paradox involved in the notion of Tao attainment or self-forgetting to which we must now turn. In the very notion
of Tao attainment there is built in the notion of a one who attains to
the Tao and a Tao to which one attains. This is a subject/object distinction which the very definition of Tao would appear to disallow. In the
very notion of self-forgetting there is built in the notion of a self who
would forget the self. But this is paradoxical, since a self who would
exist to forget the self would therefore be a self, and the self would not
have been forgotten. Tao attainment would appear to be an impossibility, for its attainment would appear to require the integration of
terms which are said not to exist. Self-forgetting would appear to be
impossible; for the self to forget the self requires the existence of the
forgetting self.

How can we talk about losing the self? Who would be losing the
self? If there is no one to lose the self, then plainly the self cannot be
lost. If there is one who loses the self, then the self is not lost. The
concept of self-loss seems inherently self-contradictory.

If there is someone who attains to the Tao or Heaven, then there
is no Tao or Heaven, for the very existence of the one who obtains the
Tao rules out the possibility of there being a Tao. On the other hand, if
there is no one to attain to the Tao, the concept also appears to be
impossible to maintain. If a self exists who becomes enlightened, then
ipso facto, there is no enlightenment. If there is no self which exists to
attain to enlightenment, *ipso facto* there is no enlightenment. The concept of the Tao seems inherently self-contradictory.

But the Tao or self-transformation cannot be impossible to obtain
or the entire project of the *Chuang-Tzu* would appear to be a bogus
project. Surely, the project of self-transformation and the goal of a state
of transformation or Heaven or the Tao must have some kind of reality or
else the entire project of the *Chuang-Tzu* would be hyperparadoxical.

I would like to suggest a twofold solution to the hyperparadoxicality of the central project of the *Chuang-Tzu*. While the twofold solution cannot remove the entire aspect of paradoxicality from the *Chuang-Tzu*, it can, I submit, remove the hyperparadoxical element. The paradoxical residue which cannot be totally removed is a necessary feature of the explanation structure of the *Chuang-Tzu* and ought not to be removed.

The first part of the solution which I would propose to remove the hyperparadoxicality of the project of the *Chuang-Tzu* is the analysis of the temporal context of the Tao attainment or self-forgetting. The concept of Tao attainment can be referred to as a viable heuristic concept for the moments leading up to the realization of the Tao. From the foregoing, we have ascertained that the concepts of Tao attainment or self-forgetting are not viable as descriptive concepts for the moment of their fulfillment.

We may use the concept of the Tao as a lure for the subject seeker in the sense of a regulative idea as in the philosophy of Kant. The concept of the Tao or self-transformation can exist as goals for the subject seeker to pursue. They make no sense, however, as descriptive concepts for the moment of the accomplishment of the goal. In the later chapters of the *Chuang-Tzu*, we find a very poetic expression of this idea:

> The fish trap exists because of the fish; once you've gotten the fish, you can forget the trap. The rabbit snare exists because of the rabbit; once you've gotten the rabbit, you can forget the snare. Words exist because of meaning; once you've gotten the meaning, you can forget the words. Where can I find a man who has forgotten words so I can have a word with him?[16]

Once man has been trapped by the concept of the Tao or of self-transformation, there is no longer any need for the concept. Whether or not the bait is false, all that matters is that you are able to catch the fish.

Analyzing the concepts of Tao attainment or mind forgetting into discrete temporal stages and arguing that the validity of the concepts is restricted to their regulative use removes the hyperparadoxicality of the project of self-transformation. The project still makes sense for the subject seeker as a goal to pursue. The only part about it that does not make sense is that there is no problem-free mode of describing the goal insofar as the goal is actualized. The goal makes sense as a goal; the language we have at our disposal becomes unusable as a language of description for the goal when the goal is no longer a goal, but a state of actuality. The concept of self-transformation can still function as a heuristic concept to enable the subject seeker to aim for self-transformation as an end result, but once the seeker has achieved self-transformation, there is no further use for the heuristic device. A heuristic device need not possess any descriptive value; however, its function as a regulative idea for the subject seeker can remain intact even though it possesses no validity at all as a descriptive concept of the end state that it posits as one to be sought.

Have we removed the hyperparadoxicality that belongs to the concept of self-transformation? If the central arguments for the attainment of self-transformation through self-forgetting are based upon the concept that the self is an illusion, then what sense can it make for an illusory self to even seek transformation, not to speak of obtaining it? The dream argument and the argument from the relativity of all values both seem to conclude that the self—or at least the self that we thought was the self—is an illusion and must be transcended. In the dream argument, the dream self is recognized as unreal after awakening; by analogy, the waking self will be recognized as unreal after the Great Awakening. In the argument from the relativity of all values, one must go beyond the subject/object dichotomy to reach a level of understanding. To transcend subject/object requires *ipso facto* that one transcend the subject. If one has transcended the subject, then who may be said to have achieved the level of true understanding?

There seems to be a built-in paradox in the concept of obtaining enlightenment or higher understanding if the very meaning of being in the Tao or being transformed means that one is beyond the self. It is one thing to say for the subject seeker that the concept of self-transformation is of use as a regulative but not as a descriptive concept. But if there is no self, then how can the concept of self-transformation function even as a regulative concept?

If we again apply the concept of restricting the validity of the application of the concept of self-transformation to certain temporal stages, we can say that the concept of self-transformation has only a prospective and a retrospective validity. When the subject is not in the state of transformation (the state in which there *is* a subject), the concept of self-transformation may be said to be validly applicable. Prior to one's reaching the state of transformation, the concept may function as a goal. After one has passed through the transformation, the concept may be said to be applied backwards, as a description for that which was but no longer is. Just as Antonio Cua has argued is the case with the concept of harmony in the *Chuang-Tzu*, we can say that the concept of self-transformation can be known only negatively, once it no longer is.[17] In one of the later chapters of the *Chuang-Tzu*, we find this description of the state of realization:

When the shoe fits
the foot is forgotten
When the belt fits
the belly is forgotten
When the heart fits,
"Right" and "wrong" are forgotten.[18]

In this way, we can say, with Cua, that the concept of harmony can only be known retrospectively and negatively. Could we not also apply this concept of negative and retrospective knowledge to the concept of self-transformation?

But how can this be? If the self to which the concept of self-transformation is addressed is an illusion, then who is being enjoined to seek transformation? Likewise, who can be said to have achieved — but no longer is in the state of achieving — transformation? It matters not. If the self is an illusion, it cannot be said to have found but lost the state of transformation any more than it can be said to seek the transformation in the first place.

What sense is there in speaking of the self as an illusion? The point is that the recognition of the self as an illusion is a valid recognition only from the standpoint of transformation. When one no longer occupies that standpoint, it makes no sense to speak of the self as an illusion. The self is recognized as an illusion only in the very experience of self-transformation. In fact, the experienced state of transformation is nothing other than the recognition of the illusoriness of the self. Outside of this experience, it makes perfect sense to refer to the self. If we once more restrict the use of concepts to a circumscribed temporal frame we may say that the concept of the self (and self-transformation) make sense only when applied to a pre-awakened and a post-awakened state. During the actual state of realization, there is no self which is transcended and no self which transcends. In fact, at the moment of realization, since there is no subject/object distinction possible, no language is available for the description of such a state. This does not imply that the language of self and self-transformation is not valid prospectively and retrospectively. It only implies that the language of self and self-transformation is not valid as a description of the realized state at the time of the realization.

The self is not an illusion from the standpoint of time future and time past. It is only an illusion from the standpoint of time present. Time present, which is the time of transformation, is a time in which there is no subject and no object. Such an application of the restriction of certain concepts to an exclusive temporal frame would appear to remove hyperparadoxicality from the *Chuang-Tzu*. Nevertheless, we cannot be said to have totally removed all paradox from the *Chuang-Tzu*. We refer to a self and a state of transformation which the self can achieve and in the same breath say that from the standpoint of such a state of transformation there is no self, or, the self that we thought existed was an illusion. This is a paradox which, though alleviated by the introduction of discrete temporal frames for the valid application of the concepts of self and self-transformation, is not totally eliminated.

The reason that we cannot totally eliminate the aspect of paradox from the *Chuang-Tzu* is that any language is by definition dualistic as it involves both subjects and objects. It involves a separation between the language speaker and the language hearer. It involves a separation between what is described and the language of description. Any attempt to use language to describe the state of unity is bound to involve paradoxical elements. Such paradoxical elements are non-eliminable.

Approximation and Myth

The answer of the *Chuang-Tzu*, inasmuch as it is an answer, is not a literal truth. It is an approximation. Just as a myth is neither absolutely true nor absolutely false, the concept of self-transformation — or the state of self-transformation, the Tao — is a concept which is not absolutely true nor absolutely false. The concept of the Tao is, if you like, a kind of myth. Whatever we say about the Tao must contain some element of falsity, since all talk about the Tao requires our separation from the Tao and the essence of the Tao is the absence of separations.[19] Whatsoever we say about the Tao must always be from the standpoint of separation from the Tao. This is what is meant by interpreting a dream while one is still in a dream.[20] We can speak of the self as seeking transformation from the standpoint of the subject seeker or the subject realizer who is no longer in the state of realization. We cannot say very much about the actual state of self-transformation except to say that it is a state which is beyond the self.[21] This cannot make complete sense as, strictly speaking, the concept of the self belongs to the pre-realized and post-realized state only. In this sense, to speak of the state of the Tao as being beyond opposites is, at best, only a kind of approximation of the truth,[22] a likeness of the truth rather than the truth itself. This is what can be meant by saying that the concept of the Tao, or self-transformation, is a myth. It is not absolutely false, but neither is it absolutely true. It is not absolutely false, since this description of the Tao is more true than to say that the Tao consists of a state of subject/object dichotomy. But to say that the Tao consists of a state in which there is neither subject nor object is not absolutely true either. It may be a statement which is close to the truth, but it is not a statement which is the truth. It is this close approximation to the truth, this good likeness of the truth that we may call myth.

Why do I insist upon calling the concept of the Tao or of self-transformation a myth? We must keep in mind that whatever description we come up with for a description of the ultimate goal to be reached is still, after all, a description from the standpoint of subjects and objects. The Tao does not even call itself Tao. The Tao is, of course, absolutely silent. We must speak, but any description we come up with must be false. Any description involves the subject/object dichotomy, so anything we say about the Tao must be false. We can only call the concept of the Tao a myth. A myth is that which is not absolutely false nor absolutely true. It is that which is the best possible story we can come up with to explain the way things are, a necessary fiction. Or, in the words of Picasso's definition of art, it is the lie which states the truth.

The achievement of self-transformation, or of the Tao, is a kind of unity. All speech adds to unity and destroys that unity. Philosophy exists, as it were, after the fact. The only way of not destroying unity altogether is through the use of empty words: it is all right to go on talking about self-transformation and the Tao so long as we use empty words. Once words have been forgotten, we may use them again. We may interpret the dream while we are dreaming. It is a dream that we are interpreting, for even our description of it as reality or as Tao is only our image. Tao does not call itself Reality. Tao does not speak. But we may and in fact cannot help but interpret the dream, and we can only do so while we are dreaming. It is in this sense that we can understand the question of Chuang Tzu, who asks, as a philosopher, "Where can I find a man who has forgotten words so that I can have a word with him?"[23] Chuang Tzu, was, after all, not silent.

11 *The Case of Meng-sun*

In my first ten chapters, I have set out some basic modes for interpreting the text of the *Chuang-Tzu*. Most basic to all of these modes has been the underlying *motus* of the *Chuang-Tzu*, the project of self-transformation. With the understanding of this project, much if not most of the seeming paradoxicality of the text becomes understood if not wholly resolved. In the early chapters of this volume, I argued that the use of such literary devices as myths, monsters, and double-headed interrogatives had the function of appealing directly to the aesthetic or preconscious mind of the subject reader for the purpose of effecting change. In the middle chapters, I introduced the dream arguments in particular as techniques for displaying to the intellect the justification of change and as cognitive models of description for the type of change that would take place. Most recently, I have alluded to basic paradoxical residues that seemingly cannot be removed due to the very nature of language itself. Despite all of these attempts, it cannot be said that the *Chuang-Tzu* then becomes a problem-free text. It still remains chock-full of obscure references, nearly totally ambiguous passages and opaque sayings. It would be impossible in a work of any length to deal individually with each and every obscure and seemingly unintelligible passage. I would like, however, to select at least two examples of seemingly difficult passages to complete this investigation of the *Chuang-Tzu*. These two last examples shall comprise the contents of the two last chapters of this book. While even this cannot be said to have solved all remaining puzzles in the *Chuang-Tzu*, I believe that all the basic keys for understanding the puzzles have now been provided. What remains is applying the basic techniques of interpretation to the special cases that lie before us. I will take out two of these. The first special case is that of Meng-sun. The second, which will be the subject of our last chapter, is the case of the cackling goose.

It is especially useful to explore the case of Meng-sun because it combines a number of techniques, some of which we have not yet discussed. The story of Meng-sun appears in the sixth of the inner

156

chapters of the *Chuang-Tzu*, towards the end of the chapter. Thus, from the order of its appearance in the inner chapters, we may take it to be a very late and a highly developed story, one which is well worth considering. In addition, it takes on special importance due to its immediately preceding a late reference in the inner chapters to the questioning of the reality of the 'I' and the raising of the question as to how we may tell whether we are awake or dreaming.[1] But even more to the point is that Meng-sun is described as "alone having awakened".[2] This ascription of a state of awakening to Meng-sun demands our attention.

One of the difficulties that besets our attempts to understand the Meng-sun passage is the fact that the story of Meng-sun is recited by Confucius. This fact complicates our interpretation enormously. One's first impression is that this is an example of the use of 'imputed words' (the title of the twenty-seventh chapter of the *Chuang-Tzu*), a device whereby, according to Watson, words are put into the mouth of historical or fictional persons to make them more compelling.[3] The problem with taking this passage to be an example of imputed words is that Confucius represents a philosophical position with which Chuang Tzu would not normally identify. Confucianism, with its emphasis upon correct social relations, correct behavior, and decorum would in many respects seem to be virtually the opposite type of philosophy to that which is embraced by Chuang Tzu. If Confucius (or whatever sayings are attributed to Confucius) represents something to which Chuang Tzu is opposed, then whatever Confucius would say about Meng-sun should by rights be something with which Chuang Tzu should disagree. This, however, cannot be completely correct either, since some of the descriptions of Meng-sun would appear to be statements of which Chuang Tzu would approve.

If we take the passage concerning Meng-sun to be an example of imputed words, then we face the paradox of having a presumably honorific position being described by someone with whom Chuang Tzu would have significant philosophical differences. On the other hand, to some extent, Confucius is still an honored personage despite the philosophical disagreements that would exist between the two of them. It is a case of imputed words, but it cannot be solely a case of imputed words. Is it then a case of dark irony? Could it be a case in which we are to consider that the description of Meng-sun as an example of an enlightened person is really designed to mean the opposite? This cannot be wholly true since some of what is said about Meng-sun does appear to have merit. On the other hand, as we shall see below, some of what is said about Meng-sun surely cannot be taken to be that which Chuang Tzu would wholeheartedly endorse. In short, the fact that Confucius is utilized as a mouthpiece presents us with a most perplexing paradox. As the passage itself is fraught with some highly paradoxical elements, we are faced with a double paradox. A paradoxical passage introduced in a paradoxical fashion: a paradox within a paradox.

Apart from the question of the attributed narrator of the passage, we must also pay attention to the form of the passage. It is in part simple narrative and in part question and answer. If we consider the part that is question and answer, we might anticipate some developmental quality to emerge in the passage as the question tends to stimulate the answer in such a way that the level of the answer may exceed the level of the question. This is the dynamic of question and answer. An answer is not necessarily an answer only to the question that is asked. A truly philosophical answer always answers more than the question asks since the philosopher would know that the question (which reflects partial ignorance) is never the completely right question to be asked. The answer in a question and answer form always fills in the blank that any question must carry along with it.

In the story of Meng-sun, Yen Hui first describes the behavior of Meng-sun upon the death of his mother. In the eyes of Yen Hui, Meng-sun did not behave properly at his mother's funeral, and yet he has attained an excellent reputation for his management of her funeral:

> Yen-hui said to Confucius, "When Meng-sun Ts'ai's mother died, he wailed without shedding any tears, he did not grieve in his heart, and he conducted the funeral without any look of sorrow. He fell down on these three counts, and yet he is known all over the state of Lu for the excellent way he managed the funeral. Is it really possible to gain such a reputation when there are no facts to support it? I find it very peculiar indeed!"[4]

Perhaps the question is an honest statement of puzzlement as to how dissemblance can be understood as a virtue since, according to the *Analects*, Confucius would aver that any adherence to ritual without appropriate feelings would be hollow and thereby worthless.[5]

However, this is only the beginning of the paradox. In the answer of Confucius, Meng-sun is praised for achieving some level of simplicity although he is said to have not reached the ultimate level. This is still to praise Meng-sun, since to laud his achieving some level if not the ultimate level is very different from condemning Meng-sun outright for having behaved wrongly. We may take note of the beginning of the answer of Confucius:

> Confucius said, "Meng-sun did all there was to do. He was advanced beyond ordinary understanding and he would have simplified

things even more, but that wasn't practical. However, there is still a lot that he simplified.[6]

This is difficult to follow, as to praise Meng-sun at all would appear to imply that dissemblance is a virtue, or, at least a degree of virtue. Later, Meng-sun is described as one who has achieved enlightenment. In the same passage Confucius says, "Meng-sun alone has waked up."[7] Since this is in the same passage where he is said to still have some distance to cover, it is a most refractory point. In any event, it seems extremely nettling that dissemblance would be considered the fruit or the mark of enlightenment.

One may attempt to explain this seeming discrepancy by seeing all of this as a mockery of Confucius or at least of a false Confucianism — or the presumably negative view of Confucius that one would imagine would be held by Chuang Tzu. If we put a seemingly ludicrous position into the mouth of Confucius we would have a double mockery, which would successfully cancel out the content mockery of the passage. The only problem with this approach is that it is partially up-leveled while *still* in the words of Confucius. The position of Meng-sun, already acknowledged as representing a partial grasp of the truth (though why this is later depicted as an awakened view is still left unclear), is up-leveled by saying what is required to go beyond the view of Meng-sun. To go beyond the sham of the rites while not feeling anything (it is still difficult to see why this is depicted as even a partial virtue), is to realize that all of this (including the mourner) is not necessarily on the level of reality; therefore we can transcend all of this into laughter. Consider the passage which follows:

> What's more [still in the words of Confucius], we go around telling each other, I do this, I do that — but how do we know that this 'I' we talk about has any 'I' to it? You dream you're a bird and soar up into the sky; you dream you're a fish and dive down in the pool. But now when you tell me about it, I don't know whether you are awake or whether you are dreaming. Running around accusing others is not as good as laughing, and enjoying a good laugh is not as good as going along with things. Be content to go along and forget about change and then you can enter the mysterious oneness of Heaven.[8]

Laughter is suggested as the answer to the spirit of gravity (à la Nietzsche). The sense in which all of earthly changes are left behind one, I take it, is the sense of the partial praise of Meng-sun at the beginning of the passage. Meng-sun, as a ritual mourner who was not affected by earthly change, accomplished his act of mourning and this was good. However, he was still at the level of being aware that he was unaffected by earthly change and thus was aware that he had transcended. A still higher level of understanding remained for Meng-sun to achieve: a level in which he would no longer be aware of his own transcendence.

The highest understanding (which Meng-sun had not quite reached) is to know that the entire project of transcendence (when properly understood) is one huge joke since there is, strictly speaking, no one who transcends. This highest understanding is one of laughter. One could attempt to understand this as a going beyond all transformations, but since even this understanding would require a kind of transformation this cannot be the correct interpretation. The more subtle interpretation is that the last phrase referring to "forgetting about change" is also a transformation, albeit not the final transformation.

The prior description of Meng-sun as being awakened would imply that he was in a state of post-dream realization. Otherwise, if we take the statement to be an accurate one, it would make no sense why an already awakened man would stand in need of more transformation or even of going beyond transformation. Meng-sun's description as having been awakened could then be seen as a penultimate stage of awakening. The prior depiction of Meng-sun as awakened could be seen as an interim stage along the way but not as a final enlightenment. This is more in keeping with the text that he had already simplified some but had not succeeded in doing so completely.

This still leaves us with the difficulty of explaining why an apparently empty ritualism could be taken to represent a stage of enlightenment. It could be that from the standpoint of an external observer, Meng-sun would appear to be dissembling. However, if we understood the level of Meng-sun's enlightenment, what might appear to the outside observer as dissemblance would be a higher mode of understanding the meaninglessness of earthly change.[9] Meng-sun's attitude was not one of simply having no feelings of grief and holding an empty ceremony; he had transcended the state of being affected by earthly changes. The only remaining drawback was that he was still holding a ceremony and thus attributing some significance to observing the fact of change. But his inner mode of transcending his feelings was a higher mode than simple dissemblance.

We are still faced with the paradox as to why *any* of this, much less all of it, is put into the mouth of Confucius. Is Confucius used as a philosophical figure who represents the one who stands between the uninterpreted dream and reality? If so, why is dissemblance (which is hardly the true teaching of Confucius) considered on some level to be a partial understanding of the truth.

Perhaps the best sense to make out of it is that two points are being made simultaneously. One is that the idea of not being affected by external things is a step in the right direction. The other is that there is also a tongue-in-cheek reference to Confucius, as if to say that if Confucius were to make sense, the sage would be unaffected (for Confucius to say that the sage is affected does not make sense). The highest insight Confucius can reach is only possible by adopting the absurd position that dissemblance in some form is to be lauded. But then Confucius also is made to see beyond this; in his response that even this must be transcended Confucius is really going beyond himself.

It is difficult to make complete sense out of the use of Confucius in the final answer. It appears to be a very subtle dialectical maneuver, an intimation that if Confucius were to recognize the absurdity of his own position and were pushed to the logical limits, he too would have agreed with Chuang Tzu. This, however, is not completely satisfactory since the position of Confucius is too well known historically; the weight of the use of his name as stating a position which would in a very subtle sense support Chuang Tzu would probably have a greater impact in creating a dialectical puzzlement than in assisting a dialectical solution. It cannot be the case that the use of Confucius as a mouthpiece for the entire argument is meant simply to lend authority to the argument in terms of the imputed words concept, as this does not prevent the creation of the absurdities that would be present both for the position of Confucius and for that of Chuang Tzu.

Could it be said that the use of Confucius even in the final answer is designed to embrace all of the paradoxes that such a use promotes? Could Chuang Tzu actually simply enjoy the paradox? Did he put his own position in the mouth of his philosophical antagonist for the pure sake of the enjoyment and bewilderment this would occasion? This would seem to be very unlike Plato's use of the Sophists, but it might be an impish inability on the part of Chuang Tzu to resist this final mockery, this final jest, so that ultimately laughter does transcend the concern for truth. This interpretation would gather support from the ascription of the value in Meng-sun's position as that which goes beyond knowledge. Consider the part of the passage we have not yet cited:

> Meng-sun doesn't know why he lives and doesn't know why he dies. He doesn't know why he should go ahead; he doesn't know why he should fall behind. In the process of change he has become a thing [among other things], and he is merely waiting for some other change that he doesn't yet know about. Moreover, when he is changing, how does he know that he is really changing? And when he is not changing, how does he know that he hasn't already

changed? You and I, now—we are dreaming and haven't waked up. But in his case, though something may startle his body, it won't injure his mind; though something may alarm the house [his spirit lives in], his emotions will suffer no death. Meng-sun alone has waked up. Men wail and so he wails, too—that's the reason he acts like this.[10]

Meng-sun has successfully transcended the worry about life and death; he has transcended the need to know the answer to this question. His act of apparent mourning is simply to go along with the others: this is a higher act which shows the ability to be in the world while not being of the world. If only Meng-sun were to be able also to transcend the need to act like others, to transcend into laughter and beyond, then he would have successfully completed the final transcendence. Given the Confucian model, however, this is a very high transcendence indeed that he has achieved. It is the best that Confucians could aspire to.

The way of Meng-sun can be seen as a penultimate way. Despite the fact that Meng-sun has gone beyond the concern for knowledge, his need to observe the amenities of ceremony reveals that he has achieved a form of transcendence which is still aware of itself as transcendence and thus is not full transcendence or transcendence proper. Transcendence proper is even more simple than the sort of transcendence that Meng-sun has reached. Meng-sun simplified by not becoming affected by the world. The higher simplicity is to go beyond the dichotomy of Meng-sun and world altogether. This is worth a good laugh. It is simplicity itself. The best solution to a problem is to eliminate the condition for the possibility of the problem arising in the first place. What laughter![11]

There never was a problem there at all. This interpretation also coheres with the utilization of the dream analogy, particularly coming where it does, as a bridge to the highest understanding of the problem, which is not to see the problem as a problem at all. When we wake up from the dream, the dream world disappears. It never did exist at all, except as an illusion: a pseudo-problem. That there was a problem to be solved or a state of mind to be transcended was part of the dream fabric. The fully awakened Meng-sun laughs; there never was a problem to begin with. This makes sense out of placing the dream story where it is: immediately prior to the statement of the highest understanding of the problem, as if to indicate that the highest understanding is obtained as a result of awakening from a dream. This interpretation also makes sense out of the highest simplicity alluded to in the immediately prior passage. The most simplified solution (which

Meng-sun had not yet reached) would be one in which there was awareness neither of a problem nor of a solution. This can only be accomplished, so it seems, by waking up from a dream illusion. The dream (or illusion), just as in the second chapter of the *Chuang-Tzu*, is the belief in the reality of the individual subject.

The use of the dream in the story of Meng-sun is not as as example of an ordinary form of transformation among others. If it were simply another case of transformation among others, it would have no cognitive explanatory power and it would not be placed in the critical location immediately preceding the statement of what the highest understanding consists. If the dream were simply another example of the transformation of things, then there would be no point in referring to any view (such as the view of the belief in the 'I') as a possible dream. If any and all views can be seen as putative dream contents, manifestly the dream/awakening model is a more ultimate form of explanation than simply another example of worldly change. If the dream were only another example of transformation, there would be no point in including all of the other views within it as possible illusions. The entire dream/awakening metaphor is too all encompassing as a model of explanation to be used simply as an example of change. It would be like using an earthquake as an example of motion.

Finally, the positioning of the dream analogy is a strong argument in favor of its special status. It immediately precedes the view of leaving all transformations behind, and it seems to imply that one should not be too caught up in the processes of change or the dialectic between change and non-change as all changes or permutations might be equally the subject of a dream. What is required is the Great Transformation of chapter two, which recognizes that all that has come before may be but dream so that we should not take any of it all that seriously. This is the insight that is the occasion of laughter in chapter six. It *is* a transformation since it reflects a different view than what has been held before, but it is achieved by leaving behind all preoccupation with physical transformation and even with the Great Transformation. It is a transformation, but a transformation of a quite different order. It is a transformation that is not (and cannot be) aware of itself as a transformation and hence cannot label itself as such.

Nevertheless, it is still not completely clear how or why we can put all of this into the speech of Confucius. It is facile enough to say that since all of it may be part of a dream it does not matter who the interlocutors are. But apart from the concept that all may be illusory, illusions do differ from each other. Dream contents may not be reality, but they are still dream contents. And there must be some rationale for the selection of these particular dream contents, where

Confucius is both part of the dream content and the narrator of the dream.

Could the use of Confucius simply be part of the final joke? If it does not matter ultimately what is the identity of the participants of a dream, and if the narrator may also be part of a dream, then why not use Confucius? A joke is, after all, a joke and is not meant to be taken seriously. If there is no humorous element at all, it will cease being a joke at all. And if the proper response to an illusion is to see it as a joke then we must include a jocular element.

But we cannot leave it simply on the level of a joke. It is a joke which is used as part of a philosophy. If it were simply a joke then the book of *Chuang-Tzu* would be a joke book, but it is more than that. A philosophical joke is still a philosophical joke and carries with it, willy-nilly, a philosophical meaning.

The only sense of the use of Confucius as a mouthpiece is ultimately to confuse. The use of Confucius addresses the philosophical mind. The content of the message is to go beyond philosophy, but going beyond philosophy is nonetheless a philosophy. To use a philosopher with whose position one disagrees as a voice for going beyond philosophy cannot help but leave us with some confusion. And this is as it was meant to be.

Confucius and the weight his name carries with it have a certain authority that transcends the message of the text. At the same time, his position is at least partially mocked in terms of its contents and mocked again as implicitly endorsing a view which surely would be attributed to Chuang Tzu. While all of this is a true occasion for laughter it also leaves behind a sting of shock and puzzlement that no amount of analysis can remove. This unremovable paradox is not meant to be removed.

In the end, a certain element of paradoxicality is intrinsic to the text. This paradoxical residue is intentional. Any and all solutions cannot be addressed to the analytic mind alone. To do so would be to imply that the position of the *Chuang-Tzu* is the advocacy of one intellectual viewpoint among others. This would leave the message of the *Chuang-Tzu* on a purely theoretical level. But the prime theme of the *Chuang-Tzu* is like that of Marx in a certain sense: not to interpret the world, but to change it. In order to effect self-transformation, there must be an element that stills the conscious, analyzing mind. If there is no such element, what is left in the end is a philosophical position that the mind can evaluate. But this is not the same as a transformed mind.

The use of Confucius as a speaker is a double paradox. The position which is ascribed to Confucius is one which Confucius would never himself have taken. This is a cancellation of the message. But

the message itself, when rightly interpreted, is not a simple absurdity;
it is an absurdity which is a step on the way to a higher absurdity, in
which a message is contained that cannot be totally cancelled out. This
is a paradox. But the use of Confucius presents another paradox, since
the use of his name—despite the wrong-headed views which are
attributed to him—still carries with it its own historical weight. This
uncancels the partial cancelling out of the message. But the use of
Confucius again as a known philosophical antagonist cancels out the
partial cancelling out of the message. We are left with affirmation, but
an affirmation which is fraught with a paradoxical residuum.

The conscious mind is not the final arbiter of the message that is
being delivered. The use of the double paradox is one of the most
sophisticated weapons in the arsenal of Chuang Tzu. The conscious
mind is addressed twice and cancelled out twice. The weight of authority associated with the use of the name of Confucius awakens the conscious mind. The realization that such a use must be ironic cancels it
out again. But what is left over is the subliminal message that what is
conveyed is of philosophical importance even though it must be paradoxical. The contents which are attributed to Confucius are the wrong
contents. This again cancels out the message and leaves the conscious
mind puzzled all over again. But within the wrong content is a more
subtle message which rectifies the content and makes it the right content in another sense. This removes the puzzle to a certain extent and
leaves the intellectual mind with a certain awareness of the right message to be delivered. This right message, however, cannot be wholly
left at the disposal of the conscious mind since to do so will be to leave
the message of the Chuang-Tzu on a purely intellectual and theoretical
level. The unconscious awareness that all of this must be intellectually
suspect (due to the incorrect use of Confucius) clouds the intellectual
satisfaction that comes with the understanding of the higher message.
The higher message, in the end, is left to work on the unconscious
mind directly. Philosophy removes itself.

The use of philosophy is to perform a self-surgery. Confucius
cannot be said to have said this but—on the unconscious memory
level—he did so. He did so mythically, since we all know that this was
not what Confucius said. But the fact that a mythical Confucius said
this is enough to assist in effecting a transformation of the conscious
mind. We may not even remember after having read the passage—and
we need not remember consciously—that it was said by Confucius.
But the subliminal mind cannot forget this fact. It is enough to make
us aware that the message, whatever the message is, cannot be fully
understood as a theoretical message. It is a story which is meant to
transform us as we read it. It does not matter to the proper functioning

of the passage that we remember that it was said by Confucius. This can be brought out by the work of analysis. But it lingers as an unconscious residue. Its lingering on is just enough to make the message indirect, just enough to cancel out the participation of the conscious mind at the end.

The artful use of the paradox within the paradox leaves the unconscious mind free to partake of the real, implicit message contained in the story. This message cannot be stated directly. It can only be stated metaphorically, which implies that the real completion of the message requires the intervening act of the subject reader. If it could be stated directly, it could be held by the conscious mind as yet another philosophical position to be compared and contrasted among others. When the *Chuang-Tzu* states it indirectly and metaphorically, it is completed only by the action of the reader, who must "forget about change and then can enter the mysterious oneness of Heaven."[12]

12 *The Goose That Cackled*

I would like to conclude this work on the *Chuang-Tzu* with the story of the killing of the silent goose and the saving of the goose that cackled. While it is taken from one of the outer chapters and cannot be considered to be one of the authentic chapters, it carries with it a message that is worthy of the genuine Chuang Tzu and merits investigation on its own. Despite its appearance to the contrary, it does not, in my opinion and argument to follow, contradict the message of the inner chapters. In addition, it is important to read along with the inner chapters as a kind of self-commentary upon what has already been said. In this latter respect, it comes as a chaser after a hard drink. After reading the inner chapters, one might think that he has grasped the message of the *Chuang-Tzu*, but one must never be too sure about this. The story of the goose that cackled provides the antidote to certainty. It is almost as if Chuang Tzu were saying not to take what he previously said too seriously or too strictly. If you think you have caught the message, think again. The story of the cackling goose is a story, if not written by Chuang Tzu, of which Chuang Tzu would have approved. It is a self-mockery of his earlier statements, but it is not simply that. It is a joke but a joke with a point to it.

The cackling goose story is a story which, on the face of it, seems to be almost the opposite of the story of Meng-sun. Meng-sun is devalued to some extent because he cackled (or wailed) at the funeral. Better (so it is implied) if he had remained silent. The goose that remains silent in this story is the one that should be cooked for supper. The goose that makes a noise is the one that Chuang Tzu advises that we should save.

Not only is the story seemingly conveying a message almost opposite that of Meng-sun, it also seems to contradict the numerous stories of the inner chapters praising uselessness. The famous story (or stories) of the tree that is useless and saves its life because of its uselessness would seem to be contradicted here.[1] Here, the useless goose is the one that remains silent and yet loses its life on account of its very uselessness! Hasn't Chuang Tzu gone too far this time? Surely, this is humour at its most perverse which will leave us in a state of too much puzzlement. A conundrum indeed!

The story of the goose is simple enough. Immediately after repeating the story of the tree, the uselessness of which has enabled it to live out its life, Chuang Tzu, referred to here as the Master, stops for a night at the house of an old friend. The friend intends to kill a goose for supper. The son of his host says that there are two geese and wonders which one he should kill:

> "One of the geese can cackle and the other can't," said the son. "May I ask, please, which I should kill?" "Kill the one that can't cackle," said the host.[2]

The next day, when Chuang Tzu's disciples ask him about this, his answer, though not completely univocal, nonetheless seems to be an endorsement of what has happened. It was correct, in short, that the silent goose be killed.

Here is a paradox worthy of the genuine Chuang Tzu. He seems to mock his own earlier position that uselessness is to be commended. Uselessness in this case comes to a bad end.

What sense can we make out of this? Is it a supreme joke—taking back with the left hand all that has been given with the right? Or is this a joke with a point? If so, what is the point?

The useless goose is the silent goose. In the interest of self-consistency, it would seem, it should be kept alive and the cackling goose, which has proved itself to be too useful, should have been killed. Although this would be perverse according to ordinary standards, it would be in keeping with the standards set by Chuang Tzu. By violating his own standards, Chuang Tzu would seem to be presenting us with a supreme paradox, a paradox that calls into question all that he has said before.

I think, on the contrary, that this story is not a paradox *simpliciter*: it is a pseudo-paradox. It fits into the category of Socratic irony. Although it seems like an irony, it is not really irony; although it seems paradoxical on its face, it is not really paradox.

One way out of the paradox is to claim that it is not really contradictory to Chuang Tzu's earlier position, for all that Chuang Tzu is really saying here is that one should not take anyone's position too seriously—even his own. In all things, one should adopt the middle way. Sometimes it may be correct to praise what is useless; sometimes it may be correct to praise what is useful. If we carefully read the answer given to the question his disciples raise, at first it would seem to permit this interpretation:

Chuang Tzu laughed and said, "I'd probably take a position half-way between worth and worthlessness.[3]

But he does not stop with this statement. If we read further, he immediately departs from the solution of the middle way:

But halfway between worth and worthlessness, though it might seem to be a good place, really isn't—you'll never get away from trouble there.[4]

Chuang Tzu does not seem to be endorsing a position halfway between usefulness and uselessness. If we read further, we can gain a deeper insight into the meaning of his answer:

It would be very different, though, if you were to climb up on the Way and its Virtue and go drifting and wandering, neither praised nor damned, now a dragon, now a snake, shifting with the times, never willing to hold to one course only. Now up, now down, taking harmony for your measure, drifting and wandering with the ancestor of the ten thousand things, treating things as things but not letting them treat you as a thing—then how could you get into any trouble? This is the rule, the method of Shen Nung and the Yellow Emperor.[5]

Here, we would gather that the only rule to follow is that there are no rules to follow; this would seem to be the real point to the story. If we are to understand the previous philosophy of Chuang Tzu aright, we must not take it as providing a rule to fit each and every situation which may crop up. If we did that, we would have turned the philosophy of Chuang Tzu into rule following, and that would be to misunderstand the thrust of the foregoing.

The joke of the story is that we expect Chuang Tzu to give us an answer that he does not. We expect him to disapprove of the slaughter of the useless goose, but he does not. Contrary to expectation, he laughs at the decision of his host, thus tacitly approving of it. In what follows, he seems to praise spontaneous action: action that does not follow from any rule, including his own seeming rule to value what is useless. While the story has the form of a joke, of a paradox, it is not a paradox. It is a vehicle for his admonition against rule following of any sort. It is a philosophical joke but not on himself; it is a philosophical joke designed for the wrong-headed reader.

The solution of the middle way is really no solution at all. The middle way does not tell us which goose should be killed. It would be totally arbitrary to save the useless tree and kill the useless goose. It would be a variation on Solomon's offering to slice in half the baby the possession of which two women are debating. The solution of the middle way would lead to further absurdities. Should we save one useless tree for every useful goose? Should the next useful goose be saved for the last useless goose killed? And does not the very idea of a middle way sound unlike Chuang Tzu, whose way, though in the end very sane, does not appear to be operating through a methodology of rational decision making?

Who is to say that killing the silent goose is the middle way? It seems totally arbitrary to choose which goose should be killed. The useless always serves a use. The tree provides shade: it is not, after all, totally useless. We cannot be too tied to formal application of rules. For to be tied to a formal application of a rule is not freedom.

There are no rules to be followed. To follow rules is not to rejoice in the useless; it is to use the useless as another category to be applied, to make a utility out of the principle of the useless. But then it is not really useless, is it?

The really useless knows no categories. But it does not follow that it makes stupid decisions. It follows the wisdom, not of the rule of the middle way, but of spontaneity. In this case, the cackling goose simply acted out of its own ignorance, not to serve any useful purpose. But in the end, its action turns out to be very useful, for itself. The silent goose, trying hard to follow the message of the *Chuang-Tzu*, misunderstood the message. It misunderstood by *trying*. In its very attempt to be purposeful by being purposeless (silence is to be preferred), it erred.

It is the nature of a silly goose to cackle. A goose that does not cackle is not following its own real nature; it is following the premeditated plan of trying to follow Chuang Tzu's rules for geese. Better to be a real goose. Cackle away. You can trust the goose that follows its own nature; it can be relied upon. What, after all, does the silence mean?

We cannot only examine the actual written answer of Chuang Tzu. We must also take into account the story contents. Chuang Tzu did, after all, tell us a story about a goose that cackled. And the goose that cackled is the goose that saves itself. He does not, in his long-winded answer to the question of his disciple, go back on the story that is related. It is what happened: the silent goose was killed; the goose that cackled was saved. The actual written answer of Chuang Tzu seems to commend the path of spontaneity, of not conforming to rule, but we cannot take this answer as a complete answer in itself. To fully understand this answer we must also take into account the materials of the story that is used.

In the end, Chuang Tzu is the goose that cackles. Chuang Tzu is not silent. Silent geese are not to be trusted, for we do not know what the silence means. Chuang Tzu offers us words that are empty, but not no words at all.[6] The trick is to find the correct words that lead us to a state of awakening. These are the words that will save us, just as the Roman geese awakened the Romans and saved them from an invasion. Silent geese are not really useless; they are very useful from the point of view of the invaders!

The useless goose, the one that follows its own goose nature, cackles. It then becomes the useful. But it becomes the useful not because it intends the useful but because it follows its own nature. It is nature that is to be trusted in the end, not plan or premeditation. Even in the early chapters, the useless is not honored for its own sake but because it is following its own ends to be what it is.[7] Of course, in the early chapters, Chuang Tzu is stressing uselessness, but that is as medicine to correct the disease of plotful practicality. If one latches onto the useless as a formula, one has mistaken the fingers for the moon—or, in the case of Chuang Tzu, for the horse.[8]

The silent goose is a metaphor, if you like, of the wrongheaded mystic. The wrongheaded mystic is the one who sees all words as useless. Nothing can be spoken, so it is best to say nothing at all. But this is silly mysticism; this is the truly silly goose. A truly silly goose is one that is silent. Such a goose deserves its fate because it is precisely in not being a goose that it is silly. An ordinary silly goose is not silly, because it is in its nature to be silly. To poke fun at a cackling goose is to poke fun at rabbits for being timid. The brave rabbit who meets his predator head on is the truly silly rabbit. The ordinary silly rabbit who runs is the non-silly rabbit.

Chuang Tzu's goose is not a silly goose; it is a natural goose, nothing silly or foolish about it.It lives because it cackles. But it does not cackle to live (that would be a doing, a forced action). The goose that does not cackle is doing nothing. It is forcing itself to do what is against its nature: it forces itself to repress its innate urge to cackle. The true non-doing goose simply lets itself be. It cackles away, and so it is saved. If Chuang Tzu had the cackling goose killed, he would be truly insane. Chuang Tzu's philosophy does not lead us to insanity; it leads us to sanity. There is no paradox in the killing of the silent goose. It is right and proper. To understand it as a paradox is to fail to understand that there is no paradox here at all. It is a pseudo-paradox. It only appears to be a paradox but in fact is not really a paradox. The psuedo-paradox traps the unwary reader. The reader who, by now, understands Chuang Tzu aright, sees no paradox here but a perfect illustration of Chuang Tzu's philosophy.

Is this too much interpretation? Have I carried such a simple story to an overly embellished conclusion? Subliminally, in the text itself,

having the cackling goose live is all that is required. Such an elabora-
tion as I have given is necessary only for philosophers who demand
explicit explanation. In reading that the cackling goose lives we know
that *talking is all right*. It is silly talk (it is the talk of a goose), but that is
also all right. Talking geese (philosophers) are much better than non-
talking geese (mutes). The natural silliness of philosophers is not silly;
it is their native habit. If a philosopher were to be silent, *in toto*, that
would be truly silly philosophy.

Philosophy, as the chattering of geese, seems like totally useless
stuff. But it is not. It is the saving of the human race.

Chuang Tzu's philosophy is like the goose that cackled. It seems
terribly silly and terribly useless. It certainly seems funny. And it certainly clamours for our attention. But it can save our lives (the meaning of our lives, that is).

The goose that cackles is the metaphor of metaphors. Chuang
Tzu is not talking about silence as opposed to non-silence. He is talking
about how to talk about silence. What better metaphor can there be of
this than the cackling goose whose message is to alert us? For we need
to be alerted, to the dangers of both simple talking (descriptive talk
with no wake-up call to it) and not talking (which allows us to fall asleep).

The cackling goose is the message of Chuang Tzu. It is a message
with a meaning. It is not pure nonsense. The silent goose, like the
brave rabbit or the timid tiger, would be pure nonsense. Chuang Tzu's
goose is not silent. The not-doing is not for the sake of falling into a
mystic trance, the silence in which there are no distinctions at all. There
is a difference between Chuang Tzu and the butterfly. There is a difference between the silent goose and the cackling goose. And when
the goose cackles, we listen.

Notes

Introduction

1. Arthur Waley, *Three Ways of Thought in Ancient China* (London: 1939), p. 163.
2. Watson attempts to capture the concept of the unrestricted movement of the mind with his, "Free and Easy Wandering", but this is still open to the interpretation of a walk taken for pleasure. Fung Yu-Lan's, "The Happy Excursion" is perhaps the least apt as it is easily confused with travel taken for the purposes of recreation. (B. Watson, *The Complete Works of Chuang Tzu* New York: Columbia University Press 1968 and Fung Yu-Lan, *Chuang-Tzu*, 2nd edition, New York; Paragon Book Reprint Corp., 1964).
3. Mikisaburō Mori, "Chuang Tzu and Buddhism," *The Eastern Buddhist 5, no. 2 (October 1972): 44-69. cf.* also, Robert E. Allinson, 'Zen in the Light of Taoism: An Exercise in Inter-Cultural Hermeneutics,' *Zen Buddhism Today*, No. 6, Kyoto, November, 1988.
4. One may wonder why the historian of religions' approach to ancient philosophical texts has achieved such prominence. The history of the history of religions may be said to have begun with Joachim Wach's *Religionswissenschaft* (Leipzig: 1924) which included both the history of religions and comparative religion. Deprived by the Nazis of his teaching post at Leipzig, he imigrated to the United States. In 1945 he came to the University of Chicago. The term 'history of religions' has its origin as the English translation of *Religionsgeschichte* which, in German, due to the nature of the German language, refers to a singular object. At the beginning, there was only one religion that was studied and thus no problem was created by the singular object. 'History of religions' would concern itself with the genesis and the development of a practice within a particular religion, while comparative religion would cut across all religions to analyze a religious theme such as prayer or sacrifice as it appeared in various traditions. Eliade was brought to Chicago from Paris in 1957 as Wach's successor and founded the *Journal of the History of Religions* shortly afterwards. (For some of the biographical information, *cf.* Eric Sharpe, *Comparative Religion*, London: Gerald Duckworth and Co., 1975, pp. 213, 238. One can go back, of course, to Max Müller, as Sharpe does. But Wach seems to receive only a late reference in Sharpe's account.

It is important to point out that the term 'religion' is not found anywhere in the Orient, but is a purely European term which was first translated into Japanese and then into Chinese in the late part of the nineteenth century. If the body of writings that are classified as religions by Western scholars were to be referred to as teachings or as ways of thought, many misunderstandings could probably be avoided. For a history of the adaptation and translation of the term 'religion' into Japanese, *cf.* Tatsuo Hayashi, 林 達夫 et al., *Tetsugaku jiten* 哲学事典 (Tokyo, Heibonsha, 1971); Shuji Suzuki, 鈴木修次, *Nihon Kango to Chugoku: Kanji-bunkaken no Kindaika* 日本漢語と中国：漢字文化圏の近代化 (Tokyo, Chuokoronsha, 1981); Gino K. Piovesana, *Recent Japanese Philosophical Thought 1862-1962: A Survey* (Tokyo, Enderle, 1963). For a fuller discussion of this, *cf.*, Robert E. Allinson, 'An Overview of the Chinese Mind,' in, Robert E. Allinson (ed.), *Understanding the Chinese Mind: The Philosophical Roots* (New York: Oxford University Press, 1989).

1. On the Chirping of Birds

1. I follow the standard practice of referring to the text—the *Chuang-Tzu*—rather than the author except when it is inconvenient to do so. The text as we have it today is a collection of thirty-three chapters, which is an edited abridgement by Kuo Hsiang, who died in 312 A. D. The first official version consisted of fifty-two chapters, the first seven of which are agreed upon to be authentic and considered to be the work of one Chuang Chou who was born in or around 370 B.C. In Wu's book on Chuang Tzu, the name Chuang Tzu is taken as a collective name for the authors of the *Chuang-Tzu*. In working with the *Chuang-Tzu* as a philosophical text, I am primarily interested in the question of how it works as a text apart from the historical question of authorship. The substance of my argument will be drawn from the authentic or inner chapters. Reference to the mixed and outer chapters will be made whenever greater clarification is to be so achieved or, in certain instances, in light of their historical importance in previous interpretations of the *Chuang-Tzu*. However, the core of the argument that I present can be made by relying exclusively on the materials to be found in chapters one through seven. There is little question that various parts of the *Chuang-Tzu* must be composed by different authors. One can then attempt to explain contradictions by arguing that they derive from the fact that the text is written by different authors representing different schools. Such is the tack taken by A. C. Graham in his work on the *Chuang-Tzu*. However, there are many seeming contradictions that appear within the first seven chapters that require explication that the multiple authorship hypothesis does not address. In addition, in my opinion, certain contradictions serve a vital philosophical function which would be lost if they were simply explained away as the result of the differing intentions of different authors.

For an extensive treatment of the historical question of the text and
its authorship, cf., Kam Louie, *Inheriting Tradition, Interpretations of the Classical Philosophers in Communist China, 1949-1966*, (Oxford: 1986), 110-29
and A. C. Graham's, "How much of 'Chuang-Tzu' did Chuang-Tzu write?,"
in *Studies in Classical Chinese Thought*. Henry Rosemont and Benjamin
Schwartz. (eds.), *Journal of the American Academy of Religion Thematic Issue*,
47/3 (Sept. 1979): 459-502.

2. That this is a serious obstacle that must be dealt with at the outset can be
seen by the number of commentators that take it for granted that the
Chuang-Tzu is a text that expounds relativism. To cite only two cases in
point, A. C. Graham classifies Chuang Tzu as a relativist: "For Chuang
Tzu, it only confirmed that moralists arguing from different standpoints
can never reach agreement, and encouraged him in his uncompromising
moral relativism." A. C. Graham, *Chuang Tzu, The Inner Chapters*, (London:
1981), 4. Kam Louie claims that the eminent historian of philosophy, Feng
Yu Lan considered Chuang Tzu to be a relativist: "Feng Yu Lan added
that the passage under consideration was the key to understanding Chuang
Tzu because it clearly revealed a philosophy which advocated avoiding
problems in the world and which was relativist." Kam Louie, *Inheriting
Tradition*, 116.

3. In chapter eight I will take up a detailed analysis of previous interpretations of the *Chuang-Tzu* which have considered the philosophy to be one
of relativism. In that chapter, I divide up the past interpretations of the
Chuang-Tzu in terms of either explicitly attributing to or being committed
to an interpretation of relativism of one kind or another or to one degree
or another. These various kinds or degrees of relativism make up the different typologies of relativism that characterize the standpoints of the interpreters. See chapter eight, "The Question of Relativism."

4. Kuang-ming Wu, *Chuang Tzu: World Philosopher At Play*, (New York: 1982),
xiii. This book is highly recommended as a companion volume to this
present work. For the original sources of the quotation cf., *Chuang-Tzu*,
trans. Fung Yu Lan (Shanghai: 1931), 3.

5. *Ibid.*, xiii. cf. H. G. Creel, *What is Taoism?* (Chicago: 1970), 55.

6. For reasons which will become important later on, I prefer this translation
of the title of chapter two (following Watson). Below, I will indicate how
differing translations of the chapter title can influence the understanding
of the chapter's content and vice-versa. (Strictly speaking, there are no
"chapters" or "chapter titles" in the original. However, my subsequent
discussion mainly concerns the historical tradition of interpreting the
Chuang-Tzu. In any case, it is a good example of the influence of philosophical interpretation upon translation and vice-versa.)

7. Burton Watson, tran., *The Complete Works of Chuang Tzu*, (New York and
London: 1970), 39.

8. There are, in total, about seven different modes of responding to the seeming contradictions that emerge in the text of the *Chuang-Tzu*, some of
them hypothetical and some of them actually adopted by commentators.
We can classify them in the following ways: (i) the *Chuang-Tzu* is a relativ-

istic text and the author was simply unaware of the untenability of relativism; (ii) the multiple authorship hypothesis; (iii) the author was aware of the self-cancelling nature of relativism but was perversely minded; (iv) the author intended the *Chuang-Tzu* to be a philosophical joke, somewhat along the lines that some have claimed Plato was perpetrating in his dialogue, *Parmenides*; (v) that the *Chuang-Tzu* is not meant to be philosophy at all but is a work of poetry or literature and hence has no responsibility to be self-consistent; (vi) that the *Chuang-Tzu* is a work of relativism but that it is defensible as such — this response characterizes many of the commentators whose interpretations I have divided up into differing kinds and degrees of relativism in chapter eight; (vii) the response of the present volume. The first six responses, in my opinion, do not do full justice to the profundity and the brilliance of the *Chuang-Tzu* any more than the hypothesis that Plato was perpetrating a philosophical hoax in the *Parmenides* does justice to the philosophy of Plato.

9. A. C. Graham, 52. Emphasis mine.

10. The difficulties that translators face are immense. In the case of the *Chuang-Tzu*, the problem is acute; so much so that in a private conversation with me, D. C. Lau has asserted that he would never attempt a translation of the *Chuang-Tzu* because the text is so corrupt. One way out is that of Wing-tsit Chan, who has commented in his plenary address to the International Research Conference of the Society for Asian and Comparative Philosophy that he finds it best to consult a variety of English translations as an aid to philosophical interpretation (Honolulu, 1984).

11. In Graham's interpretation, we must transcend the inadequacies of logic in spontaneous action. The problem remains, if Chuang Tzu is a relativist, how is he justified in endorsing spontaneity? In any event, as readers of the *Chuang-Tzu*, we must be expected to make sense out of the statements that make up the *Chuang-Tzu*. If statements are without meaning, then how can we even pretend to understand that Chuang Tzu is enjoining us to spontaneous action? It would seem that a certain amount of logic must be presupposed if we are to understand anything at all from the *Chuang-Tzu*. However, according to Graham, "Chuang-tzu sees it as the lesson of disputation that one is entitled to affirm or deny anything of anything." *Op. cit.*, p. 53. It seems to me that if what you affirm you could just as easily deny, then any predication is either equivocal or nonsensical. Graham would like, presumably, to except from this implication Chuang Tzu's attribution of a special illumination to the sage which makes sense of everything. As opposed to the predications of Confucians and Mohists, ". . . the Illumination of the sage is a vision which brings everything to light." But as soon as this is predicated it becomes meaningless. If this vision is private and never communicated, perhaps it can be free from the demands of consistent utterance. But even to attempt to meaningfully state that ". . . the Illumination of the sage is . . . " is to affirm. And if all affirmation is equally negation then this too must be pure gibberish. For Graham's notion that Chuang Tzu is urging us on towards spontaneity, *cf.* his essay, "Taoist Spontaneity and the Dichotomy of 'Is' and 'Ought',"

in Victor H. Mair, ed., *Experimental Essays on Chuang-Tzu* (Honolulu: 1983), 3-23.

12. The point is that if language is relativistic, then this applies to all language affirmations and not only language claims as lodged by Confucians and Mohists. This historical reference makes sense only as an example since the problem of language is not limited to Confucians and Mohists but applies to anyone who is a language user. The point I make in the chapter is that we could not even understand the example as a historical example without relying upon the integrity of language.
13. Watson, 39.
14. *Ibid.*
15. *Ibid.*
16. A. C. Graham, 52.
17. Watson, 39.
18. Wing-tsit Chan, *Sources of Chinese Tradition* (New York: 1960), 70.
19. Watson, 38.
20. *Ibid.*, 39.
21. *Ibid.*
22. *Ibid.*, 39-40.
23. *Ibid.*, 40.

2. Myths and Monsters: On the Art of Metaphor

1. The notion that there are two separate cognitive functions is a time honored one in philosophy. Kant must be given credit as the first major philosopher to emphasize this in his first *Critique*, although he does not proceed to develop this insight to its fullest purpose. While the two separate functions to which I refer here are not by any means identical to the two sources of knowledge in Kant, there is a significant parallel. However, the concept of intuition to which I make reference is not at all like the concept of intuition in Kant and should not be confused with it. As it will become clear in the course of the present chapter, intuition in my usage has the function of providing understanding, a function which is not attributed to it in Kant's usage. The analytic or conceptual function, which provides understanding in Kant's sense, would function as providing explanation rather than understanding in my sense.

Of course, these two functions are not completely separable. Some level of understanding (in my sense) is required in order to grasp the meaning of explanations. However, and here the divergence with Kant is most extreme, what I am arguing is that there is a pre-conceptual level of understanding which falls under the province of the intuitive or aesthetic function (in my terms). I am utilizing the concept of aesthetic cognition in a wider sense than Kant's in that I am not referring thereby to the capacity of cognizing in some special sense of space or time. I am also not referring to the capacity of enjoying artistic experience or the production of the works of art. I am using the concept of an aesthetic function to stand for a pre-conceptual mode of understanding which understands its proper object of understanding as a whole. I am also not using the concept of intuition in its popular sense of standing for the capacity for knowing something which cannot be known empirically or through the five senses. In my usage, the concept of intuition, like aesthetic apprehension, refers to the ability of grasping the *cognoscendum* holistically, in one piece, all at once. What is in common with Kant is the notion that there are two separate sources of knowledge and that the rules of one do not apply to the other.

2. While there has been an animus in philosophy against what has been referred to as "faculty psychology," there has been some scientific evidence that the brain is itself divided up physically in terms of its mental functions. Whatever the merits of this analysis, the division possesses a certain metaphorical value. The right hemisphere of the brain has been found to be related to imagination and the left hemisphere of the brain has been found to be related to conceptual formation. For the analysis with which this book is involved, the physical correlation is not of crucial significance. We do not have to think of these two functions as referring to separate faculties of knowledge; however, I see no harm in understanding the mind as possessing separate cognitive capacities. Whether or not these correspond exactly with what science is discovering is not the point. The point is that the metaphor of separate cognitive capacities is not so likely to be disposed of as an unscientific idea given the empirical discoveries of science. For a scientific explanation of this, one may be referred to Howard Garner, *Frames of Mind* (New York: 1983).

3. I think that the uniqueness of beginning with the idea of myth rather than introducing it in the middle or at the end of the work deserves our special consideration. We might consider the implication that while some fictional quality is introduced at the beginning (what I have called a necessary fiction), the conclusion to which one is brought is more akin to what we think of as reality. The progression, then, is from the unreal to the real. In Plato, by contrast, (we may think of *Timaeus*), if we are left with a myth in the end, the overall impression might be that philosophy did not develop toward reality. It may be noted that, for the most part, I make no references to the content of the myth as it relates to its possible appearance in traditional Chinese folklore. My concern throughout is with the function of the myth in the text at hand as a literary/allegorical and cognitive device rather than with the particular content of the myth as it may appear in Chinese tradition. This is not different from analyzing Plato's use of myth apart from how he may draw his images from traditional Greek culture. The reader may be directed to the first footnote of the subsequent chapter for a fuller discussion of the place of myth in Chinese tradition as it would be treated in the works of historians of religion.

4. For a very extensive and admirable treatment of the use of metaphor in the *Chuang-Tzu*, one cannot do better than to read Kuang-ming Wu's *Chuang Tzu: World Philosopher at Play* (New York: 1982). For the use of metaphor, dissociation and other cognitive strategies in hypnosis, one may

be referred to Stephen R. Lankton and Carol H. Lankton, *The Answer Within: A Clinical Framework of Ericksonian Hypnotherapy* (New York: 1983) and Stephen G. Gilligan, *Therapeutic Trances: The Cooperation Principle in Ericksonian Hypnotherapy* (New York: 1987).

3. The Content of the Myth

1. My treatment of the content of the mythical materials is concerned with how such materials function intra-textually. This approach differs from that taken by historians of religion or anthropologists who may have an interest in tracing the appearance of the content of the mythical materials in Chinese literary sources in general or who may have an interest in examining the role of myth *per se* in the evolution of Chinese culture. For example, in Norman Girardot's article on "Mythic Themes" in the section on Chinese Religion in Mircea Eliade (ed.), *The Encyclopedia of Religion* vol. 3, (New York: 1987), he is preoccupied with the question of how myth functions in general in Chinese religion. One conclusion to which he is brought is that, "Myth to some extent always refers to the issue of "beginnings" or world foundation" (p. 298). While such a conclusion may have a very general level of application it does not seem to apply to the fish-bird myth which I am examining, which, as far as I can tell, does not have to do with world foundation. This notion of a returning to the beginning figures strongly in Girardot's writings. A bit further in the same article he writes, "The inner structure of all forms of existence, it seems, is mythic in nature since change is fundamentally understood as a constant series of new beginnings or sets of structual permutations, that return to the [sic] recapitulate the 'first' processes of creation" (p. 303). Again, the myth of the fish-bird does not have to do with creation, and what is more important, the concept of transformation with which the *Chuang-Tzu* is concerned is not a "constant series of new beginnings" but a one-time and one-way transformation in an evolutionary direction (as in fish transforming itself into bird — from lower to higher). Girardot's work is a good example of the methodology of the historian of religion (he is a former student of Eliade's and Chairman of the Department of Religions [sic] Studies at Lehigh University): here, a comparative theme (the notion of creation), is utilized as the search principle to find parallel notions in Chinese religion. It is interesting to note that Eliade (the editor of the *Encyclopedia*) is also professor of the history of religions, and, in fact, was brought from Paris to be Wach's successor at the University of Chicago (*cf.* my introduction). It is not surprising, then, that the approach taken by historians of religion should have risen to such prominence given the support by such figures.

   In Girardot's, *Myth and Meaning in Early Taoism* (Berkeley: 1983), he enlarges upon the above themes. Some of his material is based on the story of Emperor Hun-tun found at the end of chapter seven of the *Chuang-Tzu*, a chapter which, I concur with Graham, is one for which Chuang

Tzu did not much care. Girardot treats this story as a myth and it is the story on which he focuses, rather than the fish-bird myth which I single out for special attention. In fact, I can find only one oblique reference to the big bird in Girardot's book (p. 91). In the end, he concludes that the keynote of the *Chuang-Tzu* is endless transformation (which he takes from chapter 33 of the *Chuang-Tzu*) [p. 111]. He couples this with the confusion hypothesis as well (p. 163) both of which I examine in great detail below in chapter six.

Ironically enough, if we indulge in the methods of comparative religion for a moment, we can find support in extra-textual materials for Chuang Tzu's literary images of superior knowledge as opposed to shallow understanding in the *Huai Nan Tzu*, translated by Charles Le Blanc (Hong Kong: 1985), where Dragons and Phoenixes are contrasted with mud-eels and sparrows (pp. 148-9). This reminds us of Chuang Tzu's contrast of the vision of the big bird as over against the narrow outlook of the cicada and the dove. (*cf.* above, pp. 42-44 *et passim.*)

2. While no one would deny that this is the beginning myth of the *Chuang-Tzu*, it is my singular claim that it is the central myth (*cf.* n. 1). Again, if we indulge in comparative religion for a moment, we may find an example where a philosopher (Chuang Tzu) has influenced the evolution of mythical content. We find Chuang Tzu's metaphorical figure of the distance of 90,000 *li* (about 30,000 miles) that the big bird flies repeated in the myth of P'an-ku is devised in the Three Kingdoms period (220-265 A.D.), the philosopher's figure of 90,000 (literally nine ten-thousands) may have played a role in influencing the content of a later myth. *cf.* David C. Yu, "The Creation Myth and its Symbolism in Classical Taoism," *Philosophy East and West*, 4:31 (October, 1981), 479. It is controversial whether Chuang Tzu's myth of the fish-bird influenced or was influenced by the image of the Sacred Bird of the Mountain of Heaven which appears in the *Shan-hai ching*, composed in late Chou (403-222 B.C.). *cf. ibid.*, 481.

In any event, what is important is the use to which this image is put textually in the *Chuang-Tzu* and not the role it might play in earlier or later texts. If one looks closely at the fish-bird myth in the *Chuang-Tzu*, one can see that it is an earlier version of the butterfly anecdote, and as such is not as highly developed. Nonetheless, both the fish-bird transformation and the butterfly anecdote are stories of transformation. In the *Chuang-Tzu*, they are exemplars, not of world creation, but of the theme of self-transformation which is the central theme of the *Chuang-Tzu*. Other references to or examples of transformation which appear in the *Chuang-Tzu*, as I argue below, are metaphors of the self-transformation which is our central objective. The butterfly anecdote, however, has progressed from the form of the myth or the legend to the form of the co-temporary anecdote, the highest form of the metaphor. This is not to say that the myth is a less important form. It is only to say that the myth is more primordial or primeval and serves a different philosophical function in the drama of the raising of the levels of consciousness. One can utilize the fish-bird myth to illuminate the butterfly anecdote and vice-versa. There are, of course, obvious differences. But the central idea of self-transformation is common to both. We can also see

elements in common with the Great Awakening of the Great Sage anecdote of chapter two of the *Chuang-Tzu*. This discussion can await the
formal discussion of the butterfly and Great Sage anecdotal stories below.

3. Graham avoids the problem of repetition through the traditional choice
   of referring to the contents of the second version (as I have labeled it) as
   part of T'ang's questions to Chi. This way, it does not so much appear to
   be a simple repetition as the same story appearing from a different perspective. *Cf.* A. C. Graham,*Chuang Tzu, The Inner Chapters* (London: 1981),
   44. This expedient, however, still leaves the content of the material as
   repetitious and thus, to my mind, suspect. Graham also seems aware of
   some problem, as he has placed the entire portion of the second version
   within parentheses. In any event, there is no notice taken of the most
   significant difference between the two versions (a problem he shares with
   Girardot). This is the key issue and one which is not addressed by having
   it reappear in question form.

4. Burton Watson, tran., *The Complete Works of Chuang Tzu*, (New York: 1968),
   29 (emphasis mine). There are some issues of translation which center
   around the name Northern Darkness which can also refer to the name of a
   lake. But these sorts of issues do nothing to affect the points at issue.

5. I have omitted an intervening example to maintain narrative continuity.

6. This was said prior to the reaction of the cicada and the dove. *Cf.* Watson, 30.

7. *Ibid.*

8. *Ibid.*

9. *Ibid.*

10. Despite such statements as this, a great majority of commentators have
    seen fit to view Chuang Tzu as an unqualified relativist. We will discuss this
    in detail in a later chapter. Suffice it to say for the present that the practice
    of viewing Chuang Tzu as a relativist is most likely due to the overwhelming
    influence of Kuo Hsiang, who in his commentaries on the *Chuang-Tzu*
    develops his own philosophy in addition to being responsible for editing
    the text which we rely upon. So that one can be aware of how even these
    passages referring to the small minded insect and the small bird are con-
    strued as being of equal worth to the big bird, consider this passage from
    Kuo Hsiang's commentary:

    > Although the great is different from the small, yet if they all indulge
    > themselves in the sphere of self-enjoyment, then all things are follow-
    > ing their own nature and doing according to their own capacity; all
    > are what they ought to be and equally happy. There is no room for
    > the distinction of superior and inferior. (Fung Yu-lan, *Chuang-Tzu, A
    > New Selected Translation with an Exposition of the Philosophy of Kuo
    > Hsiang* [New York: 1964], 28.)

    With reference to the choice of the creatures themselves, we may be
    reminded of the fact that both are well known to keep up an incessant
    and, to some, irritating stream of noise. I find the dove's constant crooning
    irritating although the cricket has always seemed soothing to me. The
    important factor, however, is that both are constantly making noise or

chattering and in this respect can be seen as gossips, which does cohere with their role as narrowminded skeptics who debunk the alleged feats of the big bird.

11. Watson, 33.

12. *Ibid*, 34-5.

4. The Monster as Metaphor

1. Burton Watson, *The Complete Works of Chuang Tzu* (New York: 1970), 74.

2. *Ibid*., 84.

3. The story of Cook Ting is of a cook, not a butcher. However, the cook performs functions which we would understand to be those of a butcher. For example, Cook Ting carves up a whole oxen. In any event, the story of Cook Ting is completely about butchery or carving as is the famous story in Plato. The fact that he is a cook is nearly incidental to the story since there is not a word about cooking in it. *Cf. ibid.* 50-1. As there are excellent discussions aplenty about Butcher Ting, I will not add to them. I would refer the reader to Kuang-ming Wu, *Chuang-Tzu: World Philosopher at Play* (New York: 1982), 73, for such an excellent discussion. (I am very pleased to discover that Wu shares my analysis about the story so much that he refers to Ting as Butcher Ting.) Graham, who, as is the usual case, refers to the figure as Cook Ting, discusses the point of the story in his essay, "Taoist Spontaneity and the Dichotomy of 'Is' and 'Ought'," in Victor H. Mair, *Experimental Essays on Chuang-Tzu* (Honolulu: 1983), 8. I do not completely agree with Graham's analysis but will save my analysis of Graham for a later chapter. Wu hits the nail right on the head.

4. In the case of Plato, he is more likely to refer to shoemakers and packasses rather than actually giving them speaking parts in his dialogues. But this is a difference in literary gambit. The cognitive function is very much the same.

5. One is reminded of Socrates' self-description as a sting-ray (*Meno*) and a horse-fly (*Apology*). Both images carry a *literal* shock value.

6. Wu makes reference to Chuang Tzu's use of historical figures as philosophical mouthpieces (my phrase) for positions different than or even opposite to their own (Wu, 19).

7. Paradox will be discussed separately in a later chapter. Paradoxical views, when expressed by a monster figure, are enhanced in their paradoxicality quotient. I will discuss this below.

8. Benedict de Spinoza, *Ethics* 5, Prop. 42, note.

9. Watson, 52.

10. Watson speculates that the ex-commander may have had his foot amputated as a punishment. This would still be consistent with its having been a part of his destiny or the work of Heaven. *cf. ibid.*, 52, n. 5.

11. This progressive softening is characteristic of the philosophical method of the *Chuang-Tzu*. If the *Chuang-Tzu* had simply begun with the shoutings of a madman, it would not have had much credibility to it. A simple

observation such as this is helpful to the understanding of the integration of content and form that is so characteristic of the work.

12. Watson, p. 84.

13. *Ibid.*, 66.

14. The archetype of the tree story which repeats itself through the *Chuang-Tzu* has been thoroughly discussed by previous commentators. It is about as well known as the story of Cook or Butcher Ting. Actually, the tree story requires little elucidation as it is very self-explanatory in any case. What perhaps has not been discussed is the number of times it is repeated. The first appearance of the tree archetype is as early as chapter one of the *Chuang-Tzu* (Watson, 35). The second exemplar of the tree archetype, which is the one which has received the most attention by commentators but in fact is only one of many, occurs in chapter four of the *Chuang-Tzu* (Watson, 63-4). The third instantiation of the tree archetype is actually in a dream of the carpenter who appears in the second version (Watson, 64). The fourth version comes soon after the tree in the dream and is remarkably like the first version of chapter one (Watson, 65). The fifth version, which is the one which immediately precedes the story of Shu, is the story of multiple trees. Since these are usable trees they do not count in *sensu stricto* as exemplars of the tree archetype except in a negative sense. Thus, we can say that it is the fourth appearance of the famous tree archetype that immediately precedes the story of Shu. This is of special interest since the fourth version is so much like the first version, in which the tree is actually named SHU.

15. The basic point of the tree story is that uselessness turns out to be very useful. What has not been sufficiently noted, however, is that it has been monstrosity, or a significant deviation from the norm, that has accounted for the uselessness. In addition, the concept of the tree as an archetype has not been brought forth. The importance of conceiving of certain repetitive stories as exemplars of basic archetypes is that it furthers the notion of literary devices as serving progressive cognitive functions.

16. Watson, p. 35.

17. This particularly lugubrious reference to the use of trees is a wonderful indirect reference to the fact that the most useful of us will doubtless sacrifice our lives early. We can take this to be an early reference to the Type A personality who courts death by virtue of his stressful life style.

18. Watson, 65-6. The reference to sacrificial animals, again, may be an indirect reference to the life-sacrificing nature of the useful man.

19. *Ibid.*, 66. The injunction is indirect. Just as it would have been better for him if he had crippled virtue, so it would be for us. Told in a story form, it will be assimilated by our intuitive mental functions rather than being debated by our analytic functions if it is brought up directly in direct prescriptive discourse.

20. *cf.*n. 1.

21. Watson, 75.

22. Watson, 72-3.

23. Watson, 82 (chapter six of the inner chapters).

24. This is a most effective use of indirection. If Chuang Tzu had placed the position he was advocating in his own words, the natural reaction would

be to think of objections to it. For, if a thesis is put forward as his own set of values, there is always the probability of a contest of wills between reader and author. The analytic, critical mind, confronted with a set of directives, naturally conceives of alternatives. To place a set of treasured values in the mouth of a madman immediately puts the analytic mind at ease. Obviously, no one needs to listen to the speech of a madman. Thus, the speech of a madman can be taken in without impediment by the intuitive, holistic, pre-conscious mind. A better example of the cognitive function of a literary ploy could not be found.

One thinks immediately of Western analogues such as the great speeches given to the Fool in the works of Shakespeare and the madman in Nietzsche. Who, for example, has read Nietzsche who does not recall the speech of the madman who shouts out that G-d is dead? Perhaps, not a great deal of the rest of *Zarathustra* will be remembered, but such a speech cannot help but be remembered. (It is repeated in a compact form in *The Joyful Wisdom*, [New York: 1960], Aphorism 125, 167-169). If it had simply been a prose statement in an atheistic philosopher's argument, such as, "There is no G-d," would this be particularly memorable? How many philosophers have made such a claim, and who remembers them? But who can forget that Nietzsche proclaimed that G-d is dead?

In fact, to make the point even plainer, while Nietzsche is given credit for coining this phrase, he is not the first to have done so. The honor belongs to Hegel, who uses this statement much earlier. (Cf. Hegel's *Phenomenology of Mind*, trans. J. B. Baillie, [London: 1964], 753.) Hegel himself, ironically enough, takes the phrase from a hymn of Luther's (cf. his footnote, p. 753). But the point is that Hegel uses the phrase in a philosophical paraphrase. Therefore, he is not much remembered for it. This strengthens my thesis that it is not the fantastic content of the utterance alone that is striking but the form in which it appears that accounts for its power.

25. This translation is a combination of Watson, 66, and Gia-fu Feng and Jane English's version found in *Chuang-Tzu*, Inner Chapters (New York: 1974), 89.

26. I have omitted discussion of Robber Chih, partially because he appears in a later, probably spurious chapter and partially because the robber, as a social deviate, is a sub-set of the madman in my classification system. He disobeys the laws of society. Of course, unlike the madman he does so quite knowingly, and insofar as he does, his statements are not as cancelling of the analytic dimension of the mind as those of the madman. But the madman, it must be remembered, has a certain logic to his utterances. Both the robber and the madman share in common their intransigence to conforming and come in for an equal measure of social opprobrium.

5. The Beautiful as Metaphor: The Symbol of Metamorphosis

1. A. C. Graham, *Chuang-Tzu: The Inner Chapters* (London: 1981), 60. The intricacy of this parable bears special mention. While the Great Sage may

make his appearance only once in ten thousand generations, it nonetheless seems like it is the passing of a single day. This points up the difficulty of the conundrum which he solves while at the same time dramatizing the enormity of his skill in solving it. The difficulty is so great that it requires the passage of ten thousand generations for a sage to emerge who can explain these perplexities to us. However, once he emerges, his skill in explanation is so great that the passage of time is eclipsed by the power of his explanations. His power of explanation is so great that he makes the passage of ten thousand generations appear to be a single day. The difficulty of the problem is so great that it is only one man in ten thousand generations who can solve it. But when he does so, it is in the twinkling of an eyelash.

2. The butterfly may in fact be a more hardy creature than we realize. According to Chinery's, A Field Guide to the Insects of Britain and Northern Europe, (London: Collins, 1976), butterflies can even live through winter, (p. 17). Nonetheless, butterflies are perceived as delicate and transient and there is no reason to believe that Chuang Tzu thought any differently.

3. It cannot be denied that Chuang Tzu was a very playful philosopher. The importance of his playfulness is pointed up in the title of Wu's exemplary book on Chuang Tzu, Chuang-Tzu: World Philosopher at Play (New York: 1982).

4. For example, one is put in mind of ancient Greek where the word for soul is synonymous with the word for butterfly, psychē. Strictly speaking, the butterfly is taken as the personification of the soul, or to be precise, the wings of the butterfly are taken as the image of the soul. But the point of the association remains. How amazing that Chuang Tzu would have chosen the butterfly as the counterpart of Chuang Tzu's consciousness! Or, perhaps, it is not so amazing. Perhaps it is a further indication of the appositeness of the image — a cross-cultural synchronicity rather than a bizarre coincidence. This would further strengthen my thesis that the image is not casually chosen. One may find other cross-cultural parallels within the Orient. For example, in Burmese, the word for butterfly, Hlepa, literally stands for the souls of the dead. The Burmese were thus dismayed when British colonials captured these souls of the dead in their butterfly nets.

5. The very choice of a butterfly as the alter-ego of Chuang Chou, in addition to its other characteristics, also reflects a certain playfulness.

6. The Butterfly Dream: The Case for Internal Textual Transformation

1. There are at least two separate reasons why we should not take the conventional order of the textual fragments as sacrosanct. First, Chuang Tzu himself may not have had a definite order for his fragments. Thus, any rearrangement has to do with following a superior logic rather than some psycho-biographical incident. A. C. Graham writes that the order of the episodes in the Inner Chapters "... is not sacred, since there is no reason to suppose that Chuang Tzu ever did put his jottings in a definitive order.

The occasional passages which break recognizable continuities may be moved to more suitable contexts" *Chuang-Tzu, The Inner Chapters,* (London: 1981), 32.

  Secondly, our version is itself an edited version which has gone through the hands of Kuo Hsiang, who lived some six hundred years after Chuang Tzu. In the above book, Graham reports that our present *Chuang-Tzu* is an abridgement of fifty-two chapters into thirty-three chapters by Kuo Hsiang, ". . . who may be suspected of having tacked the more interesting parts of discarded chapters on the ones which he retained" (*ibid.,* 26). For both reasons, there is nothing to argue against the possibility that the modifications that I have introduced are more in keeping with the real meaning of the text.

2. This is the butterfly dream anecdote with which chapter two of the *Chuang-Tzu* conventionally ends in the raw version of the butterfly dream (to be discussed in the following chapter). It may be noted that sometimes I have referred to the butterfly dream story as a story, sometimes as an anecdote, sometimes, for short, as an image (the story itself functions as an image of awakening in addition to including the butterfly character which is used as an image), sometimes as a metaphor, sometimes as an analogy and sometimes as an argument (as a short form of an analogical argument). Which is it? It is all of these, depending upon both the *context* of the references and the *function* of the use of a multinonymous denotator in the first place. In respect to context, I may wish to point the reader to one or another of the different functions of the butterfly image/story/analogy/argument. In respect to the specific function of a multinonymous denotator, the mind of the reader is being moved out of the one to one, one name — one reference mode of thinking into a many-named — one reference mode of thinking. This is not to be confused with the Fido-Fido problem of Ryle's. Ryle was concerned that if there were one name we would then be moved to think that an entity existed as a referent for that name. Here, the function of the multinonymous denotator is not to lead the mind away from (or towards) existential referents but to bring the mind to the realization that one thing (butterfly) can have many denotators, each one of which is valid depending upon context and function. The mind is thus predisposed to allow a greater interflow between cognitive functions such as naming, imagining, analogizing, arguing and so on. In so doing, the mind is learning to cognize more holistically. The multinonymous denotator moves language away from its strictly denotative function and closer to its cognitively liberating function. The function of the multinonymous denotator is to free the reader's mind from attempting to fix the butterfly story *simply* as a story or *simply* as a story that contains an image — it is that, but it is simultaneously something more. It is an image that functions within a story and a whole story-image that functions as an analogical argument. One of the purposes of this reading of the *Chuang-Tzu* is to expand the notion of argument beyond that of explicit analytical deductions designed for the conscious mind. While the butterfly anecdote is not an argument proper in the sense of a syllogism, it is an argument in the sense of being a means of both

persuasion and a means of assisting the movement of the mind. It is a narrative device designed to very subtly figure into an entire transformative strategy. As a result, it can be fairly referred to as an argument in a broader sense. We continually alter the mode of reference because it is in keeping with the spirit of the *Chuang-Tzu* to force shifts and accomodations in our cognitive capacities and assimilations and our concepts of our cognitive capacities and assimilations. An anecdote is a valid argument in the context of the overall meaning structure of the *Chuang-Tzu*. The butterfly anecdote is image, story, anecdote and argument all at once. It is not limited to any of these. And, in terms of the operational strategy of the *Chuang-Tzu*, it could not be any one of these without being all of them. (*cf.*, chapters two and three of this volume).

3. Even if it were proposed that this is all meant as a joke, it is not at all clear how it would work as a joke, even a bad one. Even jokes must possess a certain logical coherence to function as jokes. If the story were designed to be jocular, why would it end with the no-nonsense conclusion that there must be a distinction between Chuang Chou and the butterfly? All confusion hypotheses (including the joke, which is a species of the confusion hypothesis) seem to disregard the strong statement that there must be a distinction between Chuang Chou and the butterfly.

4. Fung Yu-Lan, *Chuang-Tzu, A New Selected Translation with an Exposition of the Philosophy of Kuo Hsiang* (New York: 1964), 64. Incidentally, it can be seen that the hypnogogic state of consciousness (in which the borderline between reality and dream is not clearly marked even though one has physically awakened) is, for all intents and purposes, part of the dream state. Even if it were seen as a state of awakening, it most certainly would be seen to be a species of the confusion hypothesis.

5. A. C. Graham, "Chuang Tzu's Essay on Seeing Things as Equal," *History of Religions* (Chicago: 1969-1970), 9:2, 3, p. 149.

6. A. C. Graham, *Chuang Tzu, The Inner Chapters*, 21-2.

7. *Ibid.*, 61.

8. Mark Elvin, "Between the Earth and Heaven: Conceptions of the Self in China," in M. Carrithers, S. Collins, and S. Lukes, eds., *The Category of the Person* (New York: 1986), 166. Watson's translation also captures the force of Elvin's "assuredly a difference" as he renders: "Suddenly he woke up and there he was, solid and *unmistakably* Chuang Chou. . . . Between Chuang Chou and a butterfly there must be *some* distinction!" (First emphasis is mine; the second is Watson's.) Burton Watson, *The Complete Works of Chuang Tzu*, (New York: 1970), 4. It would seem that the importance of emphasizing the distinction and the certainty of the awareness of the distinction would not be so important if the transformation were an endless or continuous one, but it would be if the transformation were one-way and one time only.

9. Elvin, 166.

10. Graham, *Chuang Tzu, The Inner Chapters*, 61.

11. The *Chuang-Tzu*, chapter twenty-two.

12. While Elvin does not make specific mention of a transcendence, it would seem to be implied in his concept of achieving great or true knowledge.

My reasoning is as follows. If, according to Elvin, we are unaffected by endless transformation in the state of great knowledge, then I presume that we are affected by it in the state of ordinary knowledge. In this sense, if I have read Elvin's subtle and erudite article correctly, one must rise above ordinary or pedestrian knowledge in order to reach superior knowledge.

13. Elvin, 167.
14. *Ibid.*
15. In view of these difficulties, we may wonder why the endless transformation hypothesis has gained adherents. One reason for this may be the unfortunate reliance upon the spurious chapter thirty-three. For example, Girardot refers approvingly to the: "Butterfly Way" of *creatio continua*, a life that is "blank, boundless, and without form, transforming, changing, never constant" which he quotes from Watson's translation of chapter thirty-three of the *Chuang-Tzu* (Watson, 373). And again, Girardot applies the model taken from thirty-three to the butterfly story of chapter two when he writes: "In the spirit of the 'butterfly parable' from the *Chuang-Tzu* where dream and reality are constantly blurred in the great transformation of things . . ." *cf.* N. J. Girardot, *Myth and Meaning in Early Taoism*, Berkeley: University of California Press, 1983, pp. 111, 163. (This adds a bit of the confusion hypothesis into the pot).
16. Kuang-ming Wu, *Chuang Tzu: World Philosopher at Play* (New York: 1982), 7.
17. *Ibid.*, 20.
18. Kuang-ming Wu, "Dream in Nietzsche and Chuang Tzu," *Journal of Chinese Philosophy* (Honolulu) 13:4 (1986): 379.
19. This is not a problem that is peculiar to English language translations as it is clear from the context in the original that the reference for things is plural. In the Chinese language plurals are not given by suffixes (as the English 's'), as nouns are indifferent to singularity or plurality (and are called mass nouns). However, it is a useful principle to consult English language translations as a guide to interpretation, and in this I follow Wing-tsit Chan's practice as a principle of interpretation (stated on the occasion of his plenary address for the International Research Conference for Asian and Comparative Philosophy, Honolulu, 1984).

7. The Butterfly Dream: The Case for External Textual Transformation

1. *Cf.* pp. 85-87 above and n. 5 at the end of the previous chapter.
2. This is not contradicted by what is also said later in the same passage, that "when I say you are dreaming, I am dreaming, too." If this passage were indicative of still being in a dream *after* the ultimate awakening, this could be an argument for the two stories making the same point, viz., the point of the confusion hypothesis. But Graham does not make this argument. He says that they are making different points. Presumably, he would interpret the Great Sage dream story in a way which would grant veridical vision to the awakened sage (*cf.* A. C. Graham, *Chuang-Tzu, The Inner Chap-*

ters, 21). There is no reason to equate the statements that are made about reality with the great non-verbal cognition that "someday there will be a great awakening when we know that this is all a great dream." Further, in a statement which follows the "I am dreaming" statement, there is an implication that this is possible of explication: "a great sage may appear who will know their meaning." If the "I am dreaming" statement is capable of explication, then it is not a statement which is to be taken as simply part of the contents of a dream. All dreams, being illusions by definition, cannot be explicated in any sense as being comprised of veridical statements about reality or veridical comments upon the correct interpretation of reality. The issues involved with the limitations of language to completely state what is real will be dealt with in a later chapter. (Translation by Watson, 47-8.)

3. As I have indicated above, there is no reason to take the present edited order as sacrosanct whether we are considering the internal order within a specific passage or we are considering the order of the passages themselves within a chapter. *cf.* n. 1 to chapter one, p. 174-5 and n. 1 to chapter six, p. 185-6. For further arguments which relate to the questionable current ordering of the text, *cf.* also A. C. Graham, "The book Chuang-Tzu and the Problem of Translation," in *Chuang Tzu, The Inner Chapters,* 27-39, and A. C. Graham, "How Much of Chuang Tzu Did Chuang Tzu Write?" in *Studies in Classical Chinese Thought,* Henry Rosemont and B. Schwartz, (eds.). *Journal of the American Academy of Religion* 47/3 (September, 1979): 459-502. Additional arguments for the fact that the text as we have it has already been rearranged may be found in Livia Knaul, "Kuo Hsiang and the *Chuang Tzu," Journal of Chinese Philosophy* 12 (1985): 429-47.

4. The translation is that of Wing-tsit Chan in Wm. Theodore de Bary, *Sources of Chinese Tradition* (New York: 1960), 74.

5. This translation is by Burton Watson in *The Complete Works of Chuang Tzu* (New York: 1970), 47.

6. Chan, 74.

7. *Ibid.*

8. Watson, 47-8.

8. The Question of Relativism

1. H. G. Creel, *Chinese Thought from Confucius to Mao Tse-tung* (Chicago: 1953), 112.

2. Lars Jul Hansen, "An Analysis of 'Autumn Floods' in Chuang-Tzu," in Arnes Naess and Alastair Hannay, eds., *Invitation to Chinese Philosophy* (Oslo: 1972), 132.

3. Chad Hansen, "A Tao of Tao in Chuang-Tzu," in Victor H. Mair, ed., *Experimental Essays on Chuang-Tzu* (Honolulu: 1983), 35.

4. *Ibid.,* 50-51.

5. *Journal of Chinese Philosophy* 12:4 (December 1985): 436.

6. Wing-tsit Chan, article on Chuang-tzu in the *Encylopedia of Philosophy,* ed., Paul Edwards (New York: 1967), 2:110.

7. Anthony S. Cua, "Forgetting Morality: Reflections on a Theme in Chuang-tzu," *Journal of Chinese Philosophy* 4, (1977): 311.
8. David B. Wong, *Moral Relativity* (Berkeley: 1984), 214.
9. A. C. Graham, "Taoist Spontaneity and the Dichotomy of 'Is' and 'Ought'," *Experimental Essays on Chuang-tzu*, ed. V. Mair (Honolulu: 1983), 12.
10. *Ibid.*, 14.
11. *Philosophy East and West*, July 1983, 242-3 (emphasis his).
12. *Ibid.*, 242 (emphasis his).
13. A. C. Graham, "Chuang-tzu's Essays on Seeing Things as Equal," *History of Religions* 9:2,3 (November 1969/February 1970): 138.
14. It is of note to come to the realization that someone of the stature of Graham has in effect altered his interpretation framework for understanding Chuang Tzu in the course of his intense research on Chuang Tzu. If I am correct in my positing at least two different interpretation stances for Graham, this is a testament to the richness of the possibility of interpretations to which the text is liable and at the same time an illustration of the difficulty in fixing on a choice.
15. *Ibid.*, 149.
16. Russell B. Goodman, "Skepticism and Realism in the *Chuang-Tzu*," *Philosophy East and West* 35:3 (July, 1985): 231-2.
17. *Ibid.*, 234.
18. *Ibid.*
19. *Ibid.*, 236.
20. Burton Watson, trans., *The Complete Works of Chuang-tzu*, 48.
21. For a fuller discussion of the linguistic issues involved in being committed to relativism in some limited sense while at the same time endorsing non-relativistic values, see my article, "Having Your Cake and Eating It, Too: Evaluation and Trans-Evaluation in Chuang-tzu and Nietzsche," *Journal of Chinese Philosophy* 13:4 (December 1986): 429-43.

9. The Origin of the Relativistic Thesis

1. For the distinction between the genuine and the non-genuine chapters, *cf.* chapter one, "On the Chirping of Birds," n. 1. What is a bit strange is that while there is a widespread if not a universal acceptance of the distinction, there seems to be no hesitation in lumping chapters from the authentic and the inauthentic sections together. The problem with the indiscriminate grouping of materials is the consequent misinterpretation to which it gives rise.
2. For example, *cf.* Fung Yu-Lan's classic, *A History of Chinese Philosophy*, vol. 1 (Beijing: 1937), 220-45. Fung's discussion of the *Chuang-Tzu* commences with a quotation from ch. twenty-two (*A History of Chinese Philosophy*, 223) and continues with quotations from chapters seventeen, twenty-five, and two, which receives the primary attention (*A History of Chinese Philosophy*, 224-5). There is some discussion of chapter one (*A History of Chinese Philosophy*, 226-7) but it is followed by a discussion from chapter nine which in turn is followed by a discussion of Lao Tzu. Since Fung was discussing both Chuang Tzu and what he terms his school, part of the

problem lies in the requirements of the sort of text he is writing. But in any case there is no significant correlation noted between chapters one and two of the *Chuang-Tzu*. In his later and more sophisticated, *The Spirit of Chinese Philosophy*, Fung continues the same practice. In discussing Chuang Tzu and Lao Tzu together, he begins with chapter thirty-three of the *Chuang-Tzu* and goes from that directly to chapter two of the *Chuang-Tzu* with no discussion of chapter one at all. *Cf. The Spirit of Chinese Philosophy* (London: 1947), 65-72. Later, Fung does discuss chapter one (*Spirit*, 76), but there is no connection noted between it and chapter two of the *Chuang-Tzu*. The habit of neglecting chapter one of the *Chuang-Tzu* continues in more recent literature. *Cf.* Chad Hansen, *Language and Logic in Ancient China* (Ann Arbor: 1983), 88-97. Here, Professor Hansen commences his discussion with chapter two of the *Chuang-Tzu* and remains essentially with it throughout. In all fairness, this is in keeping with the needs of the particular hypothesis he is framing, but nonetheless such a custom further strengthens the impression that one may skip over chapter one of the *Chuang-Tzu* and get on directly with the more weighty matters discussed in chapter two. The custom is continued in most essays contained in the recent *Experimental Essays on Chuang Tzu*, ed. Victor H. Mair (Honolulu: 1983). *Cf.* the first essay by A. C. Graham, "Taoist Spontaneity and the Dichotomy of 'Is' and 'Ought', " where the quotations commence with those from chapter two (*Experimental Essays*, 5-6), thus continuing the impression that these arguments may be examined in isolation from any development which may have preceded in chapter one. When such a practice is engaged in by someone with the erudition and standing of Graham, it is difficult to overestimate the influence of the comparative neglect of chapter one.

3. *Cf.* my own chapters two, three, five, and six, above.

4. Burton Watson, *The Complete Works of Chuang Tzu* (New York and London: 1968), 36.

5. *Cf.* the confusion hypothesis which I discuss at length in my chapter six, above.

6. *Cf.* above, chapter eight.

7. *Cf.* above, chapter six.

8. In the Great Sage or Great Awakening dream anecdote which I have referred to in my chapter seven above (*cf.* p. 104), there is no mistaking this meaning. Condensing the relevant remarks one may read: "He who dreams of drinking wine may weep when morning comes; he who dreams of weeping may in the morning go off to hunt. . . . Only after he wakes does he know it was a dream. And someday there will be a great awakening when we know that this is all a great dream."

9. According to Graham, it is unlikely that Chuang Tzu titled his pieces. The titles were introduced by a later editor. Graham includes the notorious "Evening Things Out" in his view that it is not original with Chuang Tzu: "The terms 'even things out', the 'ultimate ancestor' and 'emperors and kings' do not occur in the *Inner Chapters* themselves, only in the latest, the Syncretist stratum of the book. Probably Chuang Tzu left behind only disjointed pieces, mixed up perhaps with his disciples' records of his oral teaching, and it was a Syncretist editor of the second century BC *who*

devised the headings." Cf. A. C. Graham, *Chuang Tzu, The Inner Chapters* (London: 1981), 29 (emphasis mine).

As the title of a chapter naturally directs the reader's attention to the point that will be addressed, the selection of the title itself is of importance in addition to how it is translated. Even if one becomes convinced that the appropriate title should be "The Equalization of Things," rather than the "Discourse on Relativism," the point is that it is appropriate only to a title selected by a later editor. The influence of the title, however understood, is enormous. I should note that the difficulty in understanding the title that is supplied obtains whether the reader is reading the original or a translation. As the Chinese is capable of either interpretation (as discussed above), there is no need to translate the title into English or any other language to become aware of the difficulty. It is only by so doing that an English reader can become aware of the difficulty that besets every Chinese reader who is reading the work in the original, classical Chinese. I have emphasized the influence of the choice of translation only to make a point that would be more familiar to a non-Chinese reader.

In any event, the habit of referring to the various chapters in the *Chuang-Tzu* by the utilization of the titles is now endemic. Thus, when one by shorthand refers to chapter two by a title such as, "The Equalization of All Things," one tends to sum up the contents of the chapter in its mode of reference. Given the extraneous nature of the titling to begin with and the ambivalence of the title in its natural language, the custom of title usage and its consequent influence has been, in my opinion, completely blown out of its proper proportion. This is particularly important when the title proves, as I argue, to be systematically misleading. For this reason, I have followed the practice, in the main, of referring to the chapters of the *Chuang-Tzu* by simple enumeration.

10. *Ibid.*, 48. This title selection leaves no doubt as to the probable direction which is so indicated. The "sorting" or classification has as its result the evening out of the differences between things so that they are leveled or equalized. The insertion of the word "which" heightens the effect by highlighting a causal relationship between the grading and the putative resultant leveling out. It is by this very act of grading or sorting that one arrives at the presumably desired outcome of reducing all differences between things. Thus, no doubt is left in the mind of the reader as to the eventual outcome of the chapter. In fact, the inclusion of the word "which" referring to the sorting process makes clear the (putative) intent of the author to establish the ontological and/or axiological equalization as his conclusion. Unlike more neutral titling choices which maintain either neutral or ambivalent interpretations, this choice leaves no ambiguity in the possible interpretation choice.

11. Wing-tsit Chan, *Sources of Chinese Tradition* (New York and London, 1960), 70. By itself this title choice does lend itself to the impression that the equality of things is more likely than not going to be the desired demonstrandum of the chapter. However, by comparison with Graham's it does, on a subtle level, contain a certain implicit ambiguity which is totally removed by Graham's choice. With the choice of Chan, there is a certain

tacit openness, however subtle, that this is either a conclusion that the chapter will attempt to establish or a possible theme that the chapter will discuss without taking a position as to whether this will be a theme that the chapter will affirm or deny or take no position on whatsoever.

12. Ibid., 64

13. Fung Yu-Lan, *A History of Chinese Philosophy*, 231.

14. Chad Hansen, *Language and Logic in Ancient China*, 89.

15. Kuang-ming Wu, *Chuang Tzu: World Philosopher at Play* (New York: 1982), 93.

16. Liou Kia-hway, tran., *L'oeuvre complète de Tchonang-tseu*, Paris: Gallimard, 1969, p. 35.

17. Max Müller, ed., *The Sacred Books of the East* 39 (Oxford: 1891).

18. Wing-tsit Chan, *Sources of Chinese Tradition*, 65-87.

19. Here, there is no indication of any chapter breakdown whatsoever so that the reader has no idea which passages come from authentic and which from inauthentic chapters. Graham refers to this act as an act of good sense, but to my way of thinking it popularizes strong possibilities of misinterpretation and hence is careless. In Graham's argument, Arthur Waley, the greatest of translators from Chinese and the only one who always knew what he was doing, was a lover of Chuang Tzu who had the good sense to offer only carefully selected extracts embedded in exposition, in his *Three Ways of Thought in Ancient China*. (Graham, *The Inner Chapters*, 31). Here is at least one case where I would aver that Waley did not know what he was doing and his act of indiscriminate mingling of authentic and inauthentic material rather than representing good sense was an exercise of poor judgment.

20. Watson, *The Complete Works of Chuang Tzu*, 177.

21. Ibid., 181.

22. Of the so-called outer chapters (chapters eight to twenty-two), in which chapter seventeen is obviously included, A. C. Graham has this to say, "None can be plausibly ascribed to Chuang-tzu" (*Chuang-Tzu, The Inner Chapters*, 28). Why chapter seventeen has received such undue attention is unclear. It is not that being inauthentic it is thereby unimportant. It is only that one would thereby be forewarned that it may contain material or points of view that might be at variance with the inner chapters (one to seven). One would be on the lookout for evidence of such possible disagreement with the outlook presented in the inner chapters.

23. What I attempted to indicate is some solid philosophical basis for why chapter seventeen violates the spirit or intention of the interior chapters. It is not that by being inauthentic alone that evidence from the outer or the mixed chapters (twenty-three to thirty-three) should be disallowed. It is only if such evidence contradicts the central thematic development of the inner chapters that it should be subject to question. The arguments that I present in this volume could be (and for the most part are) made by relying upon the inner chapters alone. If any material is drawn from the other chapters it is only if it further clarifies and enhances the message already contained in the inner chapters that it is permissible. If one is interested in the historical and literary bases for the inauthenticity of the outer and

mixed chapters one may be referred to Graham's chapter, "The book *Chuang-Tzu* and the Problem of Translation," *ibid.*, 27-38.

24. Literature on "Autumn Floods" abounds. To take only two examples one may note that one of the essays in Naess and Hannay's *Invitation to Chinese Philosophy* is devoted to "Autumn Floods" (Lars Jul Hansen, "An Analysis of 'Autumn Floods,' in Chuang Tzu," [Oslo: 1972]). As an example of a more recent treatment one may be referred to Russell B. Goodman's essay, "Skepticism and Realism in the *Chuang Tzu*," *Philosophy East and West*, 35:3 (July 1985), in which supporting material for some of his main arguments is drawn from the "Autumn Floods" chapter.

25. Watson, *The Complete Works of Chuang Tzu*, 189 (this is material drawn from the nefarious chapter seventeen, "Autumn Floods"). This, to me, represents further evidence why this argument should not be taken as representative of the thought of Chuang Tzu. To say this might be said to be begging the question if I both use the inauthenticity of the chapter to disallow the evidence drawn from it and to also argue that such material is therefore inauthentic. My main argument would be to argue from the incompatibility of the types of conclusions reached with those of the interior chapters for the inadmissibility of evidence from the outer or mixed chapters. In this case, one may use historical and literary methods to delineate this chapter (seventeen) as spurious (in the manner of Graham). It should not be surprising then that one could find philosophical evidence to support this conclusion. In fact, we should be surprised if this were not the case. What remains troubling is why this chapter in particular is continually referred to as a source for extrapolating the view of Chuang Tzu.

26. *Cf.* n. 8, above. It is clear that veridical evidence is obtained in the awakened state which corrects the corrigible evidence obtained during the state of the dream.

27. That it is agreed upon as spurious should at the very least set us on guard to look out for possible misleading materials. If, after a careful examination, it is evident that such misleading materials do in fact exist, it is of importance to treat the chapter and its contents with a certain degree of circumspection. The custom of treating the chapter as an unquestioned and unquestionable source of the thought of Chuang Tzu is widespread even in recent literature. *cf.* Benjamin I. Schwartz, *The World of Thought in Ancient China*, (Cambridge: 1985), 219.

10. The Paradox of Self-Transformation

1. One may refer to the objective of the *Chuang-Tzu* in a variety of ways and Chuang Tzu himself does so. Watson posits freedom, by which I take it he means liberation, as the central objective of the *Chuang-Tzu*. (Cf. *The Complete Works of Chuang Tzu*, [New York: 1970], 3.) Sometimes Chuang Tzu depicts the objective as a great awakening (Watson, 47); sometimes Chuang Tzu refers to the goal as entering into Heaven (Watson, 89), frequently as attaining the Way, sometimes as becoming one with Nature

(Watson, 40). *Cf.* Watson's footnote where he identifies Heaven with Nature or the Way for Chuang Tzu (Watson, 40). All of these expressions are of course metaphors for achieving the state of enlightenment. The basic key to achieving enlightenment is the transcendence of the ego or the 'I', which I have referred to throughout as the transformation of the self. Forgetting the self and transforming the self are more or less the same thing.

2. For an excellent discussion of self-forgetting, *cf.* Anthony S. Cua, "Forgetting Morality: Reflections on a Theme in Chuang Tzu," *Journal of Chinese Philosophy* 4 (1977): 305-28. Note Cua's etymological breakdown of the character *wang* 忘 :

     亡 = to lose

     心 = mind

3. Watson, 133.
4. *Cf.* my chapter six, above.
5. Watson, 49.
6. *Ibid.*, 88.
7. *Ibid.*, 47-8.
8. This dream story is, as I have argued in earlier chapters, extremely sophisticated and compresses at least three levels of analogy into one. On one level, there is the evidence of the illusory nature of physical dreams. On another level, even philosophical interpretations are included as parts of a possible dream. Here, the concept of dreaming is expanded to include the mental acts of a philosopher (including Chuang Tzu), whose philosophizing might just as easily be taking place during a dream as a dream about imbibing wine. The point of including philosophers as dreamers is to imply that not only are philosophers possibly dreaming on a physical level, but what is more important, that their claims to reality and truth are possibly illusory. At this point, Chuang Tzu's story exceeds Descartes' dream in subtlety and sophistication since even Descartes' conclusion that he is thinking or that he exists could just as easily be the conclusion of a dream subject in a dream as that of a waking subject while awake. Of course, Descartes makes use of the concept of a non-deceiving Deity as an ontological *Deus ex Machina* to avoid this possibility. Chuang Tzu stays strictly within the limits of an epistemological analysis. Chuang Tzu's story also makes use of the dream analogy to stand for the possibility of an ultimate awakening, a use to which Descartes does not put his dream anecdote. For Chuang Tzu, the dream story is not used simply as a device to show how far we must go to satisfy a thorough going epistemological inquiry, but also as a teaching story to illustrate that no matter how sophisticated and seemingly certain we may become, we may not have achieved a complete awakening. In this sense, Chuang Tzu may be taken as being even more epistemologically rigorous than Descartes, who satisfies himself, finally, that he is certain of something. On another level, of course, Chuang Tzu also wishes to keep his subject reader aware of the omnipossibility of an inner awakening which, like the awakening from a physical dream, could happen at any moment, including the present one.

9. Watson, 48.
10. *Ibid.*, 29.
11. *Ibid.*
12. *Ibid.*, 26.
13. *Ibid.*, 25.
14. To say that there is no 'I' cannot be an exact rendition of a true state of affairs because it is a negative description. It says what there is not, but it does not say what there is. The closest we can come to truth is a negative description. Any positive description will require descriptive terms which *ipso facto* rule out the possibility of being in the state being described (this point will be addressed more completely below). It is important to note here that the best Chuang Tzu can do is to come close to the truth, to give an approximation of what there is.
15. Wing-tsit Chan's translation of Chuang Tzu in Wm. Theodore de Bary, ed., *Sources of Chinese Tradition* (New York: 1960), 71.
16. Watson, 302. The reader may raise the objection that I am now turning to the outer chapters to support my point of view. I think that this chapter, however, is one of the few exceptions among the outer and mixed chapters which is consistent with the internal message of the inner chapters. Thus, even though it may not be one of the genuine chapters, it in no way contradicts the genuine chapters and only, like one or two others, makes the message a bit more explicit.
17. *Cf.* Anthony S. Cua, "Forgetting Morality: Reflections on a Theme in Chuang Tzu," *Journal of Chinese Philosophy* 4 (1977): 305-28.
18. *Cf.* Kuang-ming Wu, *Chuang Tzu: World Philosopher at Play* (New York: 1982), 136. I have used Wu's modified version of Merton's translation in Thomas Merton, *The Way of Chuang Tzu* (New York: 1965), 66, 112.
19. *Cf.* n. 14, above.
20. *Cf.* n. 7, above.
21. Again, this is a negative description. Since there is no subject/object distinction which is possible during this state, the least and the most we can say about it is that such a state is beyond the concept of the self. In the attempt to "describe" such a state we can say that it is beyond the subject/object duality. This is a pointer to the state rather than an objective description of the state. The justification for the use of the term "beyond" is that it is also an attempt to describe the ontological change that has taken place. There has been an experience of a transformation of the subject knower.
22. To say that there is no 'I' can only be a statement that is close to the truth; it is not a statement which describes what is. It is, however, not totally false to say that the Tao is a state in which there is an absence of contraries.
23. Watson, 302. 'Forgotten words' are similar to 'no-words' which are discussed in the notes to chapter twelve. Forgetting words means to forget the descriptive function of language so that words may be used freely without the cavil and carping that comes from attempting to pin language down precisely to denotative objects. Chuang Tzu delights in the prospect of a conversation with one who has also "forgotten" words.

11. The Case of Meng-sun

1. Burton Watson, trans., *The Complete Works of Chuang Tzu*, 88.
2. *Ibid.*, 88. The sense of this remains whether we translate this as Meng-sun alone as having awakened or as Meng-sun as being especially awakened. In either case, he is singled out as being a special case and this singling out deserves our attention.
3. *Ibid.*, 303. This presents a case where we can draw inspiration from a later chapter which is not authentic but which does nonetheless offer a valuable clue for the interpretation of earlier and authentic chapters. This clue can be found by interpolating the inner chapters and one need not have recourse to the later chapter for the finding of this clue. But this presents a case for the helpfulness of a later chapter which, while not authentic, does not contradict the message of the earlier chapters and indeed provides an explanatory supplement. In this respect, one may use some later chapters— although not all—as commentaries upon the inner chapters. The argument for which of the outer and mixed chapters may be used as supplemental and which ought to be avoided as misleading is the subject of a study in itself. For a thorough discussion of the use of imputed words and other forms of discourse in the *Chuang-Tzu* that are the subject of chapter twenty-seven ("Imputed Words"), I recommend Kuang-ming Wu's, *Chuang Tzu: World Philosopher at Play*, especially 28-38.
4. Watson, 88.
5. *Cf. Analects* 3.4, 26.
6. Watson, 88.
7. *Ibid.*
8. *Ibid.*, 88-9.
9. It is nonetheless difficult to escape the feeling that this is a type of dissemblance. One can contrast this to the highest form of behavior that is commended at funerals, which is described as either a brief expression of genuine grief or as a celebratory transcendence. Compare, for example, Chuang Tzu's expression of regret upon the death of Hui Tzu, that he no longer has any one with whom to talk (chapter twenty-four), Chuang Tzu's banging on a drum and singing upon the death of his wife (chapter eighteen) and his humorous comments on the care of his own body after his death (chapter thirty-two). Of the last, Chuang Tzu's answer reminds us of that of Socrates. When Chuang Tzu spurns burial and his disciples complain that the birds will eat his body, his answer is that if he is buried he will deprive the crows and kites in order to provide for the moles and the ants. *Cf.* Watson, 269, 191-2, 361. While all of these may be said to be taken from the later and inauthentic chapters, the views toward death can be said to be more characteristic of Chuang Tzu.
10. Watson, 88.
11. In this context, one is reminded of the attitudes of both Kierkegaard and Nietzsche. One thinks, for example, of Kierkegaard's dream in which he is granted whatever he wants by the assembled gods and he chooses always

to have the laugh on his side. ("Diapsalmata," 5.1, *Either-Or*). In Nietzsche, one may think of Zarathustra, where laughter is pronounced holy and is called upon to kill the spirit of gravity. (*Zarathustra* 1: "On Reading and Writing,"; Part 4, "The Awakening," no. 1; "The Ass Festival," no. 1, *et passim.*
12. Watson, 89.

12. The Goose That Cackled

1. *Cf.* notes 13, 14, chapter four, above ("The Monster as Metaphor").
2. Watson, *The Complete Works of Chuang Tzu*, 209.
3. *Ibid.*, 209.
4. *Ibid.*
5. *Ibid.*, 209-10.
6. One is reminded of several passages in Chuang Tzu. Perhaps the most notable comes from the inauthentic but helpful chapter twenty-seven: "But the unity and what I say about it have ceased to be a unity; what I say and the unity have ceased to be a unity. Therefore, I say, we must have no-words! With words that are no-words, you may speak all your life long and you will never have said anything." (Watson, 304) The meaning is that one realizes that one's language is always destructive of the unity of being in that it creates duality where there was unity. However, once one realizes this one may continue to use language, knowing that the language that one uses is empty in terms of being descriptive of reality. Words that are words constitute the language of description. Any language of description re-creates the subject-object dichotomy and *ipso facto* destroys the unity of realization. Words that are no-words can be used as a special language that is not intended as a language of description and therefore may be used freely without destroying the unity of being.
7. *Cf.*, n. 1, above.
8. *Cf.* Watson, 40. While this passage has been taken as a direct reference to the famous discussion of the white horse in chapters two and three of the *Kung-sun Lung Tzu* (*cf.* Watson's footnote, p. 40 and Chan's footnote in Wing-tsit Chan, *Sources of Chinese Tradition*, p. 71), it may also have a more general application. Be careful not to use attributes or, in Gia-fu Feng's translation, fingers (*Cf.* Gia-fu Feng and Jane English, *Chuang Tzu, the Inner Chapters* [New York: 1974], chapter 2) to stand for that which is not an attribute. Or, in other words, be careful not to mix up the signifier with the signified. In an even wider application of the idea, do not mistake the sign system for the reality which is signified; do not confuse the language which we are using for that which is spoken about.

Here the contents are taken as a formula when Chuang Tzu means them as an illustration. The concept of the useless is praised early on in the text, but only as an indicator of where to look for the most useful (that which contributes to the longest lived). There is a value in the useless, to be sure, but to stay with the example of the useless is to miss the point. It is as if we were to use as an example of the useless being of the highest value certain useless (cancelled or out of date) postage stamps which, for their size, are the most valuable things on earth. We would then conclude that the subject of our discussion was postage stamps. In the language of Chuang Tzu: "To use a horse to show that a horse is not a horse is not as good as using a non-horse to show that a horse is not a horse" (Watson, 40). Here, if we insist upon uselessness, as a formula to show that the useless is not really the useless, we will mistake the reality which is signified by the concept of the useless with the useless. The reality which is signified by the useless is now, in fact, being signified by the useful goose. This could be taken as a case of using a non-horse (a useful goose) to show that a horse is not a horse (the useless goose is not a goose).

*I*ndex

Ai T'ai-t'o, 65-66
Analogies. *See* Metaphors
Aristotle, 11, 52

Big Bird, 41-42, 43, 44, 139, 180n 2
Butterfly: beauty of, 71-72; internal change of, 74-75, playfulness of, 75-76; as symbol of transformation, 71-74, 76-77; transience of, 75
Butterfly dream: amended version, 82-84; arguments for amendment of, 78-79, 185n 1; compared with the Great Sage dream, 103-10; confusion hypothesis, 79-80, 84-87, 93-94, 97-98; endless transformation thesis, 79-80, 87-93; as metaphor for self-transformation, 79, 80-81; as preceding the Great Sage dream, 99-103, 105-6; raw version, 81-82, 83-84; retaining the raw version, 96-99; similarities and differences of amended and raw versions, 83; similar message to the Great Sage dream, 96-99

Cackling goose, 167-72; Chuang Tzu as the, 170-72; self-mockery by Chuang Tzu, 167; usefulness and uselessness, 167-71
Chan Wing-tsit, 19, 112, 114, 134, 137
Chieh Yu, madman, 69
Chirping of birds: differences between words and the, direct textual evidence of, 18-22; differences between words and the, indirect

textual evidence of, 17-18, 19; differences between words and the, logical proof of, 15-17; double-headed questions, 25-27: meaninglessness and meaningfulness of language, 15-22
Ch'i Wu Lun, second chapter, 15; translation of title, 133-37
Cicada, 48, 139; and the Little Bird, 42-47
Confucians, debate with Mohists, 17, 19
Confucius: madman as critic of, 68-69; as mouthpiece, 7, 157-66
Creel, H.G., 14, 112-13
Cripples, 51-52, 59-65
Cua, Antonio, 115, 152-53

Elvin, Mark, 87-89, 93, 183n 12
English, Jane, 7

Fung Gia-fu, 7
Fung Yu-lan, 14, 84, 134

Gia-fu Fung. *See* Fung Gia-fu
Girardot, Norman, 179n 1, 188n 15
Goodman, Russell, 120-21
Graham, A.C., 7, 9-10, 88-89, 134; confusion hypothesist, 85-87; neither relativist or non-relativist, 119-20; on the chirping of birds, 16-19; soft relativist, 115, 116-17
Great Awakening dream. *See* Great Sage dream
Great Fish, 41-42, 180n 2. *See also* Big Bird

201

Printed in the United States
760800003B